Nothing Extenuate

Fox Cooper in 1847

Nothing Extenuate

THE LIFE OF
FREDERICK FOX COOPER

BY
F. RENAD COOPER

BARRIE AND ROCKLIFF
LONDON

Contents

Abbreviations

The following abbreviations have been used in this book:

A.N.   Allardyce Nicoll: *A History of English Drama.*

B.M.   British Museum.

Dicks'   Dicks' edition of *Standard Plays* (*circa* 1875–1908).

D.N.B.   *Dictionary of National Biography.*

Figaro   *Figaro in London.* 1832–39.

Illustrations

Preface

I HAD always rather envied people who could write books, especially those who did so in their spare time, since the hours in a day are all too few for me. Thus the task of producing something about my family history was saved up for my retirement, and when this took place it was almost the first job I set my hand to. But the scope of what I have written has proved to be very different from my expectations.

Never before having attempted a lengthy piece of composition I looked into an authors' dictionary to find out what was said under the heading of "Preface", and was interested to learn that this is the place in which the author explains the purpose and scope of the book. That, indeed, is what I had intended to do. The next piece of advice in the same dictionary is worth quoting: "It is as well to make this *thoroughly* explanatory as cases are not infrequent where this is the only part of the book read by a reviewer." Whether or not this book ever gets to the length of being reviewed by a professional reviewer, I feel that advice to be excellent, and I shall try to follow it without going into too much detail which even an assiduous reviewer might not have the time, or the desire to read.

When beginning this task I was aware that the background on the paternal side of my family was largely theatrical. I possessed one framed playbill, a book on Dickens and the Drama, a few family notes, and a theatrical travelling trunk which had belonged to my father and which I had not properly examined when it came into my possession at his death in 1939.

The object I set out upon was to prepare a family tree to which some kind of story would be attached; I was minded to do this mainly for my own instruction and amusement, but also because it might some day be of interest to my three children, and to other members of the family. I naturally started with the Coopers where there was good evidence of four past generations; and I toyed with the idea of the title: *From Footlights to Headlights*, to honour the achievement of my cousins in the world of rapid motor-cars.

One of the most intriguing indications in the family notes that were left to me was that we were descended from an Isaac Cooper, who had been a very wealthy stockbroker. In view of this—shall we say Christian?—name, one of my uncles was quite convinced that we came of Jewish stock, and that the sequence was: Isaac, Henry Fox, Frederick Fox, Frederick Harwood, the last-named being my grandfather. My first steps, therefore, perhaps unwisely as I see it now, involved direct enquiries into the life and family of Isaac Cooper. This took me to the Stock Exchange where I was kindly given particulars linking up with various press cuttings preserved among the family notes, or pasted in the almanacks of my grandfather which I found in the theatrical trunk. (These form a complete run from 1860 to 1905, but the information they contain is somewhat sparse as they were not intended to be a guide to posterity.) My researches in the Stock Exchange, however, and into various parish records to which they led, failed to convince me that we were descended from, or related to, an Isaac Cooper. The fruit of this diversion is given in Chapter 11.

The next step was to join the Society of Genealogists where they were most helpful, and I put in a good deal of work; but little progress was made because my ancestors moved about too much, did not seem to leave Wills, and possessed no property. I must here emphasize three points: (1) it has been no part of my object to try to find out whether there may be a large sum of money waiting to be claimed by a member of the family; (2) I have not set out to establish that we are remotely related to any member of the peerage, or descended from distinguished forbears; and (3) I have not been afraid of the truth into whatever avenues this has led me. The latter has been a vital principle at times as will be recognized by anyone who reads through this history.

Some of the notes in my possession had been prepared by Barry Duncan, the theatrical antiquarian, who was well known to two of my uncles, and who lives in a sort of Aladdin's cave, but above ground. I therefore went to see him, and he promised to dig out whatever he could to help in my writing. There and then he showed me an article in the *Theatrical Times* of June 1847 containing a lot of information about my great-grandfather, and a portrait, which forms the frontispiece to this volume. In due course he produced a veritable reservoir of material, some of which had clearly been sold by a member of the family. Included in this haul was a book of press-cuttings prepared by my grandfather and relating to his own father, Frederick Fox Cooper. These acquisitions completely altered my outlook. I realized that Fox Cooper, whose first name it is convenient to drop, was probably the most exciting character within the scope of my research into the family background, and that traces of his passage through this life could be found in a variety of ways. I ascertained that the monumental work of Allardyce Nicoll on the nineteenth-century drama mentions a number of his plays, and I was stimulated by a memorial in the *Glasgow News* written about Fox Cooper after his death in January 1879 by E. L. Blanchard, a well-known pantomime author and theatrical journalist. From this I quote: ". . . his history if truly told would serve as another example of the utter uselessness of intellectual gifts without the ballast of strong moral principles." This struck me as a challenge and an entice-ment, with the result that I decided thenceforth to concentrate upon writing a biography of my great-grandfather, and in general to include only so much family history as would contri-bute to the story of his life. Another story might come later. Genealogy, meanwhile, took second place except in so far as I was to learn a lot more about Henry Fox Cooper, my great-great-grandfather, concerning whom a chapter is included by way of prologue.

Briefly, I have obtained evidence of the incarnation of Fox Cooper as dramatist, journalist, theatrical manager, actor, critic, and poet. He edited and published newspapers, and became the lessee of theatres; he also claimed to be a

parliamentary reporter and shorthand-writer. Last, but not
least, he was habitually if not persistently insolvent, and found
himself in gaol for debt on seven or more occasions. He never
pursued any one operation for much more than a year: he was
nearly always on the move, and as will be seen from Appendix
III there are records of about fifty different private addresses.
Fortunately many of his adventures were of a nature that
normally claims the attention of the public, and there was
thus a wealth of information in newspapers and other publications, although this has not always been easy to find. Nor has
it always been free from inaccuracy.

Having got thus far I resolved to have printed this biography
of Fox Cooper, primarily for personal reasons, but possibly
for the interest of theatrical historians and others who like
reading about the stage, and the people on it. I realize fully
the risk of venturing into the arena of theatrical history, where
a reputation is easily lost. Fortunately, I have none to lose.
Writing it has been an exciting adventure, and I have set down
much, but by no means all, of what has come to light, yet
omitting no essential feature. It may not be accounted a very
accomplished book, but one of the secrets of life is to enjoy
doing things indifferently well, and this I have enjoyed.

Another feature deserves a special explanation or apology.
Throughout this record will often be found references to the
source of my information. This may seem tedious to the general
reader, but it may prove of value to those who contemplate
delving into their family past, and of benefit to those who are
acquainted with the problems of reconstructing events in the
history of the theatre. (Not infrequently one has to make
a choice between conflicting pieces of evidence from the
printed word.) The alternative of placing all references at the
end of the chapter, or by way of footnotes would in my opinion
have been cumbersome. Of the latter I have tried to be sparing
in my use.

I must conclude with a few words about the means of access
to original material, and proffer thanks for all the assistance
so freely given. My main avenues have been—not in any strict
order of their importance, but rather as they come to mind—
The British Museum, including the Newspaper annexe at
Colindale, the State Papers room, and the Department of

Manuscripts; the Public Record Office; the General Register of Births, Deaths, and Marriages at Somerset House; the Enthoven Collection in the Victoria and Albert Museum; the House of Commons' library; the National Trust; the Press office of the Royal Opera House, Covent Garden; the Rectors of several churches who have found time in a busy day to show me their parish records; the Stock Exchange; the Archives at County Hall, Westminster; the Guildhall library; the Westminster library; the Harvard University library; the Alexander Turnbull library, New Zealand; and various other London, provincial, and overseas libraries, all of which through their librarians and archivists have been unfailingly helpful.

To write down the names of individuals who have helped me is an invidious task, for in any short list there are bound to be important omissions. Barry Duncan has already been named: through him I met George Nash and his assistant, Miss Johnson, of the Enthoven Collection. In this manner I came to know Malcolm Morley, himself already fascinated by the subject of this biography of whom he had written critically on several occasions in *The Dickensian*. Sir St Vincent Troubridge kindly wrote me a very informative letter which added a lot to my knowledge. Most of the helpful and patient folk at the various libraries and at the British Museum in London are unknown to me by name, but at Colindale one becomes acquainted with Mr W. D. Wilson who has an intimate knowledge of most of the newspapers published in the nineteenth century. I cannot omit to mention the valuable research voluntarily undertaken by Mrs P. M. Wilson of the Alexander Turnbull library, and the help of Mrs Saunders, archivist at Marylebone. Finally, ending in the local village I place on record my thanks to Miss Purser, Marlow's librarian, and Mrs O'Brien who has typed from my almost illegible hand.

Marlow-on-Thames   FREDERICK RENAD COOPER
1963

Prologue: Henry Fox Cooper

I AM fairly confident that my great-great-grandfather was called Henry Fox Cooper. Whether he was christened Henry Fox is another matter, as will be seen below. From the certificate of the baptism of my grandfather, who was born in 1826, I know that my great-grandfather was named Frederick Fox Cooper; but being unable to find a formal record of his birth in 1806, or subsequent baptism, I have to rely in the first place upon a strong family tradition, and a statement in the *Theatrical Times* in 1847, that the father of Frederick Fox Cooper had been Editor of *John Bull*. Evidence from the newspaper *Paul Pry* in 1830 supports this conclusion.

Now a Henry Fox Cooper certainly edited *John Bull* in 1821 because it is on record that he was committed to Newgate by order of the Speaker of the House of Commons for publishing a libel against an M.P. The prison register happily preserved, if happily is the right word, describes him upon being brought into custody on 11 May 1821 as "5 feet 8 inches, dark complexion, grey hair, hazel eyes and stoutish made. Born St Marylebone, gentleman." (He was discharged when the House rose on 11 July.) His age was then recorded as forty-five, but at his death in August 1838 his widow reported his age as sixty-five. On this evidence he was born *circa* 1773–76.

Thereafter I discovered in the register of baptisms of the parish church of St Marylebone entries relating to the following children of Henry and Phillis Cooper:

born on: 9 Aug. 1766 William
         3 Feb. 1768 Elizabeth
        26 Nov. 1771 Henry
        20 Feb. 1774 Samuel Fox
         7 Sep. 1778 Harriet

It is quite possible that there were other children, before or after, but it seems a fair assertion that great-great-grandfather was born on 26 November 1771, and probably interpolated the name Fox at a later date: it may have sounded better in the world of journalism. As an alternative it is conceivable that Henry Cooper died young, and that Samuel Fox altered his name to Henry Fox, perhaps because the former may have sounded too crafty. But I can find no evidence to support this conjecture. Of the parents, Henry and Phillis, nothing further has come to light, but according to the rate-books of the parish of Marylebone there was a Henry Cooper living at 2 Little George Street (now Gosfield Street, W.1) in 1769–70. I cannot say definitely why the name Fox came to be given to one of their children.

My knowledge of H. F. Cooper is fragmentary. The first event is the publication of a book of poems in 1805, of which a copy is in the B.M. where there is also a third edition of 1811. The dedication of this volume, by permission to the Duchess of Manchester, evidently the fifth Duchess, offers some confirmation that the poems were written by the same H. F. Cooper, because children of the fourth Duke and Duchess were being baptized at the parish church of St Marylebone in the 1770's. It is quite probable that the Coopers were known to Their Graces, perhaps by reason of some contract for service. Manchester Square is within that parish.

The fifth Duchess of Manchester, who married the Duke in 1793, was Lady Susan Gordon, and she bore him two sons and five daughters. But the marriage was unhappy and a separation took place in 1805. The Duke subsequently became Governor of Jamaica, and the Duchess ran off with a footman in 1812. It would be interesting to know more about the reasons for the patronage of the poems.

Although the dedication is a courtly piece of prose, the poems are not outstanding: they clearly belong more to the eighteenth century than to the nineteenth, and they sing of love, and death, with a fair seasoning of moral sentiment and the pathetic fallacy. An extract from one which enjoys a greater latitude is quoted at the end of this prologue.

In the preface the author says his aim is to inculcate the divine precepts of Christianity, and to disseminate the godlike attributes of Charity, Benevolence and Humanity. He is also unfriendly to War, which he describes in lurid terms. It is a little curious that they were printed in Birmingham (by Knott & Lloyd) and I have thought that this pointed to some family association with that city in view of a subsequent event in 1824 which is mentioned hereafter. The City of Birmingham reference library has a copy of the 1805 edition of the poems, and the librarian (who kindly enquired into the matter) told me that the printer Lloyd was Robert Lloyd, younger brother of Charles Lloyd, the poet. The latter was a friend of Wordsworth, Coleridge and Lamb, and possibly acquainted with H. F. Cooper. But Knott & Lloyd were well-known printers with a wide range of publications in addition to poetry, so a family connexion in that city is not established by this particular fact.

According to an article written by H. F. Cooper in 1826, he was engaged on a newspaper in Macclesfield, Cheshire, in 1813–14. This might have been the *Macclesfield Courier*, founded in 1811, but confirmation is lacking.

On 4 August 1815 H. F. Cooper was arrested for debt, and detained in the Fleet Prison until the middle of December that year. In the register of the Insolvent Debtors' Court he is described as a translator of languages, and his incarceration arose from a sum of under £100 due to one John Henderson.

In January 1817 he started a Sunday paper entitled *The Legislator*, which survived until the end of March 1818. Unfortunately only the issues for the last three months have been preserved in the B.M. at Colindale: each was priced eightpence-ha'penny, duly impressed with a fourpenny stamp, and containing eight pages. The first article on the front page was headed *The Political Legislator*, and was mostly the focus of some worthy cause; the second was often a sketch of a theatrical character. The general tone of the journal was radical, and it stood for the rights of the working classes. There were short summaries of current events, and longer accounts of

B

proceedings in Parliament; some financial topics, police court news, theatrical brevities, and a sprinkling of advertisements. A glimpse of H. F. Cooper is afforded by the first issue for 1818, from which the following is extracted:

> In availing himself of the opportunity which the season of the year affords, the Editor of *The Legislator* presents his warmest acknowledgements to his Friends and Subscribers for their support. He assures them that he considers himself entitled to it; not from any abilities he has manifested in conducting the Literary Department of this Paper, but solely from his anxiety to advocate and elicit Truth, and his desire of maintaining those Principles of Independence, which are the offsprings of an Independent Mind, unconscious of party bearings and actuated by a desire to correct, as far as in him lies, the Evil Propensities in certain classes of Society. In this line he will unceasingly persevere, notwithstanding he has met with almost insurmountable obstacles, his endeavours being opposed by means, which, in less civilized States, would incur the charge of Tyranny; at least, they present Uncharitableness and a want of Fellow-feeling.

My opinion is that *The Legislator* was attempting a siege against the privileged classes without big enough guns, or a sufficient sense of humour. Although no indication of the end of the paper is given in the last issue, it is clear that it was unprofitable, since the proprietor was again in the Fleet Prison within two months of that journal's sudden end. The commitment book states that he surrendered himself in discharge of his bail at the suit of a gentleman named Thomas Hague to whom he owed a little over £100. His release by order of the Court for the relief of Insolvent Debtors took place five months later, in October 1818.

We next come to *John Bull* and certain well-documented events of 1821. That weekly paper was founded in December 1820 with the object of defaming the characters of all those socially connected in any way with Queen Caroline, or, put in other words, the extinction of the Brandenburgh House Party. Priced at sevenpence a copy, a large proportion of the eight pages was devoted to its political cause. It even listed the clergy who prayed for the Queen, and as an example of its satire may be quoted a leader protesting against her coronation, and making reference to the mother of William the Conqueror who had the honour of bequeathing her name to such a numerous sisterhood. Essentially a weapon of the Tories, *John Bull* claimed that the Whigs had provoked the chastisement, and history states that Theodore Hook* was the person chosen —or perhaps suggested by Sir Walter Scott—to run the paper, though his name was not to appear. H. F. Cooper has been described as the nominal editor: to occupy his leisure by correcting the proofs, and to act as a sort of legal lightning-conductor to the concern for a salary of three guineas a week. And thus it came about that he together with a young printer (Weaver) took the rap when the Whigs pressed home the advantage derived from a rather innocuous and inadvertent libel against Mr H. G. Bennett, M.P. in the edition dated 5 May 1821. Many references of a much more scurrilous nature seem to have been passed over, and it is safe to say that no journal of this character could possibly survive today.

So H. F. Cooper and Weaver were ordered to attend at the Bar of the House. The proceedings, in which Arrowsmith and Shackell (men associated with the proprietorship) were also examined, suggest that all four had something to hide; H. F. Cooper admitted that he wrote the paragraph containing the libel, which he obtained from general rumour, but now, finding it false, he regretted his action. Not one of them admitted the complicity of Hook even after bribery to the tune of £500. Andrews' *History of British Journalism* remarks that ". . . in this lay all the honour we fear we can award them. Cooper afterwards (in 1826) started a spurious paper called *Cooper's John Bull* but it proved a failure, and he died in embarrassed circumstances 21 August 1838."

It is of interest that the motion for committing H. F. Cooper to Newgate on 11 May was opposed by the Marquis of Londonderry, but it was carried by a majority of eighty-three. Weaver was committed similarly by a narrow majority of seven, only half the number of members voting. The House was evidently

---

* At this time Theodore Hook was subject to charges in connexion with a deficiency which arose when he was Treasurer of Mauritius. He was arrested out there in March 1818, and was not finally discharged until 1825, but he enjoyed much freedom in the intervening years.

becoming tired of the whole matter. Whether or not H. G. Bennett had any suspicion as to who was really the culprit, it is not possible to say, but it was he who six weeks later moved for an enquiry into the defaults of Theodore Hook in Mauritius.

The first leaders printed in self defence in the two following issues of *John Bull* are inscribed Newgate, 12 May and 19 May, 1821, respectively. There is no proof that they were written by H. F. Cooper, since at this stage Hook may well have taken the helm, and impudently put Newgate at the end of his articles. Incidentally, an advertisement in the issue of 19 May respectfully informs the public that owing to the imprisonment of Mr Cooper and Mr Weaver the publication of the *Journal of Literature* is unavoidably suspended. The first two numbers had appeared in the first half of May, but there is no evidence of any resumption.

This London literary journal is mentioned in Barham's *Life of Hook* as being instigated by him, but it was consistent with his subterfuge that he should imply that H. F. Cooper was the Editor, although the latter may have acted in some professional capacity. The two numbers preserved in the B.M. at Colindale show that it was intended to be a periodical of some literary pretension. There were sixteen pages at a cost of one shilling. Most of it was devoted to current literary reviews, with sections on the Theatre, and Fine Arts; the former suggest the authorship of someone at least as erudite as Theodore Hook.

A short political paragraph appeared in the second number in which it was stated that the only news of importance that week were the proceedings in the House of Commons in respect of a breach of privilege printed in *John Bull*, the details of which could be found in all the daily papers. Finally the back sheet announced that it was printed and published by Shackell & Arrowsmith from 11 Johnson's Court, Fleet Street, where communications to the editor were to be addressed.

The later history of *John Bull* shows that Arrowsmith, Shackell and Weaver were all fined on more than one occasion, and paid damages on another for a libel on the Queen. The basic defence was that the "facts" of the libel were common knowledge. H. F. Cooper was not involved in these legal proceedings, which *John Bull* reported in November 1821, on three occasions in 1822, and in subsequent years. This may well be to his credit, especially as he later claimed to have been the editor of *John Bull* from its inception until December 1825. It is also relevant that for the purpose of an action in the King's Bench in November 1821, Weaver put in an affidavit to the effect that the control of the paper rested with Mr Cooper, the editor, who alone had the power to adopt or reject any matter offered for insertion. But reading between the lines of the reports one obtains the impression that he was editor in the administrative or professional sense, and once bitten he properly declined to take any further responsibility for the anonymous adumbrations of the insidious Hook.

That the endeavours of *John Bull* were appreciated is evidenced by an extract from the *Croker Papers*, Vol. V, p. 246. "The King [George IV] ended by saying neither he nor his ministers nor his parliament nor his courts of justice all together had done so much good as *John Bull*. He then fell upon Judge Bayley for his sentence on the editors of this paper."

In spite of, or perhaps because of, prosecutions and rivalry, the success of *John Bull* continued after the death of the Queen, and Weaver upon sworn evidence gave the circulation as nearly ten thousand copies at the end of July 1821. About ten years later Theodore Hook, the malefactor, obtained £4,000 from the sale of a moiety of his share, but he continued to draw a salary until his death in 1841.

After leaving *John Bull* in December 1825, H. F. Cooper quickly brought out *Cooper's John Bull*, copies of which are nicely preserved at Colindale. It was first published on 1 January 1826 but survived for only twenty-three issues: each appeared on Sunday and Monday, the latter edition containing weekly stock prices but fewer advertisements. This courageous venture followed certain events in the last quarter of 1825 which H. F. Cooper described as dismissal from his post as editor, then reinstatement after an appeal to a person who must have been Hook.

Subsequently there was a "mutiny of the crew", and one of the marines did him a secret mischief. By the end of the year he was obliged to withdraw entirely. I cannot guess the nature of the secret mischief, but H. F. Cooper was obviously caught

between Hook and Shackell; he had little freedom of action as the latter would not publish anything with which the former might disagree. It may or may not be of significance that the publishing office of *John Bull* was removed in October 1825 from Johnson's Court to No. 40 Fleet Street.

Andrews' description of *Cooper's John Bull* as "spurious" is scarcely deserved because that newspaper made no claim to usurp the position of the original *John Bull*: in fact there had already been a Liberal competitor named the *Real John Bull*, and there was also a *John Bull's British Journal*. H. F. Cooper's effort was probably the best retort that could be made by an embittered man, but from the portions I have read it displayed no great originality. It was most loyal to the King, whose health was often the subject of a short first leader; it was Tory and anti-Catholic; and each issue contained some topical verses usually of a political character.

As with *John Bull* the price was sevenpence a copy. The last issue, however, featured a very intriguing leader in two parts, the first part having appeared the week before. Casting aside all editorial anonymity H. F. Cooper complained of his former treatment by *John Bull*, and made thinly-veiled but derogatory references to Theodore Hook. Also in this issue, Hook, described as a Putney gardener,* was castigated for allowing a young man who had abducted a girl from a boarding school to defend himself "by Hook and by Crook" in the columns of *John Bull*. In the second part of the leader H. F. Cooper averred that the reason for his dismissal had been that he was the depository [*sic*] of certain secrets; furthermore that *John Bull* on 1 January 1826 had claimed there had been no change in the editorship, which he had challenged, without response. The leader closed with a promise, or perhaps a threat, of unravelling a mystery in subsequent issues, depending upon a Mr Charles Benyon: but these were never to appear, and would-be readers were left to guess at the mystery. It is not impossible that *Cooper's John Bull* intended to announce the connexion between *John Bull* and Theodore Hook. As far as I can gather that fact did not become public property until sometime after 1830, although it was

---

* A reference to the fact that Hook had taken up residence in Putney after his final discharge from custody in May 1825. He lived in a comfortable house with a garden by the river, of which I have seen an illustration.

obviously known to quite a number, and suspected by many more.

H. F. Cooper's paper may thus have been suppressed by political action, or action by creditors may have made publication impossible. Although in its brief life the paper's advertisement duty came to £834, compared with £1,629 for *John Bull* for the whole of 1826, it must nevertheless have been a financial failure, because in November H. F. Cooper was in gaol for a trifling debt due to one Peter Fenn Bath, and his petition was heard in the Insolvent Debtors' Court on 20 December 1826. Described as a journalist formerly of Prince's Street, Lambeth, and later of Rockingham Row, Kent Road, he was discharged forthwith.

In the memorial (already mentioned) by E. L. Blanchard about Frederick Fox Cooper it is stated that his father, "editor at one time of the *John Bull*" had started a publication in Birmingham called the *Theatrical John Bull*: this seemed feasible to me in view of the printing of his poems in that city. I therefore examined the bound volume in the British Museum which shows that the *Theatrical John Bull* had a short life of only twenty-one issues between May and October 1824. I could, however, find no internal clue to the editorship of the journal, although the style has something of the vituperation of *John Bull* itself. It is also curious that it was printed for and published by a W. Cooper of Union Street, Birmingham, who, according to the City Librarian of Birmingham, was a highly respected news and advertising agent. An interesting pamphlet by the Dugdale Society entitled *Press and Public in Early Nineteenth-Century Birmingham*, when there was a spate of theatrical literature, contains references to the *Theatrical John Bull* one of which indicates that this was the first editorial venture of Joseph Allday, later editor of *Argus*. I suppose this may be true, and, without further research, I am inclined to think that the long arm of coincidence stretched forth with two hands from London to as far as Birmingham, and that E. L. Blanchard may have made a pardonable error in attributing the publication to H. F. Cooper. It would have been difficult to combine it with the editorship of *John Bull*.

I have little more to add about H. F. Cooper. Aside from the possibility of some connexion with Birmingham and Macclesfield, his world seems to have been London. There is evidence

that in 1806 he lived in Delahay Street, Westminster, which
ran North from near Storey's Gate, and the house must have
overlooked St James's Park. During the *John Bull* enquiry
in 1821, he was not asked where he resided, but another witness
said that he lived "somewhere in the neighbourhood of Blackfriars". According to the opponents of that journal this helped
to thicken the plot. It was also suggested that he was associated
with a notorious firm of doctors, who practised in Blackfriars.
This may also be true since *The Legislator* had carried advertisements by the firm of Cooper & Co., surgeons of thirty years'
experience, who specialized in the treatment of rupture.

H. F. Cooper died from dropsy on 21 August 1838 at
Shaftesbury Place, Aldersgate Street, in the parish of St
Botolph, the informant being his widow, Harriett. The *Gentlemen's Magazine* for October states that he was in his sixty-fifth
year, with the brief comment "for many years connected with
the London Press, and formerly editor of *John Bull*". His will
is not on record at Somerset House, and he was evidently a
poor man, but there is no obvious confirmation of embarrassed
circumstances.

One of the family notes in my possession states that H. F.
Cooper had six children. Apart from Frederick Fox, there was
an elder son, Henry, born in 1805, and a younger son, Foster,
who is supposed to have emigrated to Australia as editor of the
Melbourne Argus. This latter I have been unable to confirm,
but Henry (Henry Octavius William) will be mentioned
occasionally. Additionally, there were three daughters,
including one named Becky who married "into the Reverend
Newton family". There is clearly scope for more research on
these traces of information, but as the events took place before
the date from which central records commence, and in the
absence of definite knowledge of residence in a particular
place at a particular time, it is a matter of luck whether
anything of interest is found.

With nothing but the above facts and conjectures about
H. F. Cooper what can one say about the man himself? He
seems to have been essentially a writer with a leaning towards
verse; his prose style is often elaborate and complicated,
according to the fashion of the day. Unlike that of his son,
Frederick Fox, his composition lacked humour. If, as he claimed

he was the editor of *John Bull* for five years, or even if in fact
only a deputy, he cannot have found much distaste in the
writing or editing of bitter criticisms about comparatively
innocent people. Yet it must be allowed in his favour that *The
Legislator* was based on sound progressive principles, and
Cooper's John Bull was relatively inoffensive (except perhaps
when attacking *John Bull*). In some lack of flair, or warmth
of feeling, may lie the reason for these failures, and in his
resulting impoverishment. It must also be borne in mind as
regards *John Bull* that if he had six children growing up in the
early 1820's the attraction of a regular part-time salary of
three guineas a week may have been almost irresistible, despite
the editor's brief. England could not be described as a Welfare
State in the reign of George IV.

Before giving an extract from H. F. Cooper's poem "The
Victim of Slavery", (1805), the following passages from
Trevelyan's *History of England* are worth recalling:

During the Napoleonic war Britain's lead over the rest of
Europe in colonization and trade was immensely
increased. . . .

Britain held, therefore, at this critical juncture, the
destiny of the coloured races very largely in her own hand . . .

It was a turning point in the history of the world when
William Wilberforce and his friends succeeded in arousing
the conscience of the British people to stop the slave trade
in 1809, and to abolish slavery in the Empire in 1833, just
before the development of the interior of Africa by the
European races began.

The poem ends with these lines:

Then why tyrannic dart among that race,
Whose only crime is being black in face,
And drag them forth like beasts to toil the day,
And slave and wear a dreadful life away?
But 'tis not freedom can our hands restrain,
When avarice points at *any* road to gain;
No matter whether wading seas of blood,
Or plundering nations, so 'tis understood
That "laws of nations" bid the merchants sail,
Waft cargos rich in human traffic's gale;
And yet these merchants, in a christian land,
Wage the rude traffic with a sov'reign hand,

And worship GOD in *name*, but not in *deed*,
For what's religion, unless truth's the creed?
When that divine precept is set to view,
To "DO AS YOU WOULD BE DONE UNTO,"
Is thrown aside, and avarice brings the train
Of murder, rapine, plunder, and false gain,
It matters little what the creed may be,
For this is certain—'tis not SINCERITY,
And heav'n offended, sure will mark the man,
Who makes religion but a worldly plan
To fill his coffers from fair freedom's shore;
On such a man his timely vengeance pour.
Oh! then beware, this dreadful trade forego,
Which leads to gain, but ah! it leads to woe;
Let not the gentler virtues sink and die,
Virtues which take their only source from high;
But through the earth let it recorded be,
THAT AFRIC'S SONS BY BRITONS ARE MADE FREE.

Somehow, I don't think that the author would be ashamed
of those thoughts today.

Chapter 1

Early History to 1830

MY great-grandfather, Frederick Fox Cooper, was born on 4 January 1806, at Delahay Street, Westminster, according to a note in the handwriting of Uncle Harwood. The day of the year is frequently marked in the almanacks of my grandfather, and the date appears in the *Theatrical Times* of 12 June 1847. Unfortunately, I have failed to find a record of the baptism of Fox Cooper, as he came to be known, at St Margaret's, Westminster, where it might be expected, or in the registers of St John's, Westminster, or of St Giles', Camberwell, in which parish the family were subsequently living; unsuccessful also has been my scrutiny of the registers of other churches in Lambeth and Southwark. This lack of corroboration, while somewhat frustrating, is of no great consequence to the story of his life.

Of his childhood I have no knowledge, but as the son of a journalist his home background may have seemed precarious and insecure; nor can it have been improved by the occasional imprisonment of his father, as already related. I wish I knew something about his education and who taught him to write with fluency: perhaps his father. The *Theatrical Times* provides a few early glimpses, no doubt prompted by Fox Cooper himself; and I have tabulated them for the purpose of examination:

   (*a*) He received his second name after his godfather, the celebrated Charles James Fox, who with Richard

Brinsley Sheridan was the intimate friend of his uncle, Sir Edward Cooper, the antiquarian.

(b) He was intended for the Stock Exchange, and was accordingly articled to a relation, Isaac Cooper, a stock-broker, who died worth a million.

(c) Marrying at the early age of sixteen, he quarrelled with his friends, and left the omnium and scrip world to enter boldly into the arena of dramatic literature.

As the above statements have evidently been accepted partly or wholly by writers of much later date, and by his own son,* it is worthwhile looking at them in greater detail.

(a) Charles James Fox who died in September, 1806, could have been Fox Cooper's godfather, but, as related in the Prologue, his own father was already using the name Fox, witness the volume of poems published in 1805 and dedicated to the Fifth Duchess of Manchester. Now, Charles James Fox had appointed the Duke of Manchester to the Embassy in Paris in 1783, and might even have been acquainted with the Cooper family, but it is difficult to support the claim that Frederick Fox Cooper received his second name from the statesman. There is also the difficulty the H. F. Cooper was a Tory journalist. Additionally I have had the Parish Register of St Peter's Church, Chertsey, searched to ascertain if Fox Cooper had been carried to his alleged godfather's parish for baptism, but this was evidently not the case.

Sir Edward Cooper eludes me, although the *D.N.B.* gives an Edward Joshua Cooper (1798–1863) Astronomer, and William Durrant Cooper (1812–75) Antiquary. Neither of these appears to be related to Fox Cooper, and their dates of birth are rather too late to support the relationship of uncle.

(b) Isaac Cooper (1760–1825) was indeed a wealthy stock-broker, and he left about £120,000; a missing nought would mean little to Fox Cooper, to whom a million pounds was a no more fantastic fortune. I have made a good deal of enquiry into Isaac Cooper's family, because my grandfather was evidently convinced that there was a relationship, but proof I

---

* Obituary notices of Fox Cooper—various. E. L. Blanchard, *Glasgow News*, 16 January 1879. Frederick Boase, *Modern English Biography*, 1892. Malcolm Morley, *The Dickensian*, March, 1954. Frederick Harwood Cooper (son)—by implication in his almanack notes—1861 *et seq.*

have none (see Chapter 11). There is no reason to doubt that Fox Cooper may have been in Isaac Cooper's office, and it is possible that the identity of surnames was a coincidence; Cooper was by no means an uncommon name, as can be seen from the Post Office and other directories of the early nineteenth century. It may also be relevant that Fox Cooper's elder brother, Henry Octavius William, was at one time a stockbroker in London, although not a member of the London Stock Exchange (see Chapter 8).

(*c*) I have examined (at County Hall, Westminster) the original entry in the register relating to the marriage of Fox Cooper to Ann Foxall at St Giles', Camberwell on 9 August 1823. Accepting the date of his birth as 4 January 1806, he was thus seventeen years and seven months old. The witnesses were A. Fowler and W. Haywood, the latter probably the verger as his name frequently appears in the register as a witness; so there may have been at least a family quarrel, although it is a tradition that Fox Cooper borrowed a pair of his brother's breeches to be married in. His entry into the "arena of dramatic literature" was as early as June 1821, as a critic, and his work as a dramatic author first saw the light in 1827. But his theatrical baptism was possibly at the Adelphi Theatre as an occasional actor.

The rest of the potted biography from the *Theatrical Times* dealing with the stage, and Fox Cooper's other pursuits, will be referred to where appropriate, but it is clear from the above comments that while it has been to me a most valuable signpost, it is not free from error or exaggeration. Even then, as now, the printed word may be as suspect as the spoken one.

Much of what I have to write about my great-grandfather will involve a chronological statement of events, such as theatrical productions, newspaper and dramatic publications, and legal proceedings, elaborated by press comments and reviews. Often there will be intervals of time in respect of which I have been unable to trace any particular event. But I shall hope that from the enumeration of such facts as I have been able to ascertain, adorned here and there by comments (including my own), there may emerge the portrait of a man whom I have come to regard as the most colourful and fascinating personality that the family produced in the last century.

In the character of Fox Cooper it will appear not infrequently that there is more to condemn than to praise. The record of his public life leaves much to be desired, but this does not dissuade me from my purpose. The evil that men do lives after them, the good is oft interred with their bones; so may it be with Fox Cooper.

A memorandum by one of my uncles headed "Place of birth", probably copied from some lost notes of my grandfather, indicates that Ann Cooper (*née* Foxall) was born in Brecon on 2 December 1805: so that both Frederick Fox and his wife were under eighteen years old at their marriage. In the register the signature of the husband is very sloping and immature, but firm; it developed a lot in later years as can be seen from the Hughenden letter (following page 184). The signature of Ann is small and poor, with no character and almost a suggestion of illiteracy. Family tradition says that Ann was the daughter of a veterinary surgeon who married a sister of Alderman Garratt, tea merchant and one time Lord Mayor of London. Despite this she could not have been taught to write her name without an effort.

The first child of the marriage of Fox Cooper and Ann is reputed to have been a son who died in 1832—probably in the cholera epidemic of that year—and was buried in the cemetery in Blackfriars Road. This would no doubt have been the cemetery of Christchurch which largely disappeared in the Second World War, and the registers of which (partly damaged) are now at County Hall. But I have not found a record of the burial of any young Cooper who might have been a member of the family. The next child was my grandfather, born on 24 November 1826, and christened Frederick Harwood at St Mary's, Lambeth, where I have seen the record. The parents were then living in Mount Gardens, Lambeth, a street near the church, but not in existence today. For many years of my life I could see the church of St Mary from my office window; but at that time I knew none of these things.

It is tempting to conjecture that Fox Cooper may have obtained early experience as a writer between 1821 and 1825 by assisting his father in the editorship (or deputy editorship) of *John Bull*, at any rate when he was not working as a parliamentary reporter or in a stockbroker's office. It partly depends upon his statement about quarrelling with his friends—did this include his father? Stockbroking can have held little attraction for him despite the promise of financial reward. I do not believe he was concerned with the accumulation of money, although he often experienced the want of it; I think that he was a born writer, with some facility of expression, if lacking originality, who became attracted above all things by the stage and its environment. Journalism, as will be seen, ran it a good second.

A monthly publication, *Drama, or the Theatrical Pocket Magazine* made its bow in May 1821, and in the second number was found my earliest trace of the imprint of Fox Cooper's pen. Among answers to correspondents, one of whom might still have been a schoolboy: "Some of F. F. Cooper's 'Pleasures' shall have insertion, he had better send us a few more, as *we* can then make our choice of the best." In the sixth number (October) under the same heading, F. F. Cooper was thanked for his packet. "He will observe that in the list below of the catalogue he has sent us the principal articles that strike our eye are: Ancient Researches, Theatrical Anecdotes not commonly known, and Epigrams." Doubtless as a result of the young author's impetuosity, he was requested to exercise patience; but in a list of articles for publication in the near future was "Dramatic Inspector" No. 1, by F. F. Cooper. This was printed in the November issue, followed by Nos. 2, 3 and 4, in January, February, and May 1822.

Tragic Actors was the title of the first, which in fulsome language sought to correct the impression that actors do not suffer for such outward distortions necessary to portray violence, torture, grief, or madness. Quoting from *Curiosities of Literature* (by Isaac Disraeli) Montfleury was given as an example. This French comedian [*sic*] had died of the violent effects of representing Orestes in the *Andromache* of Racine. Again, the actor Bond was playing Lusignan in *Zara*, and when Zara turned to address the old man she saw him dead in the chair. Changing the subject, Baron, described as the French Garrick and an actor seen but once in a thousand years, was cited as saying that the rules of acting should be broken if passion so willed: passion knows more than art. A good article if a trifle overlaid with literary allusion.

The second diatribe, *Theatrical Quackery*, was directed against extravagant claims by theatre managers, or puffing in playbills. Fox Cooper could well have been reminded of this effusion in after years when managing the City of London and Strand theatres.

Critics were the subject of the third "Dramatic Inspector". "We have been so long biased by the mercenary writings of those who pretend to give just criticism, that for the sake of the public and the theatrical part of the community it is high time to unveil the face of these writers, and to explore the fruit of their contemptible labours." Examples of their shortcomings were: totally divided opinions on new productions, simple mistakes in the naming of players, and the description of new-comers in exaggerated terms such as *Adonis* or *Venus*. A tendency to favour foreign actors was also attacked. Quite a convincing effort.

In the next two issues of *Drama*, F. F. Cooper appears only in the answers to correspondents. Here we find an early sign of his contentious disposition. He was informed in March that it was impossible to grant his request as even the earliest contributors had never asked such a favour, and the profits on the publication were too limited to allow it. With some knowledge of the habits of my great-grandsire, I thought he had asked for a cash advance on his accepted work, but the precise nature of the demand came to light in April. Following some undisclosed correspondence Mr Cooper was now re-minded of his original letter from which an extract was given: "Having proceeded to No. 4 of the Inspector I think it but fair to request the favour of a volume of the *Drama*, and as long as I continue to contribute I shall expect at the end of the half year to have one at least sent to me." Enterprising, to say the least.

The last of the four articles was entitled *Authors*, and inscribed March 1822, two months before the date of publication. Learn-ing has now given way to emotion. From the general tone it is not unlikely that Fox Cooper had already experienced the despair of the rejected author, perhaps at the hands of Drury Lane, a theatre mentioned in the argument. In his view authors received a poor deal: "Of all the miseries of human life, authorship is the worst. If a man should wish to spend a life void of perplexity he should apprentice himself to a knife-grinder or a bellows-mender." At the age of sixteen this antici-pation of his future profession was only too prophetic.

Later volumes of *Drama* contain no articles signed by Fox Cooper. His attitude was scarcely endearing to the editor who may have discovered his age, and thought him a trifle precocious. It is probable that his efforts at dramatic criticism continued, but evidence is lacking. At this point therefore, we can conveniently enter the theatrical world itself with two plays in 1827. On the general subject of Fox Cooper's plays my starting point was a list in the writing of his son, known simply as Harwood Cooper: this contains fifty-nine titles, thirteen of which are undated and untraced. From external sources I have added eighteen, making seventy-seven in all, the complete list of which appears as Appendix II. There may well have been many others. As an example, the *Dover Chronicle* in January 1842 refers to a piece called *The Play's the Thing*, in active rehearsal and written for Dover by the lessee of the theatre, then Fox Cooper; but I have no evidence of its nature or production. For nearly fifty of the established works the first, or in a few cases a later, performance is recorded. It is remarkable that of the eighteen plays omitted from Har-wood Cooper's list three of them were printed in Dicks' edition of *Standard Plays*, of which he was the editor from late in 1881 until 1889, covering about 700 out of 1,074 numbers contained in this series.* It is stranger still that there are elements of mystery about each of these three plays, which are described in Chapter 11.

The first dramatic piece in 1827, was an interlude called *Sons of Thespis*, claimed by the author to have been performed at the Surrey Theatre, and to have introduced J. B. Buckstone to the stage. But the latter, a prolific playwright and well-known theatrical manager, had already written two plays in 1825. Moreover, it is on record that Buckstone had performed as an actor at the Peckham Theatre in or about 1821. *Sons of*

---

* This is according to the B.M. index, but an article in *The Library* in 1936 refers to a wrapper of one of Dicks' plays stating that over 1,400 were then ready; the explanation may be that some numbers contained two plays. Described as the free acting drama for the representation of which there is no legal charge, it mainly comprised re-issues of the classics and other plays that had been printed before.

Thespis is not included in the catalogue of plays prepared by Allardyce Nicoll, nor can I find any other evidence of its performance; but shortly after the death of Fox Cooper, his son, Harwood, sold the manuscript of a play by this name for a small sum to a publisher named Brett.

The second was a "burlesque Extravaganza" entitled *The Elbow-Shakers, or Thirty Years of a Rattler's Life*, in one act with seven scenes, produced at the Adelphi Theatre on 3 December 1827. Elbow-shakers played with dice and the origin of this parody was a melancholy melodrama, *Thirty years of a Gambler's Life*, adapted from the French of Victor Ducange, and previously performed at that theatre. In the cast as the gamblers were the well-known actors Reeve and Yates, and a press review (cutting preserved by Harwood Cooper) was highly complimentary to the author for the tact he had displayed both in parodying the language of the original and in the popular songs he had introduced. "This type of entertainment, if it be not too low or indecent, has a prescriptive freedom from criticism: that produced last night was as good as most pieces of this sort." But the *Theatrical Observer* said that though the idea was not a bad one, the execution was defective. It was not clever enough to revive the declining taste for low vulgarity. The *Literary Gazette*, in condescending to notice a play at the Adelphi Theatre, expressed the hope that the proprietors would never again suffer their stage to be polluted by such a compound of dullness and vulgarity.

Davenport Adams in a *Book of Burlesque* describes Fox Cooper as "a new votary of travestie, coming after Planché whose burlesques were quiet after his *Amoroso* in 1818, until 1831." He also remarks that there was a surfeit of plays on the gambler's fate, and the *Elbow-Shakers* in which Fox Cooper made fun of them, was scarcely needed to effect their overthrow. In his opinion the piece had little merit. The reviewer for Richardson who printed it in 1828 said that the French originals of plays which were produced on the English stage were often too painfully exciting for our feelings. In the present case some of the parodies had to be omitted, and others curtailed owing to the length of the performance: for the first eighteen nights the curtain never rose until after eleven o'clock. Some of the speeches took Shakespearean forms, thus: "To elbow-shake, or not to elbow-shake." It was all good fun, but the play was not reprinted in Dicks' or any other edition, possibly because the French original disappeared from notice, leaving no *raison d'être* for the burlesque.

A playbill preserved in the Enthoven Collection shows a Mr Cooper taking the part of Sparerib in the production, and there is some reason to suggest that this was Fox Cooper himself. I have traced the appearance of a Cooper occasionally in Adelphi programmes right back to October 1821: in January 1822, as "Little Jimmy" in *Tom and Jerry*, in 1825 "Master" Cooper in *Life of an Actor*, and so on to 1827. (The renowned John Cooper was usually at one of the major theatres during this period.) On this evidence the dramatic life of Fox Cooper might have started on the boards at the age of fifteen; but it could not have formed a complete occupation, and some of his time may have been spent in training as a parliamentary reporter or shorthand-writer, both of which callings he was later to claim.

In November 1829 there appeared at the Olympic Theatre another burlesque by Fox Cooper entitled *Black-eyed Sukey, or All in the Dumps*, in one act with eight scenes. This was a parody on the play *Black-eyed Susan, or All in the Downs*, by D. W. Jerrold, which had run for 150 nights at the Surrey Theatre in the same year. A.N. in a section on Burlesque says that the former (i.e. the parody) makes absurdity of the latter, but adds that, in general, these "topical pieces have no real intrinsic value and are usually very vulgar artistically and very dull." The play deals at a low level of society with insolvency, prisons, and the effect of a new act (thanks to Mr Hume) which was to render debtors less liable to arrest at the suit of their creditors. One scene is set in the King's Bench Prison, the object of which (according to a paradoxical comment) was to show what places of jollity our prisons were, and what cruel privations poor debtors received from their hard-hearted creditors.

The husband of the principal character was in gaol, his death was rumoured; there was an amorous tax-collector, and an uxorious muffin-man concealed in a cupboard. However, a contemporary critic stated in far from perfect English that "it requires all the tact of a skilful artist to make a piece which professes to be a satire upon the talents of a brother author take." He went on to add that the parodist in the present case had not given a sufficient loose to his genius, and might have produced a better thing, but for the fact that with one exception all the characters in the original were mere deadweights. The piece included "a great number of extravagant airs to favourite tunes", and it was evidently considered a successful effort by a dramatist of twenty-three.

Black-eyed Sukey was printed both by Richardson and Cumberland. Richardson's preface says that the author has selected scenes and characters not susceptible to parody, that he simply takes the social stratum one stage lower, without sufficient contrast. It adds, possibly in mitigation, that it was evidently composed in haste. Cumberland's more favourable view is that the piece is neither a parody nor a burlesque on Gay's immortal ballad. "Black-eyed Sukey owed her significant sobriquet to a blow inflicted on her sinister peeper, which put it in mourning, by one Timothy Tiphill, a recreant and tragic sailor." In my opinion the course of the play is lugubrious and fitful, and the humour is somehow gruesome, but all ends well with brimming potations of blue-ruin and black strap, meaning sweet port and gin, respectively. I think also that this piece shows the beginnings of Fox Cooper's natural feeling for the unfortunate. His later sympathy for the persecuted sprang from his own experience.

The next enterprise I can date with certainty is the publication of a Sunday newspaper in 1830 with the arch title: *Paul Pry*, which had been used by three dramatists in the years 1825–7. A contemporary advertisement (headed "I hope I don't intrude") states that it had created an unprecedented sensation, and that the Proprietor would spare no expense to make it the first Sunday Newspaper in the world. The bound volume in the British Museum at Colindale lacks the first number, but the second is dated 28 February 1830. It was printed and published by Fox Cooper from 13 Wellington Street, Strand. Claiming to possess political spirit, humour, wit, fun, and eccentricity, it combined a radical outlook, with a Tory flavour. On the whole it was of general all round interest, with a tendency to be flippant, but although a high moral tone was another of the claims, broadminded readers were treated to details of divorce court proceedings. I expect that Fox Cooper would aver that a little seasoning of spice was necessary to spread the message of the radicals to the public who stood by their King and Country. A typical issue contained eight pages devoted to:

Advertisements; general items.
Gazette and Parliament; Courts of law, accidents, etc.
Pryism (a gossip column); more advertisements.
Correspondence, and Leaders.
Poetry; theatricals.
Lettres de Paris; foreign correspondence.
Literary; more advertisements.
Latest news; the funds; still more advertisements.

As the stamp duty on newspapers* was fourpence a copy, and other taxes came to three-halfpence, it is not surprising that the paper was priced at sevenpence. To us this may seem to have been an expensive luxury at a time when eggs were less than one penny each, and beef was fivepence a pound, but one copy probably passed through many hands for a diminishing consideration.

The seventh and eighth issues contain articles defending the moral character of the Duke of Cumberland, whose valet, after an attack upon the Duke, had committed suicide under somewhat unsavoury circumstances. The ninth issue, dated 18 April 1830, has an interesting account of the laying of the foundation stone of Hampton New Church. This was performed by the Duke of Clarence, with whom were Prince George of Cumberland, the Duchess of Clarence, and others. After the ceremony the general company (excluding the royalty) repaired for dinner at the Lion Inn, and the chair was taken by a Reverend Mr Merewether, Chaplain to the Duchess, supported by the Dean of Carlisle and a Mr Lapidge, perhaps the local parson.

When the loyal toasts had been drunk, the Chairman proposed the success of the *Paul Pry* newspaper, the original proprietor of which excellent and talented print he was happy to observe seated near him. The toast was received and drunk with cheers, but a Mr Guy thought it was somewhat unfair

* Broadly speaking, a newspaper was one which contained any remarks or observations upon public news, intelligence, or occurrences, and was published weekly or oftener. *Paul Pry* would come within the definition, but some of the copies I examined were not stamped.

to single out one newspaper, especially on the part of a minister of the church, whose duties were confined to another place. (Cries of Hear, with hisses.) Fox Cooper said in returning thanks, though not to the last speaker, that he would never omit to cherish a decided feeling in the columns of *Paul Pry* in support of the Established Church in such a spirit of religious uniformity as should render it no disgrace to its highest dignitaries to express their approbation, etc. . . . (loud cheers from the Chair, and from other clerical gentlemen).

Another speaker praised *Paul Pry* for rejecting a masterly satire because it contained obscene and immoral passages, and made reference to the graceful condescension that day of the heir apparent to the throne of Great Britain (i.e. in laying the foundation stone of the church) to which every inhabitant of Hampton would hereafter direct the attention of his rising offspring. The account ends thus: "After the health of Mr Lapidge, and the ladies of Hampton, the evening was concluded with many toasts, and much hilarity." This shows Fox Cooper with the capacity to shine in quite unexpected company, and one may surmise that he was already known to Ernest, Duke of Cumberland, to whom he became secretary in 1833–35 during a critical period of the Orange Lodge activities.

A few other items from *Paul Pry* are of interest to this story. The treatment of H. F. Cooper by Theodore Hook is reflected in two references which suggest that either the former guided his son in the editorship of *Paul Pry,* or the son took up the cudgels on behalf of his father. Thus, on 9 May a play by Theodore Hook (described as late editor of a Sunday paper) entitled *A Joke's a Joke,* was stigmatized as a farrago of nonsense. And on 16 May a peep at Government defaulters—taken from the finance accounts of the U.K. for the year ended 5 January 1830—contained the name of Theodore Hook, Treasurer of Mauritius, opposite the amount of £12,885.*

Paul Pry attacked the Jewish Emancipation Bill in May,

---

* When Theodore Hook died in 1841 the whole of his effects were seized by the Treasury, and sold in liquidation of the Mauritius debt. Hook is stated to have left a widow and *five* children, for whose benefit his friends raised a fund of nearly £3,000. Towards this sum the Duke of Cumberland, by then King of Hanover, gave £500. From another source it is learned that Hook had not the courage to marry the mother of his *six* children. She could scarcely claim the title of "widow".

and printed an account of the trial in France of a priest for attempted murder, described as a real specimen of Roman Catholic villainy. The union of the Whigs to oppose the Wellington administration was welcomed, although the journal was favourable to the "honest and patriotic Tories of the Old School. But in the circumstances it was better to shake hands with an honest Whig than to breathe pollution in an atmosphere infected by the turn-coat Tories." On another occasion an editorial said "we have quite enough sins of our own to answer for without being bothered by the misdeeds of others", and proceeded to lay the blame for certain typographical errors on the printers. This is somewhat refreshing as Fox Cooper was editor, printer and publisher. Hereabouts was a reference to the death in the Fleet Prison of one Matthew Wasbrough who started more newspapers than anyone they knew. The word "started" suggests that he had some affinity with Fox Cooper who so often, as will be seen, launched into ventures which were short-lived. *Paul Pry* remarked that if there were no newspapers in the next world poor Matthew would be at some loss for employment.

As was the custom in *Cooper's John Bull*, the health of the King (George IV) often featured in a short leading article, and the paper went into mourning for four numbers after his death in June. The lengthy reports about the late monarch were entirely objective and I could find no comment of any political character, but some of the advertisements were revealing: thus, Mr Newton begged respectfully to inform the nobility and gentry that during the last months he had laid in an unusually large stock of mourning, which he pledged to sell on the usual terms. Subsequently, on 22 August 1830, every purchaser of the paper was entitled to a splendid medal representing an admirable likeness of Their Most Gracious Majesties, William and Adelaide. I wonder if one of these is in existence today?

At the end of September, after thirty issues, the paper was purchased by a Mr George Cowie, who in March 1831 incorporated it with another journal, the *Intelligence*. Perhaps *Paul Pry* had seen enough.

Chapter 2

Progress, and Reverses, in the Early 1830's

I DO not know why Fox Cooper sold *Paul Pry* in September 1830, but from certain events to be related it seems that it was not very profitable. Within three months, he was in Paris, and the rest of the family followed early in 1831.* It is not unlikely that the object of this adventurous visit was to produce a play, or to obtain theatrical experience and contacts: a course that would be quite natural for a young dramatist. Colour is added to this event by the inclusion in Harwood Cooper's list of his father's plays of the title *Fiend of Many Shapes*, with word "Paris". In that gay city, however, the Cooper family did not stay very long. Later in 1831 they lived for a period in Caernarvon, North Wales, where there was a small but neat theatre.

By 21 November 1831, Fox Cooper was no doubt in London for the production of *Loves of the Lions* at Sadler's Wells. This was an operatic burlesque of Bunn's Oriental Spectacle, *Hyder Ali, or the Lions of Mysore*, produced at Drury Lane in October, in which the principal actors were described as inhabitants of the menagerie in Paris. Buckstone had burlesqued it at the Adelphi a week later. Animal-mania was raging, but the *Literary Guardian* said that after the Adelphi production, the

---

* No easy journey for a wife with two young children. A coach trip down the Dover road. Waiting at Dover for weather, tide, and sufficient passengers. A row-boat out to the cutter, possibly a steam mailboat, or a slower packet conveying cargo if cash were short. Coaches from Calais to Paris.

Loves of the Lions could not claim to much novelty. "However, Islington and the Strand are far enough apart to allow it to go down as good as new." According to the *Sunday Times* the audience at Sadler's Wells was convulsed with laughter; this was evidently too much, and after a week the cause of the convulsions came to an untimely end.

Within a fortnight Fox Cooper was no longer a free agent, as he was arrested for debt: the first (or at least the first I have discovered) of a series of imprisonments for insolvency. The Committment Book for the Fleet Prison, preserved in the Public Record Office, reads as follows:

No. 27442. F. F. Cooper on 19 Jan 1832 was committed for want of bail by Hon. Mr Baron Garrow upon a writ of Habeas Corpus directed to the Sheriff of Middlesex, and by the return it appears that on 8 Dec 1831 F. F. Cooper in the said writ named was taken by the said Sheriff and under his custody detained by virtue of a writ of *Capias** returnable before the Barons of the King's Exchequer at Westminster on Wednesday 11 Jan next to answer the King touching certain articles wherein he is Impleaded by an information lately exhibited against him before the King's said Barons by the King's Attorney-General for the recovery of the sum of £256. 4. 0. mentioned in the said information.
Bail £256.4.0.　　　　　　　　Davis.　Clerk in Court

A note at the side of the above entry reads: "Discharged by warrant of Solicitor of Stamps. 8 June 1832."

Despite the elegance of this composition, which Fox Cooper may or may not have read, a sentence of six months in the Fleet must have been an unpleasant experience, as well as a professional calamity. I do not think his family were actually resident, as was often the case, in that institution, where in 1776 there were 243 prisoners with wives and children numbering 475: over 700 souls in all. Since the year 1824 prisoners had been allowed to lodge within a certain radius of the prison, and a random note by Harwood Cooper suggests that his father may have stayed in Surrey Street, Strand, while the family spent Christmas 1831 and Easter 1832 at Union Row, Kent

---

* The discharge warrant shows this was a writ of *Capias ad respondendum*: to enforce attendance at Court.

Road.* Stage folk look forward to Christmas for employment as well as festivity; that in 1831 was one to forget. Unfortunately no record remains of the information exhibited against Fox Cooper, and in the absence of corroboration it seems a fair conclusion that the Attorney-General caught up with him for using unstamped paper in the publication of *Paul Pry*. As the duty was such a savage impost it was properly resented by the writing community, and by all who favoured the free expression of opinion. There were many prosecutions before its reduction in 1836, and eventual abolition in 1855.

In addition to the possibility that Fox Cooper had by now become a theatrical manager, about which the dates are somewhat uncertain on the available evidence, it is clear that after 1830 he began to devote more time to writing for the stage. In 1833 four plays were produced.

The first of these, because it was completed by 1828, was a farce: *The Spare Bed, or The Shower Bath*, a contrivance that must have been a novelty in the Georgian era. It is not clear, however, that the shower bath was actually seen by the audience: one of the characters shrieks "murder", struggles with an adversary and, according to stage directions "runs into the shower-bath, pulls the string, which he takes for a bell, and the water rushes upon him". Later he enters from the bath "half drowned". This play was submitted to and, after some initial encouragement followed by much delay, rejected by the management of Drury Lane, which occasioned a letter from Fox Cooper to *The Times* in June 1828, in which he complained of his treatment by a Mr Price.

It is a well-written piece of pleading which occupies nine inches of the closely printed column and concludes with these words: "I respectfully request to know . . . what remedy I have for the loss of time incurred in obeying the mandate of, and in dancing attendance upon, this paragon of American politeness." This paragon was Stephen Price who had come from the Park Theatre, New York, to be the lessee of Drury Lane at a rent of £10,000 a year. He has been described

---

* For the above privilege the prisoner would have provided a surety for keeping within the boundaries, and paid a percentage on the amount of the debt for which he was detained. This also enabled him to transact his affairs during the day.

elsewhere as a boastful, uneducated man, unpopular with his own countrymen, and with no knowledge of dramatic literature. Macready, who met him in New York in 1826, said he was not a gentleman, and on reading of his death committed himself in his diary thus: "He is gone—unpitied, unlamented; he had no friend."

The Spare Bed was subsequently described as one of the wittiest and most amusing original productions that had been seen for a long period upon its presentation on 8 July 1833 at the Victoria Theatre, the predecessor of what became the "Old Vic".* But within a fortnight, as luck would have it, there was an accident on the stage due to the explosion of a property pistol which had been thrice charged. In a letter to the press the Actor (Wm. Besson Wood) who had held the pistol said in his own justification that there must have been "scandalous neglect" on the part of those responsible; it would have been more understandable if he had accused them of being over-zealous. A further piece of publicity resulted from the dramatic critic of the *Morning Chronicle* confusing this play with another entitled *Damp Beds* by Thomas Parry (1832). In a letter to that newspaper Fox Cooper pointed out the error, adding that he was anxious to prevent the sheets from being considered damp; they had met with a warm reception from the public for many nights, and as he made his own bed, so he wished to lie on it.

The action of the play takes place at Brighton. Dorval, a retired and eccentric General, has advertised in the London newspapers and in the local press for a gentleman of honour and integrity to become the husband of his wealthy and attractive niece, Clarinda. His sister, Mrs Hurricane, who is also his housekeeper, has advertised for a footman. The General's renegade son, and his friend, Captain Ardent, have just arrived in the town, and they reply to the respective advertisements. Ardent, who is in love with Clarinda, is engaged as footman. Young Dorval manages to upset everybody. Another applicant for the hand of Clarinda is a prosperous wax and tallow

---

* I have a playbill for the second performance, which included Sir Henry Bishop's opera, *Clari, the Maid of Milan*, with Miss Jarman in the title part, and the song, "Home, Sweet Home". This was plugged, as we might say today, throughout the work.

chandler from Watling Street, London: a veritable cockney named Peter Pigeonwiddy.

The General mistakes Pigeonwiddy for an officer, approves of him, and invites him to occupy the Spare Bed. It is not long before Ardent, disguised as a lawyer, comes to draw up the delicate preliminaries for the engagement. Amidst all the resulting confusion Ardent succeeds in convincing Pigeonwiddy that Clarinda is penniless, and young Dorval plans to attack him with pistols in the night. After the drenching in the shower bath Pigeonwiddy decides to retreat, leaving Ardent to gain the hand of Clarinda. But Ardent confesses his deception to Pigeonwiddy who, realizing that it is all a flam*, asks the audience if any kind creature has a bed disengaged, but if not he would hope on some future occasion to occupy the Spare Bed.

The Spare Bed was published both by Cumberland and Dicks'. Cumberland's reviewer (probably George Daniel) said that, although the play entertained many disguises, plots, tricks and droll contrivances, it was written in such a happy vein, that the inconsistencies and anomalies are overlooked. He refers to *The Times* in 1828 and marvels how Mr Price let slip the play, adding the illuminating remark that the original manuscript contained, in pencil written by Mr Price, the names of well-known actors against the characters to be played:

Jean Jacques (a French valet)	.	Mr Matthews
Dorval		Mr Farren
Pigeonwiddy		Mr Liston

while a part was to be found for Miss Foote (who had become the Countess of Harrington). In his opinion it would certainly have ensured for the author a long run. He further stated that Keeley (a lesser actor) made a great success of the part to have been played by Liston, and it was no disparagement to say that the latter never displayed the manners of a cockney to such advantage as Keeley in this farce.

Unfortunately it was Keeley who was shot in the eye when the pistol exploded, and the run of the play was interrupted. But a Dr Millingen, author of a play entitled the

---

* Flam was a trick or a false story. Formerly Standard English, it had become a colloquialism by the nineteenth century.

King's Fool, which had been produced in the same theatre in July, was on the spot and afforded every professional assistance. In April 1834 *The Spare Bed* was produced at Sadler's Wells, and in the course of my study of playbills it has come to my notice on many occasions. It is still quite an amusing piece to read, although it must always have owed a lot to the production, and the performance of the cast.

A copy of the print by Cumberland is bound in a volume in the Department of MSS. in the B.M., where I have been unable to find the actual manuscript of the play. In this print the introductory remarks are different from (and probably earlier than) those in the bound volume of Cumberland's plays in the library of the B.M., since the reviewer states that the farce was accepted by Mr Price when lessee of Drury Lane. He adds that the play was for some reason withdrawn by the author, and produced with success at the Victoria. It would seem that Fox Cooper must have explained the matter to George Daniel, who then revised his remarks.

In all probability, this was the nearest Fox Cooper ever got to the production of one of his plays at Drury Lane, and if the reviewer's original comments are accepted, it was very near indeed.* I do not know whether he ever tried to place a play at Covent Garden or the Haymarket which, with Drury Lane, at that time constituted the three major metropolitan theatres. It was, however, recognized that there were three major 'minor' theatres, namely the Adelphi, the Olympic, and the St James's, at all of which plays by Fox Cooper were produced.

The next of the 1833 plays in point of importance, although not original, is *The Deserted Village,* a burletta in three acts, suggested by Goldsmith's poem; by such description it contained some vocal numbers, and the story is taken from a current review.

Lord Morden (Yates) plots with Text (Buckstone), the village schoolmaster, how to get Annette (Mrs Yates), the curate's daughter, into his possession and to effect it employs Mark Maythorn (O. Smith), poacher, to take her off and arrange a sham marriage between her and Lord Morden in London. This is done: satiated with his victim he abandons

---

* But if he had succeeded in 1848 in becoming the lessee (see Chapter 8) the position might have been rectified.

her. She meets Lord Fopling (Brayne) who makes advances
of a nature that cannot be mistaken, and she returns to her
distracted parents in the village, which is about to be deserted
because of Morden's spendthrift ways.

But Maythorn has contrived a real, instead of a sham, marriage, and a rich uncle of Morden's (Bennett) who has just
returned from India, espouses the cause of Annette and
threatens to blow his nephew's brains out unless he immediately
consents to marry her. The play ends happily. Mr Yates
played the reckless and vagabond Lord with great skill. Mrs
Yates was equally admirable as his victim, sustaining the pathos
of the character in an affecting manner, while John Reeve,
the pauper sexton begging a shilling from everyone he meets,
relieved the sombre tints of the drama with his light and
sketchy humour.

The *Morning Chronicle* said that the play concluded with a
tableau vivant the characters of which, including at least one
non-human, finally moved off the stage in procession. And on
the night their critic attended the performance the black
descendant of the animal "which was one of the personages
of the celebrated dialogue between Balaam and his Ass",
forgot the respect due to the very respectable company which
he kept, and strewed the way—but not with flowers—to the
great consternation of his brother- and sister-actors, and to
the roaring amusement of the folk beyond the footlamps.

The production was at the Adelphi Theatre on 28 October,
and the play was published by Duncombe in 1834, and later
in Dicks'. According to a letter to the *Globe* from Fox Cooper,
The Deserted Village had been advertised for several weeks
as a forthcoming production at the Victoria Theatre, but it
was withdrawn by him and re-presented at the Adelphi in a
form curtailed by Mr Yates, the leading actor. As to the need
for cutting the play there seems to have been some disagreement
between the management of the Victoria and Fox Cooper,
but the latter conceded that the excisions subsequently made
had been done with judgement and discretion. But after the
success of *The Spare Bed*, it looks as though the management
behaved somewhat ungratefully, as indeed was suggested by a
contemporary critic.

At this period Gilbert Abbott à Becket had brought into

existence a whimsical, satirical, but informative little paper (especially for theatrical news) published between 1832 and 1839, and known as *Figaro in London*. I shall often call it *Figaro* for short. The Victoria Theatre was then under the direction of a Mr Egerton whom *Figaro* disliked, and in the issue of 12 October 1833 there was much criticism of "this scene-shifter-cursing Egerton". *Figaro* had looked into the story about *The Deserted Village*, and it seemed that the author (having been paid for his piece) resisted a paltry effort either of the actors or the manager, to force him into making alterations to suit "the cold monotony of Warde, the whining twaddle style of Miss Jarman, or the heavy, substantial, solid, growling of the ever-delightful Egerton."

As a result of this refusal the author had been threatened with the stoppage of the money given him by bill for his piece, and (before even it was due) the lessees chose to provide for it by withholding the proceeds of a recent benefit. I do not know why this paper was so critical of the Victoria Theatre and its manager, but it may have had some moderating influence, because Fox Cooper afterwards stated that he had no objection to the alterations, and seemingly no grudge against the manager of the Victoria. It would clearly have been unwise for an aspiring author to pursue an unnecessary quarrel with any theatre.

On the whole, *The Deserted Village* had a good reception. The *Literary Gazette* said that with the exception of some stupid claptrap against rank, landlords, etc., the drama was most favourably received, and thought that it seemed likely to make crowded houses for many a day. One week later, the same journal said they omitted to name Fox Cooker [*sic*] as the young successful artist to whom the town was indebted for *The Deserted Village*. The play had since been pruned and improved to make it effective throughout. "One wishes almost for a thin house to see how it looks with a few empty seats and a trifle of standing room." In the next issue, they published an erratum in which it was desired to substitute the name of Fox Cooper for that of Fox Cooker as the successful author of *The Deserted Village*. From my reading of contemporary journals, I judge that a notice in the *Literary Gazette* was quite an achievement for a play by a young author produced at one of the lesser theatres. *Figaro* said that *The Deserted Village* fully justified the curiosity it had excited from its long announcement at, and its subsequent withdrawal from, the Victoria Theatre.

"The piece is most cleverly contrived and the interest is maintained throughout, while the acting, scenery, etc., contribute to give an excellent effect to the whole performance. It does great credit to Mr Frederick Fox Cooper, the author, and it was received at the conclusion with unmixed approbation. Only a few wretched beings contrived occasionally to raise the weak yelp of misguided malignity, as when vice falls under the lash of the dramatist." This notice went on to say that the acting of Yates, Mrs Yates, Reeve and Buckstone contributed much to the general effect of the piece, and the worthy Hemmings would have been respectable had he been more perfect in his character. Mr Hemmings led a double life, as he kept a ham and beef shop somewhere near St Paul's. And *Figaro* regretted that his heart was behind the counter wandering over the saveloys. "Moreover, if he could only carry his soul out of the beef copper and his ideas above slices of ham and small Germans, he would be a very respectable performer. The machinery of the piece was well contrived with a few exceptions. For example, the glorious beams of the sun appeared in the shape of an old bit of blazing wood besmeared with turpentine, and the moon was made to rise at the rate of at least fifty miles an hour, as if the orb of night was travelling per railroad."

The other plays in 1833 were: *Rejected Addresses* and *Mr Simpson, M.C.*

Figaro said that Mr Gray had taken the Clarence Theatre, which was in the vicinity of King's Cross, when *Rejected Addresses, or the M.P.'s lodging* was produced in August: this they regretted because the amount of pelf to be picked up in Gray's Inn Road must be very small indeed.

Mr Simpson, M.C., or Vauxhall Gardens, a Local Extravaganza, was produced for the author's benefit-night at the Victoria Theatre on 26 September. That functionary, who was no piece of fiction, was then about to retire from the position of Master of Ceremonies at the Vauxhall Gardens. He was a well-known public figure, one of whose duties was to welcome the many notabilities who frequented that place of amusement. In 1782, at the age of thirteen, he had been one of the few survivors of the battle fought by Admiral Rodney in the West

Royal Victoria Theatre.

LESSEES, Mr. ABBOTT and Mr. EGERTON.

Under the immediate Patronage of Her Royal Highness the DUCHESS OF KENT.

THE AUTHOR'S NIGHT!

Mr. WARDE AS OTHELLO!
RE-APPEARANCE OF Mr. KEELEY!
First Night of Mr. SIMPSON, M.C. of Vauxhall Gardens!

On THURSDAY, September 26th, 1833,

Will be presented SHAKSPEARE'S Tragedy of

OTHELLO.

THE MOOR OF VENICE.

THE PRINCIPAL CHARACTERS AS FOLLOW.

Othello, - - - - - - **Mr. WARDE,**

Iago, - by a **GENTLEMAN,**
(His First Appearance in that Character, and Second on any Stage,)

Cassio, - - - - **Mr. ABBOTT,**

Brabantio, - - - - - **Mr. EGERTON,**

Roderigo, **Mr. WOOD,**   Desdemona, - - **Miss JARMAN,**

Emilia, **Mrs. EGERTON.**

After which, (in consequence of the numerous applications which have been made at the Box Office for its repetition) the highly popular Farce, in Two Acts, called

THE SPARE BED:

Or, THE SHOWER-BATH.

Captain Ardent, (For this Night only) The **AUTHOR,** his First Appearance on any Stage.

Mr. Peter Pigeonwiddy, - (A Tallow Chandler from Watling Street) - - **Mr. KEELEY,**
(Who has kindly given the aid of his valuable services)

Clarinda, - - - - **Miss SYDNEY.**

EXTRACT FROM MR. SIMPSON'S ADDRESS TO THE PUBLIC AT HIS BENEFIT.

All the most illustrious Princes and Princesses of the British Empire, the most noble and puissant Princes, and other illustrious Ambassadors of the Foreign States, now residing in London, and their truly noble and accomplished Ladies; the most noble and distinguished Nobility of the United Kingdom, and their truly noble and accomplished Ladies; and also all the other respectable classes of distinguished Visitors, that so kindly honor and grace the Royal Gardens every season with their distinguished presence, and their amiable and lovely Ladies; all those truly illustrious, noble, and distinguished Visitors of the Royal Gardens, Vauxhall, are informed that C. H. Simpson, Master of the Ceremonies of those Gardens for Thirty-six Years, is one of the very few survivors, at the present day of that bloody and furious battle, that lasted from daylight in the morning until dark, fought by Admiral Rodney, in the West Indies, on the 12th of April, 1782, when the British standard completely annihilated and destroyed the whole French Fleet, and captured the celebrated Ville de Paris, a tremendously high red-sided 90 gun ship, with a gilt Lion at her head, and took their grand Commander-in-Chief, the Count de Grasse, a fine tall stout athletic man, about 5 feet 11 inches high, prisoner. When the ship was paid off, and he was, like other young gentlemen in his situation, honorably discharged in the thirteenth year of his age, and had been always much beloved and respected by all the officers on board the ship, and so much so, that Captain Stone of the Royal Navy, the brother of Mr. Stone, the Master of the ship, wrote a letter to his brother from the East Indies, stating that he would give all the world if he could have him with him on board his 74 gun ship in the East Indies. And in consequence of these achievements, he confidently hopes that all the World and his lovely and accomplished Lady will be present at the Royal Victoria Theatre, at the Benefit of his highly esteemed friend, the Author of " *The Spare Bed,*" when will be produced

(First Time) an entirely new and original Local Extravaganza, in One Act, (written expressly for the occasion by the Author of "*The Spare Bed*") called

Mr. SIMPSON, M. C.

Or, VAUXHALL GARDENS.

Mr. Makepenny, **Mr. CHIPPENDALE,**   Dicky, **Mr. ROSS,**
Captain Willoughby, **Mr. WOOD,**   Lieutenant Selby, **Mr. IRWIN,**
Ensign Montieth, **Mr. LATHAM,**   Cornet M'Gillicuddy, **Mr. T. LEE,**
Mr. Simpson, (Master of the Ceremonies) **Mr. TURNOUR.**

Mrs. Makepenny, **Mrs. GARRICK,**   Miss Eliza Makepenny, **Miss SIDNEY,**   Miss Clara Makepenny, **Miss LEE,**
Miss Georgiana Makepenny, **Miss GARRICK,**   Miss Sarah Makepenny, **Miss P. HORTON.**

In the course of the Piece will be introduced a New Scene representing

THE FIGURE OF MR. SIMPSON.

ILLUMINATED IN VARIEGATED LAMPS AS IN VAUXHALL GARDENS.

In the course of the Evening, the following Songs.

Song,	"The Bonnie Blue Cap,"	Mr. COLLINS,	New Comic Song,	"What's a Benefit,"	Mr. LATHAM,
Song,	"Come to me at Morning,"	Mrs. KEELEY,	Song,	"The Lads of the Village,"	Mr. MORLEY,
New Comic Song,	"Since I've been in the Army,"	Mr. T. LEE,	Comic Duet,	"Polly Hopkins,"	Mr. ROSS and Miss P. HORTON,
Song,	"Two a harp for my Love,"	Mr. HUNT,	Song,	"The King, God bless him,"	Mr. COLLINS.

Doors open at Six—Performances commence at half-past Six, and terminate at half-past Eleven.

BOXES, 4s. PIT, 2s. GALLERY 1s.   Second Price, Boxes 2s.   PIT 1s.   GALLERY 6d.

Tickets, Places & Private Boxes to be obtained of Mr. T. THOMPSON, at the Box Office.   No Places can be secured on this occasion after the End of the First Act.

Playbill for benefit performance on 26 September 1833

(Courtesy of the Minet Library)

Indies when (the playbill states) he annihilated the whole French Fleet and took prisoner the Commander-in-Chief, Comte de Grasse, "a fine tall, stout, athletic man, 5 feet 11 inches high." When the ship was paid off, like other young gentlemen in his situation, he was honorably discharged, and had been always much beloved and respected by all the officers on board the ship, and so much so, that Captain Stone of the Royal Navy, the brother of Mr Stone, the master of the ship, wrote a letter to his brother stating that he would give all the world if he could but have him on board his 74-gun ship in the East Indies. "And in consequence of these achievements, he confidently hopes that all the world and his lovely and accomplished Lady will be present at the Royal Victoria Theatre, at the Benefit of his highly esteemed friend, the author of *The Spare Bed*." A nice piece of mutual publicity. Mr Simpson's notoriety must have diminished after his retirement, for when the Vauxhall Gardens were offered for sale in 1840, four busts of that gentleman fetched no more than ten shillings.

The rest of the programme for the benefit consisted of *Othello*, *The Spare Bed*, and a scene representing Mr Simpson, illuminated in variegated lamps. This would occupy a period of five hours commencing at half-past six, and a box seat could be had for four shillings. Holders of tickets purchased at 13 Wellington Street, could pass Waterloo Bridge toll free. *Figaro* remarked: "Cooper indeed deserves what we trust he will meet with—the most liberal patronage." The much more distinguished and indeed sedate journal, the *Literary Gazette*, contained a paragraph headed, "The Two Authors".

By a mode of printing the announcement, the Victoria Theatre last Thursday advertised 'For the benefit of the author, the play of *Othello, or The Moor of Venice*', but after the word 'author' there should have appeared the words 'of *The Spare Bed*' by which the public would have known that it was for the benefit of that gentleman and not of Shakespeare, whose only bed in the play could not be spared as it is so necessary to the smothering of Desdemona.

I imagine that this must have been the only occasion on which Fox Cooper's name was coupled with that of the world's greatest dramatist. But notwithstanding the lack of distinction or originality in many of the plays of my great-grandsire, it

D

must be placed to his credit—and for this there is much evidence —that he had almost a sense of reverence for the work of the man he would no doubt have described as the Immortal Bard.

A different playbill of this performance is preserved in the Minet Library, to which I am indebted for permission to include a reproduction. The grace and dignity of Mr Simpson is clearly shown. It is also recorded herein that the author took the part of Captain Ardent in *The Spare Bed*, and that it was his first appearance on any stage. If this is true my conjectures in Chapter 1 about the juvenile Fox Cooper's performances at the Adelphi Theatre are mistaken; but I am not convinced.

In 1834 two plays by Fox Cooper were produced on the same night, Monday, 22 September. This marked the reopening of the Garrick Theatre then in Leman Street, Goodman's Fields, Whitechapel, and named after the famous actor who made his first appearance at an ealier theatre on the same site. The managers were Conquest and Gomersal, who announced that they had treated with authors of acknowledged celebrity in presenting new pieces written expressly for the theatre.

The first of Fox Cooper's was a broad farcical interlude entitled *The Court Jester*. For political reasons the traditional setting for adaptations of Victor Hugo's *Le Roi s'amuse* (sometimes rendered as *The King's Fool*) was an Italian one, as in the comedy by C. J. Matthews bearing the same name; but the scenes in the Garrick production were laid in Whitechapel with which locality the audiences were more intimately acquainted. Mr Conquest exhibited considerable humour as a 'Hot Baked Tater Merchant, and Court Jester': the court being in High Street, Whitechapel, represented by lamplight in Scene 2. Mrs Jefferson was making her first appearance, and Mr Cooper in a minor part could have been the author.

Fox Cooper's other contribution was *The White Tower*, a "Scotch Romantic Melo-Drama" in two acts. Several of the scenes take place in the *Castle of Glenwar*, by which title a play was recorded in Harwood Cooper's list, and marked "Garrick". The production featured both Mrs Gomersal and Mrs Conquest, the latter appearing in an incidental ballet.

The one play produced in 1835 (on 15 June, at the Victoria Theatre) was *Angelo* from the French of Victor Hugo. A.N., discussing the contemporary widespread adaptation of indiff-

erent French plays by English authors, and their comparative
neglect of the more vital efforts of the French stage, allows that
Victor Hugo was not entirely passed over, one of the notable
exceptions being the appearance of an English "translation or
adaptation" of *Angelo* so soon after its appearance in Paris,
in April 1835. This English production was the possible
consequence of contacts made by Fox Cooper during the visit
to Paris in 1830–31, and the ever-present *Figaro* contrived to
mention it on two occasions. On 13 June: "the Victoria Theatre
having just re-opened, next week there will be presented a
new tragic drama on Monday. Having perused this work we
can say it possesses a powerful interest. We only wonder
whether the fear, terror and pity which it is capable of striking
in the audience may not prove to be too much for this warm
weather." On 20 June: "*Angelo* at the Victoria is a splendid
drama, and Mrs Selby shows great merit and judgement in
her acting. The whole play abounds in original situations and
interest of the highest order. It will tell well for the
management." I have found no other trace of this adaptation,
but it was still running in July.

During the year 1835 activities of quite a different order had
occupied much of Fox Cooper's time and energies. In June
1847, the *Theatrical Times*, to which reference has already
been made, stated that Fox Cooper had been secretary to the
Duke of Cumberland (afterwards King of Hanover) as Grand
Master of the Orange Lodges in England, and further that he
had been examined for fourteen consecutive days by a committee of the House of Commons in 1835. I therefore took
some notes from the report of the *Select Committee on Origins,
Nature, Extent and Tendency of Orange Institutions in Great Britain,
and the Colonies* (House papers, Vol. 17, session 1835) and found
that the statement was approximately true, although there
is, as one might expect, some exaggeration.

That committee had been set up because of widespread
apprehension at the growth of the strong Protestant and
violently anti-Catholic Orange movement, particularly in
the Army, and its potential danger to the constitution.* Mr

* An additional reason lay in the unpopularity of the Duke of Cumberland, whose moral character was continually the subject of malevolent
attacks. The judgement of history, however, seems to be moving in his favour.
(See Willis; *Ernest Augustus, Duke of Cumberland and King of Hanover*, 1954.)

Hume was in the chair, and Fox Cooper was examined on four days in the middle of August, answering over 250 questions. His evidence was lucid, reading as the expression of a well-informed and articulate man of affairs. He admitted that he had been a member of the movement for four years;* his lodge was at Brentford where it met at the Three Pigeons, and his sponsors had been Col Fairman and Mr Bentley (a solicitor). He was a member of the Grand Committee, for which he acted as reporter, involving much sacrifice of time.

In the course of his examination it was suggested to him that a Sergeant Keith might have been a member of the Grand Committee, to which Fox Cooper replied with some dignity if not asperity, that the members of that committee were composed exclusively of noblemen and gentlemen. He was also interrogated about passwords and secret signs. Would he require a release from the Duke of Cumberland to make a disclosure? "No release whatever: it is a custom among gentlemen when they meet for particular business, to confine the nature of the business to themselves; admitted by passwords and signs, it would be exceedingly improper to disclose them to any person not belonging to the body." In answer to further questions he said that there was no complete list of members but that in his estimate there were perhaps 40,000 Orangemen in London, who might be assembled if an emergency should occur. If all dormant lodges were called into activity there might be 120,000 to 140,000 Orangemen in Great Britain. Other witnesses could give no evidence on the subject, but the Select Committee was not convinced that the numbers were quite as high as had been suggested by Fox Cooper.

From the appendix to the report it is apparent that Fox Cooper had been a member of the Grand Committee for two years. The Deputy Grand Secretary-*cum*-Deputy Grand Treasurer was (in full) the Lieut-Col W. Blennerhasset Fairman, who had long been connected with the movement and needed help with the volume of work it entailed. Thus Fox Cooper was brought in to assist, and at the end of a report on a meeting of the Grand Lodge in June 1833, the Deputy Grand

---

* His father must have been known to the movement since, at a meeting of the Grand Lodge in June 1823, thanks were offered to the editor of *John Bull* for his advocacy of constitutional Orange principles on a recent occasion.

Secretary added that he felt great pleasure in giving a minute of the proceedings furnished by Brother Fox Cooper. "His account of the principles laid down in a discussion on the constitution were so strictly patriotic as to reflect fresh lustre on the noble Lords and even the exalted personage [the Duke of Cumberland] who had the manliness to declare them."

Fox Cooper was a 'member of a committee of enquiry into various personal squabbles within the Orange lodges, and into the conduct of the Deputy Grand Secretary himself. Needless to say, the latter was completely vindicated. Of that officer's accounts Fox Cooper was one of the four auditors, and the approved expenditure of £700 contains this illuminating entry: "The D.G.S.'s life having been threatened at Birmingham, paid for a brace of pocket pistols and repairing the same, for his better security on his approaching tour through Ireland . . . £3."

Col Fairman was also called before the Select Committee and, as he declined to produce a certain book of correspondence, it was resolved by the House that he be sent to Newgate Prison; but the Sergeant-at-Arms reported the next day that when he arrived at the residence of the gallant Colonel, the latter had departed within the previous quarter of an hour. As the owner of the *Palladium*, a transient journal that traded in private scandals, he had been in trouble before, and knew when to act quickly.

It was remarked in the *Theatrical Times* that Fox Cooper's evidence did material service to the loyal party of the day which was testified by his friends Lord Kenyon and Lord Wynford, and that he had received an autograph letter from the Duke of Gordon on behalf of the Orangemen of Scotland. Lord Kenyon was a friend of the Duke of Cumberland and the Deputy Grand Master of the movement. In a letter to *The Times* he was at pains to deny that any authority had been given to Col Fairman regarding a course of action which might have resulted from the deposition of King William IV.

The final outcome of the enquiry by the Select Committee was that the Orange movement was discouraged from the highest level, i.e. by the Duke of Cumberland himself. Presumably Fox Cooper had added to his growing reputation, but not to his fortune. He lost a useful secretaryship, but inevitably it would have been terminated in 1837 when the Duke became King of Hanover, under a variation of Salic law.

On 5 December 1835 an article appeared in *Figaro* about theatrical criticism. It is preserved in Harwood Cooper's press-cutting book, which is short of the first few lines, reading as follows:

> A correspondent has directed our attention to the fact of a great portion of the present dramatic writers being at the same time theatrical critics. Charles Dance damns with faint praise (except on 'myself and my partner Joe' occasions) in the *Athenaeum*. Jerrold is, or was, the salaried critic of a Sunday paper and monthly magazine, and commands the quills of many of his brethren. Planché was eulogistic on the birth of certain bantlings in the *Literary Gazette*.

Later on, among other examples, the article mentions that "Frederick Fox Cooper Esq., who has been a critic in half the dead and living papers in London, is also a dramatic writer." *Figaro* said they would shortly return to the subject, but in the subsequent notes there is nothing worth recording.

Fox Cooper's peregrinations as a dramatic critic, which probably provided a resort in case of need, may account for a good slice of the time during which I have found no record of his occupation. There is proof enough (in Chapter 8) that in 1848–49 he was editor of the *Theatrical Chronicle*, and there were numerous other theatrical papers of this period that died an early death, with some of which Fox Cooper could have been associated. In the first half of the nineteenth century nearly 250 dramatic periodicals came into existence, over fifty of which appeared four times or less.

On this occasion in 1835, and even much later in his life, Fox Cooper is credited with the suffix "Esq.", when it is denied to his contemporaries (see also notes on *Garibaldi* in 1860). Sometimes there is a suggestion of irony. Perhaps it was a foible on Fox Cooper's part to claim such a title, or the effect on others of his insistence that he came of a wealthy family.

Lacking evidence of theatrical or journalistic failures, one must assume that being secretary to a Duke had done little to enhance Fox Cooper's financial standing, since in 1836 he was again arrested and sent to Horsemonger Lane gaol for debt. His petition for release was dated 6 February and heard in the

Insolvent Debtors' Court on 22 April. Although the petition was opposed he was discharged upon adjudication a week later, so he had spent another three months in gaol. Newspapers even at this period gave a relatively large amount of space to insolvency and bankruptcy, doubtless for the protection of the public, but often this consisted of no more than long lists of names. The absence of a report on Fox Cooper's case was probably because no interesting point of law was involved, and he was not well enough known at that time; but he was described as author, reporter, printer, and publisher.

The *London Gazette* in April 1836 giving notice of the hearing of the case, made reference to no less than seventeen addresses, ending with No. 38 Garden Row, London Road, Surrey (actually in Southwark) from which Fox Cooper had been taken to gaol. From the biographer's point of view the records of this incident and others of a similar nature provide much information that might otherwise be lost. The accounts of his removals, while possibly inaccurate in detail, contain vital clues to the activities of Fox Cooper over a period of about ten years, the first address being that at which his son, Harwood, was born in 1826. They also corroborate Harwood's rough record written from memory many years later.

One address (in Fetter Lane) is of interest because a manuscript note by a member of the family says that a Henry Fox Cooper was born here on 1 July 1830. This may have been the son who died in 1832.

The next addresses given in the *Gazette*, Rue des Marchés, Paris, and Segontium Terrace, Caernarvon, North Wales,* support the notes by Harwood Cooper. Although, as already remarked, both of these sojournings suggest some kind of theatrical venture, they could have been undertaken to elude creditors. I cannot imagine Fox Cooper, whose wife came from South Wales, going to North Wales for any different reason.

The same notice contains an office address: No. 17 Titchbourne Street, Piccadilly, with the added information: carrying on business in co-partnership with Robson Harrison, proprietors of a proposed new theatre. How typical of Fox Cooper to claim that he owned a proposed theatre! The

* Segontium was the name of the most important Roman station in the northern part of Wales,

following one is Clattern Bridge, Kingston, Surrey, which links with the period when Fox Cooper was secretary to the Duke of Cumberland, and with his registration at Brentford (not so very far away) during the Orange Lodge activities in 1833 onwards. The Duke lived at Kew. The rest of his addresses call for no special comment, but all are contained in Appendix III.

Chapter 3

Dramatic Productions: 1836–39

BETWEEN 1836 and 1839, if not before, Fox Cooper was for a brief term the lessee of one or more minor London theatres which for convenience will be discussed in Chapter 5. This period, however, covers the output of over a dozen plays, although evidence of performance is lacking for some of them. Perhaps the best known was *Hercules, King of Clubs*, a classic, sculpturesque, and rather pantomimical farce, published in Cumberland's *Minor Theatre*, Lacy, and Dicks'. The editorial remarks in Cumberland describe the play as novel and ingenious. "The dialogue is terse and the situations are full of ludicrous effect. There is nothing new in a gallant captain putting on disguise and carrying off a willing young lady; and an intriguing young valet aiding the plot with his cunning contrivances. But to treat these with any degree of novelty is a feature in farce writing; and Mr Cooper has so treated them." There is no point in outlining the plot which is, of necessity, slight. Yet it is worth noting that the youthful valet, five feet tall, is called upon to appear as a statue of Hercules, as the Dying Gladiator, as Atlas (with globe), and finally as Venus (with drapery). As this all took place in the same scene, it must have taxed the ability of the young actor, Mr W. J. Hammond,* who at the end enquired of the audience whether "clubs were trumps": the reply was unanimously in the affirmative.

* He was also joint manager of the theatre.

The production took place at the Strand Theatre on Thursday, 7 July 1836, in a heat wave which provided one critic with the 'Herculean' task of sitting out "a very agreeable trifle, well written and well acted." There seems to be some doubt about the actual date and casting of this production. A reference in the *Satirist*, and a playbill in the Enthoven Collection showing that the fourth performance was advertised for Monday, 11 July, confirm that the first performance was on the previous Thursday. Another playbill covering the period 5 July to 9 July shows that Captain Darling was to be played by Roberts, and Tim, alias Hercules, by Hammond. Cumberland's edition in 1837 gives the cast for 28 July 1836, in which Fox Cooper appears as Darling, but the playbill for 25 July, covering the sixteenth to twentieth performances makes no mention of him. This is a catch for would-be theatrical historians like myself: Fox Cooper was given a benefit performance on 28 July, at which he took the part of Darling, the playbill (reproduced by courtesy of the Westminster library archives) stating that it was his second performance on any stage.* Dicks' edition which wrongly states that the play was produced on 28 July, correctly gives Roberts as the creator of the part of Darling. Harwood Cooper's editing, perhaps relying on his memory, was partly in fault. Actually the text of Dicks' edition is slightly different from Cumberland's, and from a brief examination both of them diverge from the manuscript in the B.M.

A curious comment occurs in the *Literary Gazette* to the effect that *Hercules* (abbreviated thus) was produced in a style which promised to make its run as popular as that of *Othello*, which still continued to excite roars of laughter. The explanation appears in a later issue where it says "for those who love burlesque we could recommend nothing better than *Hercules* except *Othello*". The paper was referring to an operatic burlesque of *Othello* (possibly written by M. D. Dowling in 1834) which was given on the benefit-night at the Strand in July.

Hercules was Fox Cooper's most successful piece: by 1845, according to a contemporary playbill, it had been played over a thousand times. It was revived in 1873 with Harwood Cooper

---

* This comment is not in conflict with the claim in the playbill for the benefit on 20 September 1833 at the Victoria Theatre that Fox Cooper then made his first appearance on the stage.

NEW STRAND THEATRE

OTHELLO   HERCULES

STRAND THEATRE, EVERY NIGHT
HAMMOND'S SEEN, IN BLACK & WHITE.

MR. FOX COOPER'S NIGHT

Author of "The Deserted Village,"—"Spare Bed,"—"Hercules," &c

THE HIGHLAND FLING, BY MADEMOISELLE ROSIER.

After which 19th time, (written by Mr. FOX COOPER,) an entirely Original, **CLASSICAL, COMICAL, SCULPTURESQUE** Burletta, called

HERCULES!

Captain Darling......Mr. FOX COOPER, *(his First Appearance at this Theatre, and Second on any Stage.)*
Tim.........................(his Man, alias HERCULES)............................ Mr. W. J. HAMMOND.
In which Character he will Sing

"The BIRTH, EDUCATION, and LABOURS of HERCULES."

Mr. Christopher Granite...Mr. A. YOUNG.   Mr. Fuzby...Mr. WYMAN.   Tommy...Mr. ATTWOOD.   Harry...Mr. SEARLE.
Mrs. Ramsbottom,......Mrs. TAYLEURE.   Lavinia..........Miss FURGUSON.

A COMIC MEDLEY DANCE BY Mr SEARLE.

To conclude with, every Evening, an OPERATIC BURLESQUE BURLETTA, called

OTHELLO

(ACCORDING TO ACT OF PARLIAMENT.)

Duke of Venice,   Mr. WYMAN.   Barbantio, (a hasty old codger any senator of Venice)   Mr. A. YOUNGE.
Othello,   (Moor of Venice, formerly an independant nigger from the republic of Hayti) Mr. W. J. HAMMOND.
Iago, (Othello's officer, once a native of Gaultee mountains, County Tipperary, province of Munster, & Kingdom of Ireland, Mr. H. HALL.
Ruderigo,   (a very silly youth, and very partial to Mrs Othello)   Mr. ATTWOOD.
Cassio,   (a man of note, but still an injured man, rather in liquor or the liquor rather in him)   Mr. ROBERTS.
Ludovica,   (a very respectable Gentleman)   Mr. JOHNSON.
Montano, (caught in a row with Cassio, but not at all disposed to fight)   Mr. STOKER.   Policeman.   Mr. SEARLE.
Desdemona,   (a very good natured lady, wife of Othello, and not a bit too well treated by him)   Miss DALY.
Emilia,   (a lady in attendance on the latter)   Miss STOKER.   Ghost of Desdemona   (with a few expiring notes——

BOXES, 4s.   PIT, 2s.   Second Price—BOXES, 2s.   PIT, 1s.
Doors open at half-past 6, commence at 7.   Box-Office open from 11 till 4, where Places may be taken, and Tickets had of
Mr. MASSINGHAM.   Half-price a quarter before 9.
No Money Returned.   Vivant Rex et Regina.   J. KNIGHT, Printer, 8, Waterloo Road.

Playbill for benefit performance on 28 July 1836
(Courtesy of the City of Westminster Public Libraries, Archives Dept.)

in the name part. I found it quite fun to read, and even Malcolm Morley (no mean authority) thinks it a good farce.

Ion, Travestie, produced at the Garrick in November 1836 should be mentioned next, as it is stated to have been played for a total of 250 nights at the Garrick, Queens, and Victoria Theatres. This was a burlesque of the tragedy, *Ion,* (based on Euripides), by Sir Thomas Talfourd produced at Covent Garden less than six months before. *Eye-on* was the title of the play as advertised, and a large eye is shown in the bill for the Garrick Theatre, where Conquest appeared in the name part. In the subsequent presentation at the Queen's Theatre all the characters, with one exception were acted by "ladies", and the only male in the cast, T. F. Matthews, took the part

Garrick Theatre,

LEMAN STREET, WHITECHAPEL,

On Monday, Wednesday, Thursday, & Friday, Dec. 5, 7, 8 & 9,

The performances to commence with a new grand Asiatic Drama, of deep and powerful interest, varied by strong comic humour, and interspersed with Song's, Choruses, Dances, Combats, aided by new Scenery, Dresses, Decorations, &c. adapted for the Garrick Theatre, by Mr. FREER, and entitled,

BARMECIDE

The DOOMED OFFSPRING !

OR,

A Father's Heart---a Mother's Love.

Haroun Al Raschid, (Caliph of Bagdad) - Mr. J. R. WILLIAMS
Giafar, (Barmecide, Grand Vizier) **Mr. FREER** Isouf, (Chief of the Eunuchs) Mr. BRADFORD
Goodman, (an Englishman, attached to Giafar) Mr. PAUL, who will introduce a Characteristic Song
Hassan, (Son to the Caliph) - Miss ROGERS Nair, - (Son to Giafar and Zaida) - Miss SUMMERSBY
Aboulcassem, (Chief of the Arabs) Mr. SHEPHERD Morabeck, (an Arab) Mr. PEATHERSTON
Hafra, Mr. BECKET Zadak, Mr. LEWIS Hosein, Mr. OAKEY Octar, Mr. STARMER
Zaida, (Sister to the Caliph, and married to Giafar) **Mrs POPE** Selima, (Nair's Nurse) Miss WILLIAMS
Ebra, (a Dancing Girl) Miss ROSE Officers, Guards, Mutes, Arabs, Dancing Girls, &c.

On MONDAY, after the 1st Piece, the laughable interlude of, The

SARCOPHAGUS !

Skirts, - - - **Mr CONQUEST**
The other Characters by Messrs. WINGROVE, BRADFORD, &c. Miss MELVILLE and Miss ROGERS

On WEDNESDAY and FRIDAY, the admired Travestie of

I-ON !

---I-ON, (a Foundling cherished by Medon) **Mr. CONQUEST**

On THURSDAY, (by desire) the truly laughable Farce of,

Hercules, King of Clubs !

Tim, - **Mr. CONQUEST**

Playbill for 5–9 December 1836

of the female character, Clemanthe. The device (if that is the right word) was not, by any means, novel. The play was to have been revived in 1847 at the Strand Theatre, under the management of Fox Cooper; but it was withdrawn by order of the Lord Chamberlain, and it is possible that this interchange of cast had something to do with the decision. (See also Chapter 7.) Cumberland's *Minor Theatre* prints the play in Vol. 12, and the reviewer is highly complimentary.

> Mr Cooper has taken a few liberties with historical truth but so had Shakespeare, and so had Sergeant Talfourd.* The resuscitation of Adrastus when he is as dead as a wall, is an incident not absolutely warranted by fact. Yet the king is so pleasant a potentate that probability will pardon the bringing him back to life. The language, without affecting superior elegance and refinement, is not unclassical.

Among the quaint sounds and apposite allusions were instanced: So help me Bob; Who are you?; Hookey; Cut my lucky; Blow me tight; Mizzle; Strike me comical. The reviewer thought that in ages to come these terms might prove a serious stumbling-block to future commentators.† He finally remarks that Talfourd's play took twenty-four years for conception and completion, but Cooper's took twenty-four hours. The former was a banquet for mortals, the latter a dish for the gods!

There were three other plays in 1836:

Jewess, Travestie, a burlesque of *The Jewess* (which had been dramatized both by Moncrieff and Planché) from the French text by Eugene Scribe of Halévy's opera *La Juive,* was produced at the Victoria in September. It had poor notices and was quickly withdrawn. A reviewer said it was one of the most trashy productions that ever disgraced the theatre. "It was properly hissed throughout, and if the author, Fox Cooper, had showed the cunning of his name, he would have concealed it from the public."

The Sarcophagus is shown as a comic interlude in a playbill of the Garrick, on 30 November, but no details are provided except that Mr Conquest appeared as "Skirts". During the

---

* Sir Thomas Noon Talfourd (1795–1854) was a lawyer of high distinction as well as a dramatic poet. *Ion* was considered his most important work.

† After 125 years some of these expressions are indeed puzzling, despite valuable reference works such as *A Dictionary of Slang* by Eric Partridge.

following week *Ion* and *Hercules* were also in the programme, Conquest playing the lead in all three. (See page 59.)

Waiting for Bail: the title of this play, a timely one, was included in Harwood Cooper's list. It was probably written in prison between February and April, and the only direct reference I have found to it is in *Figaro*, 4 June 1836. A paragraph headed "To correspondents", states that "F. F. Cooper, author of *The Spare Bed*, has in rehearsal at the English Opera House [i.e. the Lyceum] a new farce: *Waiting for Bail, or Sponge in a Sponging House*,* in which Wrench is to enact the principal part. From the peculiar and exclusive source of information which *Figaro* possesses, we confidently predict that the above will prove an excellent hit to this well-managed company." But, a fairly complete set of playbills for the year 1836 in the Enthoven Collection provides no evidence of its production at that theatre. *Waiting for Bail* is also mentioned on the print of *The Queen's Visit* (1838) as another play by Fox Cooper.

The records of the Lord Chamberlain show that a licence was issued to Fox Cooper to have performed for his benefit at the Strand Theatre a Burletta, Music, and Dancing with Spectacle, on 13 March 1837. *Figaro* provided an amusing review which I have abbreviated and paraphrased:

Fox Cooper, whose cunning is considerable as his name implies, succeeded in hooking in the public to the Strand Theatre a few evenings ago to a benefit. He had ingeniously rigged together a company from the unemployed of the other theatres, and had provided a lengthy entertainment (showing just what lengths an entertainment can go to). A Shakespearean sketch of Othello and Iago was very bad, and ended in a hoot in which the orchestra and audience joined. Iago then came on and said he could act, but Othello could not. Then Fox Cooper came on and swore Othello could act, but Iago could not. We don't know whether this is true since Othello never opened his mouth. We understand the actor went through the third act of the play with Fox Cooper privately in the dressing-room, and when later he came to "death and damnation" he turned round and knocked his

---

* A house kept by a Sheriff's officer, for the preliminary confinement of debtors, and to relieve them of their cash.

head so hard against a wall that "Oh!" was the loudest thing he said during the whole evening. Mr Wilkes was Iago: doing people* is said to be his habit.

Many other mishaps occurred during the evening. A hornpipe was danced with such alarming vigour that the curtain was dropped halfway through. Fox Cooper acted a part in his own *Deserted Village* and, without flattery, we may say that he was the best of the bunch. As a friend of his remarked, he only wants ease, self-possession, a thorough concept of the part, and a knowledge of how to give it effect to make a very passable actor. Joking apart, had we criticized him, we would have spoken much more favourably of him than he has spoken of himself. He has many requisites of the stage, and as authorship probably does not engross all his precious time, we don't see why he should not try acting as some more industrious authors have done before him.

As we shall find during this tale Fox Cooper acted only infrequently, sometimes to take a part in one of his own plays, and occasionally at a special performance. He even said that he was not an actor (see Chapter 10), although I doubt if he would have welcomed such a statement from another.

It is also interesting that Fox Cooper, who wrote little tragedy, used *Othello* for the third time at a benefit performance: the attraction of something he could not himself encompass. Despite his outward show of humour he might still have admitted: "I am not merry, but I do beguile the thing I am by seeming otherwise."

The Lists of Ashby, or The Conquests of Ivanhoe, was produced at Astley's Theatre in the Westminster Bridge Road on 27 March 1837. That famous centre of amusement had been erected on the site formerly occupied by a circus-ring and, appropriately, it specialized in equestrian entertainment. *Ivanhoe* was described as an historical drama, based on the novel by Sir Walter Scott, and it returned to the same theatre over twenty years later in April 1859. Dicks' print published in 1882, makes no mention of the 1837 production, but a comparison of the two relevant playbills shows that the synopses were similar. The play is a potted version of the novel, containing

* Possibly the contemporary smart reply to the question: "What does he do?"

a series of short impressionist scenes, often accompanied by fighting sequences, both on horse and on foot, with elaborate stage settings. Towards the climax the castle of Torquilstone is engulfed in sparks and red fire, with smoke bursting into the turret apartment from which Rebecca threatens to cast herself down. But the day is finally won for the Saxons by Richard the Black Knight with the aid of Robin Hood and Ivanhoe; only the Normans are discomfited.

The reviewer for the *St James's Chronicle* was diverted because at what might be termed the psychological moment he was close enough to hear the prompter cry "the fire wants feeding"! Yet he was satisfied with the biped, and full of admiration for the quadruped, performers. The *Globe* was impressed with the scenes in the circle, a feature of which was the performance of a very young son of Mr Ducrow with the aid of four ponies. The backs of these animals provided a platform about which he walked as easily as if it had been *terra firma*, and rapturously the journal concluded the notice:

> Sure never were seen such beautiful ponies
> Other horses are beasts, but these, macaronies.*

The *Morning Post* had little to say of the literary pretensions of *Ivanhoe* but could not commend too highly "its merits as an equestrian performance, and its many pictorial beauties produced by artful stage combinations". Owing to the intensely cold weather the theatre was "anything but crowded".

A comedietta entitled *The Queen's Visit* which was produced at the City of London Theatre on 6 November 1837, antici-pated by three days the City pageant and the presence of the monarch at a gargantuan banquet in the Guildhall. This event naturally monopolized the journals to such an extent that Fox Cooper's play was almost overlooked. It was not a *chef d'oeuvre*, and could best be described as a somewhat frail *pièce de circonstance* in one act, containing the adventure of a country family on a trip to London to see the Lord Mayor's procession. They all become an easy prey to pickpockets, and are plundered right and left. But by today's standards of crime

---

* Macaroni was rhyming slang for pony, but earlier it had the meaning of a dandy, or a young man who affected the taste and fashions of continen-tal society. It suggested a preference for foreign cookery, long curls, and "spying" glasses. In 1772 there was a *Macaroni and Theatrical Magazine*.

the plundering was rather obvious, unless the acting concealed the naïvety of the text. A slight romance is interwoven as a secondary plot, but the ending is well contrived. The ingratiating pickpockets, Sam Swag and Dick Diver,* are taken to justice, the plunder is restored, and the young man-about-town successfully woos his country cousin. This piece was probably advertised as *The Queen's Visit to the City* under which title it was reviewed in several journals.

The Town on the following Saturday said that a miserable attempt to anticipate the City gala had been practised upon the audience of the City of London Theatre, and had received the rebuff it well merited. The *Weekly Chronicle* said the idea was a good one but the effect was evidently foiled owing to its having been produced on a day before the fair, and partly in consequence of Mrs Honey's absence from the seat of her own dominion. At that time Mrs Honey and Mr Cockerton, a vinegar merchant, were joint directors of the City of London Theatre, the contrast in tastes being noticed by at least one reviewer. But another critic went so far as to suggest that *The Queen's Visit* had a moral value in that it would serve to put strangers on their guard. Living up to its name the *Satirist* commended the management for "shooting folly as it flies": although the play did not rival the gilded show of the Guildhall banquet, it was vastly more amusing to all except perhaps those who obtained soup tickets on that occasion. Passably diverting, it was a trifle timely produced, and would live its brief hour amongst weightier matters.

A print (unrecorded by A.N.) of this play proved difficult to trace, but a copy came to light appropriately in the Guildhall library. It was published in 1838 by James Pattie as No. 2 of Volume I of *Pattie's Penny Play*. Since another play by Fox Cooper (*Jenny Jones*) was No. 1., there may have been some association between the publisher and the dramatist at this period, particularly as *The Queen's Visit* had received only a mediocre reception.

Some link between publisher and author of the play is also suggested by the signature to the introductory remarks:

* Messrs Vale and Norman were reported as so convincing in their respective parts that they might have been mistaken for perfect adepts in the line they had assumed.

Philo-Dramaticus, a pseudonym occasionally but probably not exclusively used by Fox Cooper. In these remarks reference is made to the last scene of the play, which represented the banquet with Queen Victoria surrounded by a distinguished company.* "It was exceedingly well acted, and all concerned were making great way with the public when the Civic powers interposed their authority, and suddenly stopped the progress of the drama." Evidently there was official objection to the representation of Her Majesty on the stage, and this might be taken to mean that the performance on Monday 6 November was not actually completed, but the play was advertised in the *Morning Advertiser* on the two following days. The chief item in the programme for that week was *Don Juan*, in which it was reported that "Mrs Honey acts and sings divinely; she meets with no petty jealousies and annoyances to depress her exertions." Very naturally—she was under the protection of Lord Chesterfield, and only a sour Cockerton would have dared.

A sidelight on Fox Cooper's mental activity at this period, and his friendship with the manager of the St James's Theatre, is afforded by a letter published in the *Observer* in January 1838:

Permit me, through the medium of your columns, to express my surprise at the various remarks which have been made, from time to time, upon Mr Braham's management of the above theatre. By some it is contended that his losses actually amount to the sum of £50 per night, whilst others take upon themselves to say that the theatre has lacked patronage ever since the commencement of the winter season. In both of these positions it is but right that Mr Braham should stand fairly before the public. With respect to the first assertion, it is a fact, which the treasurer is ready to confirm, that the receipts have more than balanced the expenditure, and as regards the second, so far from the St James's Theatre wanting patronage the box-bookkeeper's sheet will at any time negative the rumours on that head; for no theatrical establishment has enjoyed a greater share of patronage than Mr Braham's. It should be recollected that this occurs, too, at a time when the aristocracy and fashionable world are

---

* But in the *Morning Herald* it was stated that no signs of feasting were exhibited, and that in consequence the scene had more the appearance of a council chamber. Once again Fox Cooper was confused with the author of *Damp Beds* (see Chapter 2); but spare beds were often damp.

engaged spending the holidays at their country seats, and therefore of necessity absent from the metropolis—indeed, it would be exceedingly flattering to the exertions of any manager to boast of half the patronage which at present Braham enjoys.

Another ludicrous assertion calls loudly for contradiction. It is said that £4 a week is the average salary which the performers enjoy at the St James's Theatre: I do not pretend to pry into Mr Braham's private affairs, but I think I may fairly ask you, as a theatrical commentator, whether the inimitable Harley—the vivacious Barnett—the eccentric Gardner—the flexible Wright—the droll Hall—the pathetic Allison—the exquisite Stirling—and the clever Sala—members of the present company, would be content to remain under Braham's banner for £4 per week? The negative is obvious.

The above was signed Philo-Dramaticus, and a cutting from the newspaper was preserved by Harwood Cooper, providing evidence of the authorship of Fox Cooper, who did not omit to use a favourite word, "exertions", in connexion with the manager of the St James's Theatre.

It is thus not surprising that a one-act burletta by Fox Cooper, *Jenny Jones, or The Valley of Llangollen*, was produced at the St James's Theatre on 1 March 1838. In the manuscript and the print it is described as an operetta, but elsewhere as a ballad opera, with music by Sloman and Harroway, R.A.M. One unsympathetic reviewer commented that *Jenny Jones* had little to recommend her besides her name and character. But the *Idler and Breakfast-table Companion*, another short-lived fanciful journal, published in 1837–38, said it was full of fun, and made a great hit. The materials were slight but it was highly ludicrous and well wrought up. "Mr. Fox Cooper is, we believe, the author, and were this gentleman to write oftener for the theatre, we think it would be a kindness to the public." Among the actors Gardner was very funny, while Mr and Mrs Caulfield, who hailed from Birmingham, made a successful first appearance. Elsewhere a critic observed that the production (on St David's Day) was supposed to be a compliment to the Welsh saint, and that the attempt to put the ballad of the same title into dramatic shape was so far successful that the audience received it kindly. Today this would be described as damning with faint praise, but in early Victorian days, who knows?

Jenny Jones is a pleasant little offering, and the plot is simplicity itself. Jenny is the ward of Sir Watkin ap Shenkin, who wants to marry her. Edward, her lover, enters the employment of Sir Watkin as a gardener to be near Jenny. The fourth character is Bubble, an inebriated Beadle, who supplies the comedy. Finally there is Edward's uncle, Owen Owen, who is able to persuade Sir Watkin to join together the hands of the young lovers by threatening to foreclose a mortgage on Sir Watkin's property. The dedication by Fox Cooper in *Pattie's Penny Play* is to John Braham, and it again contains one of the author's favourite words in the sentence "may you long continue to enjoy the fruits of your generous exertions". He adds: "The soldier who conquers enemies abroad is not more a patriot than the manager who subdues profaneness and immorality at home. The first protects us from outward danger, the last preserves us from inward ruin." A nice and very early-Victorian sentiment, with tongue firmly in cheek. There are also three pages of introductory remarks dated 24 March 1838 over the name Philo-Dramaticus, again strongly suggesting the authorship (or at least the collaboration) of Fox Cooper himself. If this indeed be the case, the first two of the following extracts are particularly choice.

> Fox Cooper's ballad opera of *Jenny Jones*, ranks in merit next to his *Spare Bed*. It is not, perhaps, equal to that farce in point of wit; but the characters are whimsically sketched, and the sentiments and language unexceptionable. The words of the songs would have saved a hundred inferior pieces from the tomb of all the Capulets. As a poet, Mr Cooper stands confessedly high—his contributions to the magazines and papers, under the signature of F.O.X., are alone sufficient to stamp for him a fame of no ordinary or ephemeral duration. The "smile of yesterday", a song sung by Mr Caulfield, a vocalist of great promise, and new to the London boards, has already become exceedingly popular; and will, we have no doubt, rival any of our modern ballads, by Bayley, Lover, etc. It is replete with feeling and pathos.

> We are surprised that Mr Fox Cooper has not of late produced a farce at either of the patent houses. Is it because of

the great monopoly which exists in the trade of authorcraft at the Theatres-Royal? We have Fitzball working by steam at one establishment, and Planché translating like an industrious cobbler at another. Seriously and soberly, Mr Cooper employs his pen at a time when the monopolies of the theatre afford him but little chance of being brought fairly before the public.

The stage is not free, and without freedom, thank heaven, nothing nowadays can prosper. If, then, our bane be clear and palpable before us, is not its antidote equally so? Away with all monopoly, and you may enjoy new health and vigour, not otherwise.

We have thrown open the shipping trade, the silk trade, the beer trade, and the soap trade—let the catalogue be crowned and completed with the theatres, and the drama may revive, dramatic authors write well, actors increase in number and respectability, improve in quality, and augment in wealth; the public be delighted, the national fame in letters be increased; and another Shakespearean age spread its golden influence over our senses. Let every person, then, ambitious of the enterprise, be allowed to open a theatre; public competition will soon regulate the fair number of houses in that sort of business, as it does in others: let the proprietor or manager take out his licence for the performances at the stamp office, and the State will derive a benefit from the free system it never derived from the monopoly: let the said proprietor or manager be compelled to enter into recognizance with two sureties, to keep order and observe morality on his stage, and with these guarantees, and the superlative force of public opinion, which is greater than all law, we may establish a new constitution and standard system for our theatres, congenial to the spirit of the age, and permanently beneficial to the interests of the drama, and of the many who depend on its prosperity.

It will be seen that in 1846 Fox Cooper presented to the Lord Chamberlain his views on the regulation of places of public entertainment (Chapter 6).

The last two plays produced in this period are both associated with the Marylebone Theatre. Of the drama, *Cromwell*, I have no details, but a "petite" scene from it was played at Fox Cooper's benefit in December 1838, according to a handbill in my possession. A Garrick Theatre playbill advertising the *White Tower* (see Chapter 2), states that it was written by the author of the *Deserted Village* and *Oliver Cromwell*, possibly the full title of the play. The version of the latter produced at the Royal Pavilion Theatre in July 1832, with the sub-title *The Days of the Commonwealth*, may thus have been by Fox Cooper.

The Triumph of Venus was produced under Fox Cooper's management at the Marylebone in 1839. (See also Chapter 5.)

A piece entitled *King Death* was advertised for production on 23 January 1839 at the City of London Theatre, as being a spectacle from the quill of the manager (Mr Osbaldiston). A feature of this play was the interval of a thousand years that elapsed between the first and second, and the second and third acts. Owing to the indisposition of a Mr Green, the production was postponed, but after a chilly reception by the critics a later review said that the drama improved on repetition. Although Fox Cooper's authorship or contribution is by no means established, I mention *King Death* at this point because it was in Harwood Cooper's list, and because on 11 February 1839, *Figaro* stated that Mr Osbaldiston had pirated the title and plot of a piece mentioned in confidence to him by the author of *Hercules*. "As the matter is to come before the gentlemen of the long robe we refrain from commenting, but remark that it was strange that any man, especially a fox, should prove so foolish as to confide in the manager of one of the minor theatres . . ."* A further reason for believing that there was some link between Fox Cooper and the City of London Theatre at this period is that a piece of vaudeville entitled *Black Sentinel* was advertised for performance there on 12 February 1839. (See also Chapter 6.)

In my opinion a supposed passage of a thousand years between the acts of a play could well have appealed to Fox Cooper. But this order of interval has since been eclipsed in Shaw's *Back to Methuselah* which covers some thirty-five-thousand years. A story of a much more modest period, however, came to my notice in a Victorian theatrical paper, and

* I later discovered a reference in almost identical language in the *Crim. Con. Gazette* dated 26 January 1839. The same critic obviously penned both notices. It could have been Fox Cooper himself.

to me it was as fresh as a daisy. I hope it may be to others. On a wet night a lonely sailor on leave sought refuge in the pit of the local theatre, where he arrived after the rise of the curtain. The play was quite unknown to him, and when the lights went up at the first interval, he saw from the programme that there was a lapse of thirty years between Acts I and II, and between Acts II and III. It took him a little time to puzzle this out, but he finally came to the conclusion that it would be best to button on his cape and return to the public house round the corner, because quite a large proportion of the audience would obviously stand no chance of seeing the end of the show.

Other titles in Harwood Cooper's list for this decade are: *Perils of the Main* (1837) and *Irish Absentee* (1838). Both of these are untraced, but a version of the latter by J. W. Hyde was produced at the Marylebone Theatre in 1838, and printed in *Pattie's Penny Play*.

Chapter 4

A Mixture of Experiences: 1839–44

MUCH that I have related so far about Fox Cooper seems, at this distance of time, to be in keeping with the progress of an energetic, able, and ambitious young writer, subject to the financial difficulties in 1831–32 and 1836, and an urge to write vindictive letters to the press. But relatively small debts, easily overlooked by gentlefolk, could land one in gaol at that time, and ambitious young men are apt to be vindictive.

The aptitude for writing that Fox Cooper inherited from his father had developed primarily in the direction of dramatic authorship, or to be more accurate, farcical comedy and burlesque. And the output was not inconsiderable—some twenty-five plays in twelve years—bearing in mind his adventures in other fields, and the need to maintain a family sometimes met by parliamentary reporting, or theatrical criticism.

It might be suggested that his ability to adapt the ideas and inventions of others was more marked than his originality, but there was a diversity of talent. This feature, however, carried the germs of imperfection in so far as his occupation and interests changed more frequently than would be consonant with an ambition to succeed in any one walk of life. Too much variety was obviously a major weakness in his character quite apart from the habit of continually running into debt. Unfortunately I was not sufficiently interested in family affairs to ask questions of my father during his lifetime, and he was always rather reticent, except in the relating of some humorous anecdote such as the East-end story in Chapter 6. Indeed he may have known little about the life of his grandfather, who died when he was aged thirteen. My grandfather died when I was under three years old, so I could receive nothing from him direct.

This weakness which E. L. Blanchard was later to describe as lack of the "ballast of strong moral principles", was thus associated with, but possibly not confined to, instability of purpose, and a measure of looseness in financial dealings. I have put this rather mildly because my evidence, though abundant, is circumstantial; Fox Cooper may have been dogged by incessant bad luck, or incessant bad judgement. It is a family tradition that his major weakness was for cards.

I have, in consequence, seen fit to make a pause at the year 1839, since it marked Fox Cooper's second appearance in the Insolvent Debtors' Court, and his third term of imprisonment for debt. In that year he became thirty-three years of age; there is no reason to doubt he was happily married, and he had a good deal to his credit in the theatrical world. His reputation was seemingly growing, and, although of no distinguished parentage, he had enjoyed contact with some of the highest in the land, if not the most highly respected. The aim of anyone writing a biography of such a person, however imperfect the sources of information, should therefore be to find out what went astray. It is too early in this record to attempt even an interim opinion; it is enough for now to recognize that there is a question to consider.

The insolvency story in 1839, containing an important clue to another newspaper effort, is ushered in by two *London Gazette* notices, the first of which (on 2 March) comprises an order vesting in the Provisional Assignee the estate of Fox Cooper then resident in the Fleet Prison, and described as a dramatic author. A further notice orders the prisoner to be brought before the Insolvent Debtors' Court on 26 April to be dealt with according to the Statutes. The principal newspapers did not give any details of the proceedings, but the case was marked unopposed, and the Court Register shows that Fox Cooper was discharged on adjudication on 26 April, although he had been released from prison upon sureties and recognizances three weeks before. As he had been arrested on 21 February according to the Commitment book, the period of detention was some six weeks. The creditors, whose claims totalled only about £100, were recorded as William Nesbett, and Mr Levy, a gentleman we meet on subsequent occasions.

Also provided were six private addresses none of which was included in the *London Gazette* in 1836, and all of them close to central London. While at the second one: Wood Street (now Great Peter Street), Westminster, Fox Cooper made a decent pencil drawing of the corner house, from a first-floor window on a Sunday evening in the Spring of 1837. This shows a landing wharf and the premises of Thomas Hubert, coal and coke merchant,* the river in the middle ground, and Lambeth Palace with the gardens in the background. On the reverse of the drawing Harwood Cooper noted in 1894 that the building was then a public house, and that it faced Parliament House gardens (where buildings had previously existed).

From the third address in this list, namely Manor Place, Walworth, the notice states that Fox Cooper was taken to Horsemonger Lane Prison for debt: possibly the same incident as that which arose from the insolvency in 1836, although the sequence of addresses (which I have prepared from the *London Gazette* notices and Harwood Cooper's list) suggests that it was in 1837. Either the *Gazette* contained an error, or there was another spell in prison which did not lead to proceedings in the Insolvent Debtors' Court.

While at an address in Goswell Street (Middlesex), Fox Cooper was said to be renting an office at 12 Wellington Street, Strand, evidently for some publishing venture. (*Paul Pry* and a later journal, *Cerberus*, were published from No. 13 of that street.) Finally, the prisoner is described as dramatic author, editor, printer and publisher, during part of the time partner of James Turner as proprietors of the *Crim. Con. Gazette*. I had never heard of this publication but I found it in the infallible Index of the B.M. newspaper annexe at Colindale, and when the volume was brought to me it was clear that the words "Crim. Con." are short for Criminal Conversation, an expression better understood by the legal fraternity than by the lay public.† I subsequently found advertisements for this paper

---

* Robson's London directory for 1837 confirms the name with the address: Dorset Wharf, 7 Millbank Street, Westminster.

† This right of action at common law for trespass against the husband was abolished in 1858, since when the expression "Crim. Con." has become obsolete.

in *Figaro*. It was described as a "journal des amours", and was
due for publication on 28 July 1838 at the price of twopence.
Afterwards it was announced that illegal means had been
adopted by many to suppress it, with resulting delay, but it
would positively appear on 11 August.

A description was given of the features it would contain,
and the publisher promised that heartless seducers would be
held up to public indignation. On 18 August *Figaro* stated that
the *Crim. Con. Gazette* would appear definitely on that day,
and presumably no further advertisement was needed. This
weekly journal, although more in the nature of a magazine
and thus avoiding the newspaper stamp duty, eventually
appeared on 25 August 1838. (In the volume at Colindale
there are some seventy issues, the last dated 11 January 1840.)
A leading article declared that the *Crim. Con. Gazette and
Journal of the Haut Ton* had been established to arrest *as much
as possible* the progress of aristocratic vice and debauchery.
No mention is made of the names of the proprietors on the back
sheet which merely shows that it was printed and published by a
Mr G. Hucklebridge from Charles Street, Hatton Garden.

If the publication of vivid descriptions of unsavoury events
that were alleged to be taking place, or to have taken place,
was all that was needed then this newspaper should have been
a roaring success, as it certainly spared no pains in doing just
that. In the first issue the newspaper refers to the Court of
Common Pleas, Wednesday, 22 June 1836, and gives many
details about the action of Norton *v.* Lord Melbourne. Cases
of this kind—another was Lord Grosvenor *v.* the Duke of
Cumberland—were continuous features throughout the issues
I scanned. To decide whether they were all based on fact or
some of them merely fiction would take a good deal of research,
and would not prove very rewarding.

In addition to lawsuits such as the above the *Crim. Con.
Gazette* contained descriptions of disorderly houses, a lot of
personal current scandal, poems of an amorous kind, and a
theatrical column. It is in the latter that Fox Cooper's hand
can sometimes be discerned. For example, a letter is quoted
from a party in Kennington in which the writer laments that
his daughter had been provided with employment at the Surrey
Theatre, and wonders whether the paper could do anything

to help him punish her seducer. In the same column the reply is given, and it states that Mr Davidge, proprietor of the theatre, is a respectable man and would not doubt assist. The reply continued: "We have heard that he is about to revive a comedy called *Simpson & Co.*" It is evident that Fox Cooper was giving a bit of an advertisement to a friend, and possibly reaping an indirect reward. Another theatrical note in May 1839 stated that the little Marylebone Theatre had at last fallen into the hands of gentlemen, and proceeded to give quite a useful advertisement for that establishment; later issues also praised the management. It so happens that Fox Cooper became a joint lessee and the acting manager at the Marylebone in the same month, as will be related in Chapter 5.

Curiously enough the last issue of this journal was entitled the *Bon Ton Gazette*. The leading article referred to the change of name, but said there would be no change in its policy which was to please and amuse the town. Similar personnel would be employed, and their work would comprehend every topic that engages "high life". It looked as though the paper was merely making a new start under a different name, with the announcement that it would in future be stitched in monthly parts, and there was no presentiment of its impending finish. But it is possible that a warning had been given, and that some want of delicacy in a note about Her Majesty being furnished with a larger bed resulted in the descent of Nemesis. The kindest thought one can harbour about the *Crim. Con. Gazette* is that Fox Cooper was interested only to the extent of being able to say what he liked in a theatrical column. Otherwise, it is anything but a recommendation. There may have been profits from the enterprise, but Fox Cooper's share did not suffice to keep him out of gaol in the first half of 1839. Yet the paper may have provided him with some employment until January 1840 or even later, as Harwood Cooper (born 1826) has made a note in which he claims to have been engaged in the office of *Haut Ton* in the spring of 1840. A very youthful apprentice.

On 1 February 1840, another son, later named Alfred Edgar, was born to Frederick Fox and Ann Cooper. They were then living at Canterbury Place, St Mary's, Lambeth. The birth was not registered until 2 March and no names were then given to the child, but some family notes, still preserved, confirm the date of birth. Alfred Edgar Cooper lived until June 1901, the death certificate incorrectly giving his age as fifty-six years. A daughter named Mrs d'Ernst was the informant. I know little about this son of Fox Cooper, and even the above information proved quite difficult to obtain owing to the disparity in the dates and the absence of Christian names in the birth certificate. He became a musician, to wit a violinist, and at one time was the leader of the orchestra at Drury Lane. Occasionally he arranged an overture or a "medley of music" as mentioned elsewhere in this biography, and I have a manuscript for the piano entitled: "Miller and his Men, being a set of five quadrilles arranged by Alfred Edgar Cooper from the beautiful melodies of popular melodrama." (They convey little on the pianoforte today.) He married Caroline Gallagher in January 1864, and a son (also Alfred Edgar) was born in April 1871; but the boy died of variola when eleven months old, and was buried at Brookwood. Alfred Edgar Cooper is depicted as a member of a minstrel band, of which a photograph appeared in the *Illustrated Sporting and Dramatic News* on 10 June 1899, and under which Harwood Cooper has written, "Brother Alfred". It is difficult to decide which of the two violinists is Brother Alfred or bears the family likeness, as both their faces are covered with a similar flocculent growth.

By Easter 1840 the family had moved to Meads Place, Lambeth, but my knowledge of Fox Cooper's activities for the rest of that year is restricted to the production of two plays, described in Chapter 6. Christmas was spent at another address: Great Union Street, Newington, where the family was residing at the date of the national census on 7 June 1841. The return confirms the state of the family: Fox Cooper and Ann both aged thirty-five, with their two surviving children, Harwood and Alfred Edgar, aged fifteen and one year respectively. Before that event, however, a fresh adventure had loomed in sight.

Perhaps the perfect example of Fox Cooper's many changes of direction is shown by the story of the *Nelson Examiner*, a New Zealand newspaper. My first knowledge of this episode was derived from the *Theatrical Times* of June 1847, and I have pieced it together with the helpful aid of the Turnbull Library, Wellington, and the Public Record Office; I would not vouch for all the details but the main trend is established beyond doubt.

In a pleasure boat on the river Thames in the early Spring of 1841 Fox Cooper met a Mr Aglionby, Liberal M.P. for Cockermouth, and a director of the New Zealand Company.* With the best intentions the latter suggested to Fox Cooper that he should start a newspaper in the developing district of Nelson, at the northerly end of the South Island, the second colony in New Zealand.

After three insolvencies, and the notorious *Crim. Con. Gazette*, Fox Cooper could contemplate a change of air, and the idea was full of promise. So he wrote to the directors early in May outlining his reasons and qualifications for establishing a paper in the colony. Receiving an encouraging reply he set about obtaining a round dozen of letters from journalists and other friends testifying to his ability and experience for such a project. There were no half measures in this effort. One from William Maginn, the founder of *Fraser's Magazine*, said that no one appeared more capable of successfully managing every department of a newspaper. Maginn as a contributor to *John Bull* probably knew H. F. Cooper. Another from Thomas Gaspey, a former editor of the *Sunday Times*, referred to that union of tact and veracity likely to render a paper interesting to the general reader.

Alfred Mallalieu, editor of the *Courier*, said that Fox Cooper had discharged his duties with all the ability that could be desired when under his direction on the staff of the *Guardian*, and the *Public Ledger* some years since. Outside the world of journalism were personal testimonials from Lord Kenyon, and Sir Charles Aldis, a distinguished surgeon; the latter expressed the hope that Fox Cooper would continue to enjoy good health. Finally there was one from Elliott (q.v.). All these references built up an impressive volume of unqualified approval, duly submitted to New Zealand House. In June and July, Fox Cooper was still trying to obtain a decision from the directors, and this was in due course favourably given, together with an advance of £200.

To assist in this venture Fox Cooper consulted Charles

---

* Fox Cooper had been introduced to the Company, if not to Mr Aglionby, by a Mr Garratt. This could have been Alderman Garratt, an uncle of Fox Cooper's wife.

Elliott (1811–76) a friend with a established printing business in London, and persuaded him to be his partner. Elliott would provide the printing machinery, and Fox Cooper would undertake to procure and ship to New Zealand a timber house which his family and Elliott would share. A piece of land for the house was selected, the purchase being subject only to Fox Cooper obtaining from the New Zealand Company a mortgage covering the total cost. In September he made requests to the company for advertisements for a trial issue of the paper to be published in London, and a loan to cover the freight on his goods to be shipped to New Zealand; on account of the latter he was paid £100, but there arose a difference of view as to whether this sum was intended to cover a debt from Fox Cooper to a Holborn builder, Henry Manning, clearly in connexion with the timber house. The former maintained that the company had agreed to pay Manning direct, while the secretary of the company said otherwise. Some of the directors seem to have been in doubt.

During October 1841 four ships sailed for Nelson, New Zealand, with 764 emigrants, but one of these ships was wrecked. Another, the *Mary-Ann* (master, Thomas Bolton) a barque of 600 tons lying in the Downs, contained our party and their chattels. But by accident or misunderstanding Fox Cooper had omitted to discharge Mr Manning's debt of £68, with the result that a writ was served on 29 September, requiring payment and costs within four days. The *Mary-Ann* duly sailed on the fourth day, 2 October, but not before a cabin passenger, Fox Cooper, had been taken out of the ship against his consent, according to the certificate of the master. I have no doubt that the family of Fox Cooper also came ashore, and I am left wondering whether he was really enthusiastic about making his career in New Zealand.

From the debtor's side of Dover Castle, Fox Cooper at once entered into correspondence with New Zealand House, but he obtained little satisfaction apart from the return of his testimonials. After six weeks he was released from the castle on a promise to pay Mr Manning's account by instalments and he went to 46 Liverpool Street, London, from whence he hammered away at the New Zealand Company. He sought to recover his passage money, freight on goods shipped, the cost of advertisements in the trial issue of the newspaper,* and an award for the miseries he had endured. The account was resisted and Fox Cooper threatened legal action. The company replied by sending the name of their solicitors. Finally, Fox Cooper climbed down and agreed to accept the company's own judgement of what they should reimburse him, although he now considered he was owed £177. The outcome was that in early December the finance committee of the company, doubtless owing to the benign influence of Mr Aglionby, one of its members, allowed the payment of £107 12s. 6d. towards the items claimed by Fox Cooper. But the company wished for no further dealings with him, and Alderman Copeland, M.P., another director, was deputed to see Mr Garratt, who had made the introduction in the first place.

Copies of some of Fox Cooper's letters to the New Zealand Company are included as Appendix I(a). It is illuminating that he referred to the printing equipment as his own property, and that he continued to regard Elliott as his partner. He implied, too, that the newspaper would be under his control, although Elliott was on his way to New Zealand as the prospective sole proprietor. The list of cabin passengers in the *Mary-Ann* is among the carefully written records of the New Zealand Company. It contains the Elliotts with their two children, and G. R. Richardson who became the first editor of the newspaper; the names of Fox Cooper and his wife are crossed through.

The details of these incidents, which have been fortunately preserved, show Fox Cooper as the victim of delusions of a grandeur which he did not possess. He was unable to face the facts of a situation, and relied on others to extricate him from an awkward predicament. It is strange that Elliott did not— or could not—help Fox Cooper to raise the amount to pay Manning. Perhaps he was secretly relieved when his partner was taken off the ship. He was to obtain a more reliable if less colourful editor, and the newspaper became his own property, as is evidenced at its publication in April 1842.

Despite his imprisonment in Dover Castle, or perhaps because of his residence there, Fox Cooper must have found the sea air invigorating. Thus he lost no time in opening negotiations with the Theatre Royal, of which he became the

---

* Evidently printed in London as the *Nelson Advertiser*, but untraced.

lessee soon enough to advertise his Christmas pantomime in the local paper by 11 December 1841. The receipt of over £100 from the New Zealand Company provided the capital to open the season, and for much of the year 1842 the theatre at Dover kept Fox Cooper well occupied, as will be related in Chapter 5 about theatrical management.

In 1843 there appeared a newspaper by which Fox Cooper was often remembered although it survived for less than six months. It was claimed in the *Theatrical Times* that *Cerberus*, the title of the paper, had been projected in conjunction with the Chisholm of Chisholm; but Fox Cooper had also made an abortive attempt to obtain the interest of the New Zealand Company, as is shown by the following delightful extracts from his letters from the *Cerberus* office, 164 Strand:

> As the original projector of the *Nelson Examiner* which in spite of every obstacle I have firmly established, I beg leave to apply to you for the advertisements of the New Zealand Company for my new London paper the *Cerberus*, the prospectus of which I now forward to you." 12 June 1843.

> "I feel every disposition to promote the success of the proposed fourth colony through the columns of *Cerberus*, the circulation of which is now 10,000 copies." 13 July 1843.

> "With reference to the *Nelson Examiner* now carried on by my partner with much success in the second colony . . ." 19 July 1843.

The sixth issue of Cerberus did in fact carry an advertisement regarding emigration to New Zealand, where the fourth colonial settlement of New Edinburgh would be of particular interest to people from Scotland. Arrangements had been made for the foundation of a Presbyterian church.

It was also claimed in the *Theatrical Times* that *Cerberus* featured four different lines of politics under four different heads. This is, one might say, just three-quarters true: not unlike so much in the informative article in that interesting theatrical journal which itself enjoyed a life of less than three years. Alas, for it is most valuable on the minor theatres.

Cerberus was first published for the week ended Saturday, 17 June 1843, by Frederick Cooper (no mention of Fox), without reference to any interest of the Chisholm of Chisholm.

The price was sixpence a copy, it was nicely got up, and has the look of a class periodical. But it achieved only twenty-three issues according to the bound volume at Colindale, and the number of stamps issued was 21,150,* suggesting either a weekly circulation of less than a thousand or evasion of the stamp duty. For a few weeks in August and onwards Fox Cooper tried to raise the circulation by giving away with each issue a portrait of the Queen, or one of various notabilities. He then found it necessary to raise the price to eightpence, but reverted to the original figure after five weeks. It was obviously unprofitable, and Fox Cooper alluded to it in the following year as the cause of his insolvency, although one imagines that the Chisholm of Chisholm bore part of the loss.

I could best describe *Cerberus* as a weekly of political and general interest with provocative comments on current events. There were actually three political heads: Whig, Tory, Radical (in that order, which may or may not be significant) for which —and this is a Fox Cooper touch—it was claimed that three distinct editors were retained; the fourth or general head was intended to be an impartial summing up, and contained other miscellaneous items, including theatricals. Each of the first three headings of the paper is surmounted by a distinctive design incorporating the head of a dog: Whig and Radical both look like a cross between a bulldog and a pug; the Tory is a forlorn-looking bloodhound. The general heading embraces the three dogs with the Tory on top. I have made the following definitive extracts from the first issue:

Whig Head

A Whig is a friend of progressive principles. He differs from a Tory by deeming it better to aid the progress than the permanence of the institutions of society.

Toleration of religious sects in 1690, and middle-class representation in 1832, were the principles of the great epochs of Whig conflict and triumph. Against the Tories, the Whigs contend for progress. Differing from the Radicals, they fight for reforms which are practical as well as progressive.

The recent government of the country by the Whigs—

---

* House of Commons reports—Select Committee on newspaper stamps, 1851. It is a strange coincidence that there had been twenty-three issues of *Cooper's John Bull* in 1826.

F

eleven years of legislation more or less complete on progressive principles—has prevented a revolution of blood.

Whiggism we conceive to be a rational attachment to free principles and free institutions; in opposition, on the one hand, to arbitrary power and extravagant doctrines of supremacy; and, on the other, to those extreme democratical notions of liberty and the rights of man, which are apt to be generated by imperfect knowledge, or want of due reflection, or in heated and infatuated minds."

Tory Head

What, then, is Toryism?

It is this. The principle of the Glorious Revolution of 1688. A Constitutional Monarchy, the Crown having solemn duties as well as fenced rights. The Three Estates of the Realm—Queen, Lords and Commons. The Freedom of Parliament, its perfect latitude of speech, and its Annual Session. The Spirit of Magna Charta. The Bill of Rights. The Habeas Corpus Act. The Supremacy of the Law. The Independence of the Judges. The Equality of all Men in the eye of the Law.

The Liberty of the Press, and the wholesome Influence of Public Opinion in every Ramification of Government Employment, in a word—"Fear God, and Honour the King"—The Inviolability of Property—the People fairly Represented—the People Educated—the People Free;—and, if possible (humanly speaking), the People Prosperous and Happy.

Radical Head

A Whig or a Tory—despite the impulses, it may be, of a high and generous nature—is one

"Who, born for the universe, narrows his mind,
And to party gives up what was meant for mankind."

How different a being is a Radical! He is not bounded or restrained in his sympathies or his objects by any party or factious considerations. His pen and his lips give expression to the genuine impulses of his heart.

He looks upon society, not as a confederacy for the elevation and aggrandizement of a few, but as a combination for the general good. And as he believes that men generally understand their own good better than others can understand it, and would pursue it more zealously and undeviatingly than any others can be expected to pursue it, he is for putting all in a condition to do so; that is, into a condition of civil and political equality.

Confessing that our sympathies are strongly enlisted on the side of the poorer classes, we shall at all times evince due respect for the rights and property of the wealthy and the exalted. While we shall ever look with a most watchful interest at every event or question connected with the rights of labour, or affecting the welfare of the industrious classes, we shall studiously avoid all that may be likely to produce irritation and animosity, and seek to lead all classes to a sense of their common interest and social independence.

We are not bringing down those above to the level of those beneath them, but for conferring increased advantages and security upon the higher ranks, by elevating the character and improving the condition of the lower.

General Head

We give to each of the three prominent political parties a separate space for the promulgation of its peculiar tenets and intelligence, and for the free advocacy of its principles; and we have secured for each the most experienced political and the highest literary talent, which can he obtained on its side. Thus the readers of the *Cerberus* will have an opportunity of seeing all that can be urged, by any party, for, or against, any measure; and while, with every possible information before them, their judgements will be left unfettered, they will be occasionally assisted in arriving at just conclusions, from conflicting arguments by an impartial summing up under The General Head.

The walls of all London have been placarded with the query, "Who are the Editors of *The Cerberus*?" We hasten to answer the question, so far at least as we may, for we are not permitted to give their names, but to this we pledge our faith, that each department has its own *distinct* Editor, who is thoroughly in earnest on the political side whose doctrines he advocates, that each is possessed of tried and proved ability; and that independently of these qualifications each stands proudly on his high and well known private character. Each has made his profession of political faith, this day; and to these we refer in the meantime; but caring little ourselves for professions, we claim to be judged by the manner in which those professions shall be acted up to in future— and so we send our bantling forth.

The above sentiments leave little to be desired even after the passing of a century, while the aloofness of the summing up is worthy of the first leader in a great national daily.

From the last issue, dated 18 November 1843, I have made three extracts:

Whig Head

Of the three elections for London, Kendal and Salisbury, two are decided. London in the return of Mr Pattison, gave an influence in favour of Free Trade which we hope will be extended throughout the length and breadth of the land. The intelligent electors of Kendal have nobly followed the example of London, in despite of almost unprecedented efforts against it, by bribery, coercion, intimidation, and false persuasions, for which latter purpose every beer-shop it appears, was visited and drunkenness encouraged at Tory cost for the purpose of deluding; by which process a few of the weakest, the most unprincipled and the poorest were gained over. A large majority of electors, however, withstood all temptations presented; nothing could allure them from the path of integrity; even the Lowther influence was only a straw in the balance against the national good of Free Trade. The electors of Salisbury, we hope, will show a similar spirit. Mr Cobden has been there doing his duty.

Tory Head

No doubt we shall be told by the journals in the interest and pay of the Anti-Corn Law League that that *honest and patriotic* body has gained another signal triumph in the return of Mr Warburton, of Bridport notoriety, and the *fidus Achates* of the modern Cocker—Joseph Hume, for the Radical borough of Kendal. The triumph, however, notwithstanding the fact that the palaver, the artifices, and the money of the League were unscrupulously employed to achieve it, is in reality no triumph at all; for during the last ten years and upwards no Conservative candidate has ever ventured to contest the borough.

Nevertheless, although we do not regard the result of either this or the London election as being of that vital importance which is and will be ascribed to it by the adverse faction, it cannot be denied that the success they have experienced in these two essays will cheer on and stimulate the Leaguers to further exertions; and it would be unwise to depreciate the importance, nay, the positive necessity, of counteracting those exertions by renewed activity and vigour on the part of the Conservatives.

Radical Head

A great many shipwrecks have occurred recently including as might be expected, the loss of life and of property.

Unfortunately men go in sailing vessels, which ought more properly to be made *firewood* of, and, having them insured perhaps for more than their value, it becomes an object of *desire* rather than fear, to hear of their loss, and as to the lives which are so often lost too—why they cost owners nothing, and can soon be replaced! Indeed, a shipwreck is always a benefit to the owner, in respect of the sailors, whether their lives be lost or saved; because our wise legislators have so ruled it, that in case of a shipwreck, the sailor shall have no wages for the whole voyage, although it may so happen, and it often does, that the wreck occurs as the vessel is just reaching the destined port, and they may have been months, nay almost years on the voyage, but to the sailor it is all the same—whatever he may have earned, he gets nothing!

We shall soon again, however, recur to the subject and put that matter beyond dispute, and also suggest some remedies.

But *Cerberus* never did recur to the subject, simply because it was published no more.

In search of a reason for the failure of this paper—apart from Fox Cooper's remark in court that it was discontinued when he became lessee of the City of London Theatre—I am inclined to think that, other than the novelty of its approach to the political arena, it had little to offer which could not be obtained elsewhere. And even in that arena one does not expect to pay for the opinions of one's adversaries.

As if to emphasize that the insolvency proceedings in 1831, 1836 and 1839 were characteristic of Fox Cooper's normal way of life, a further period of financial embarrassment arose towards the end of 1843. *Cerberus* had landed him in debt, and was unable to protect him from his creditors. He therefore sought protection elsewhere.

A notice in the *London Gazette* on 18 December, exactly one month after the date of the last issue, contains an application by

Fox Cooper to the Court of Bankruptcy for protection under the
Acts: 5th and 6th Vic. These were recent Acts of Parliament
designed to protect insolvent debtors from being arrested
and placed in prison for relatively small amounts, and
commonly known as "the Gentlemen's (non-traders) Acts";
at that period in the development of our democratic society
it was apparently thought that no gentleman could be made
bankrupt, and *per contra* that no bankrupt could be a gentleman.
In this notice the applicant announced that he intended to present
a petition to the Bankruptcy Court praying to be examined
touching his debts, estate and effects, and to be protected from
all process upon making a full disclosure and surrender of such
estate for payment of his just debts. The notice was repeated.

It is pertinent that in the following year there was a further
enactment known as "The Private Arrangements Act 1844",
for facilitating arrangements between debtors and creditors.
I have been told by a gentleman of the law that the main gist
of it was that any debtor (not being a trader), with the concur-
rence of one-third in value and number of his creditors, could
present a petition setting forth his liabilities and assets and such
proposals as he was able to make for future payment; and for
such proposals to be carried out under the supervision of the
court. If granted, the debtor was protected from the usual
procedure of arrest. Unfortunately, the files of proceedings under
these Acts were destroyed by order at the end of 1932, under
the Public Record Office Act, 1877, and thus was lost a lot of
information that might have enriched, or enlightened, this tale.

The next entry in the *London Gazette* was on 9 February
1844 announcing that, whereas a petition of Fox Cooper
having been filed in the Court of Bankruptcy and the interim
order for protection from process having been given under the
Act for Insolvent Debtors, Fox Cooper was required to appear
in the Court of Bankruptcy on 14 February for the purpose
of being examined. Fortunately a report is contained in the
Morning Chronicle of the day following. Briefly the point about
the proceedings was that Fox Cooper contended he was not a
trader, and therefore could not be brought under the operation
of the Bankruptcy Act. It was argued by his counsel that the
editor of a newspaper was placed in the same situation as
an author or an artist, who could not respectively be said to

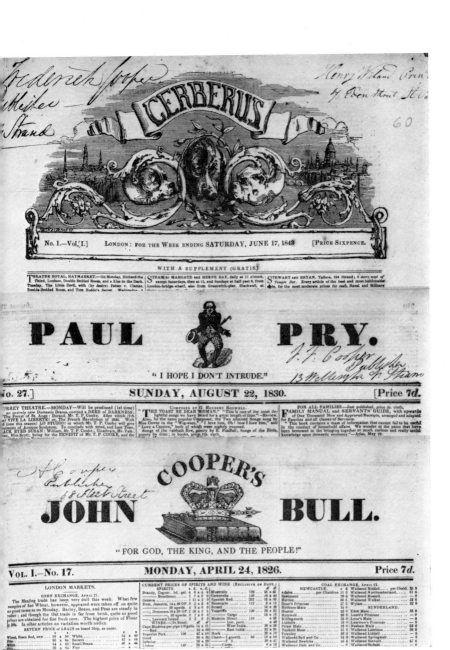

Cerberus, 1843, edited by Fox Cooper. *Paul Pry*, 1830, edited by Fox Cooper. *Cooper's John Bull*, 1826, edited by H. F. Cooper.

deal in paper or in canvas, although each must use the particular material suitable to his business but to which only the creation
of the brain gave any value. Mr Commissioner Fane did not
accept the argument, but granted an adjournment, and provided for the protection of the insolvent during the meantime.

On 1 March the hearing was continued, and again there is a
press report. This makes it quite clear that the Insolvent was
applying for an interim order (protection) under the new law.
The application was objected to on the ground that the Insolvent was a trader, and owed more than £300 (the sum limited
by the Statute which also protected small traders). He, therefore,
had no *locus standi* in that Court as an insolvent. Mr Sturgeon
on behalf of Fox Cooper, at some length and with considerable
ingenuity, proceeded to argue that the Insolvent was not a
trader by reason of using paper to convey his ideas to the world,
and cited various cases in support of the argument. Mr Fane
had no doubt that the applicant was subject to the Bankruptcy
laws, perhaps not as an author, but he had chosen to add the
occupation "publisher" and in this manner he had bought and
sold paper in his business. The petition was accordingly dismissed. Fox Cooper lost the protection he sought, and he was
subsequently arrested for debt.

In due course the Court for the relief of Insolvent Debtors
made an order on 24 July vesting the estate of Fox Cooper,
(sued and committed as Charles Frederick Fox Cooper) in the
Provisional Assignee. The debtor was described as a dramatic
author and lessee of the City of London Theatre; he was in the
Queen's prison. And there he remained until ordered to be
brought into court on the last day of September to be dealt
with according to the Statutes. There were also enumerated
seven private addresses. In the daily press the order was listed
as "original unopposed" but the proceedings were not reported.

According to the Court Register in the Public Record Office
the case was heard on 30 September, but Fox Cooper had been
discharged by D.C. (Deputy Commissioner?) on 27 September;
perhaps the ghost walked. As the date of his petition was 22
July it would seem he was in gaol for at least two months, but
why he was sued with the additional name, Charles, is unexplained. Shortly after obtaining his liberty he returned to
theatrical management.

Chapter 5

Theatrical Management—to the Year 1846

I HAVE suggested in a previous chapter that Fox Cooper may have begun his theatrical career as a youthful actor at the Adelphi, and have related how he had started to write plays with some measure of success. It is clear also that he was attracted by the idea of managing theatres possibly because he felt he would be good at spotting talent and it would thus be profitable, but more likely, or at least equally so, because this would enable him to ensure the production of his own dramatic efforts. According to the *Theatrical Times* once more, Fox Cooper had by June 1847 been the lessee of five minor London theatres: Marylebone, Olympic, Victoria, City of London, and New Strand. I will deal with the last named at a later stage because his management started only in March 1847, and because there is a relative wealth of material which justifies a chapter to itself.

In respect of two of the London theatres I have been unable to verify Fox Cooper's claim to have been the lessee. One of these is the Olympic Theatre, his tenure of which could only have been before the year 1831, when it was taken over by the celebrated Madame Vestris for quite a long period of time: but he might have been a sub-tenant for a short spell. The other is the Victoria, previously Coburg, but later the "Old Vic", and here again there is no trace of his claim, even with the help of Malcolm Morley who has done a lot of research on this theatre. A reasonable conjecture is that there may have been some kind of sub-tenancy or association in 1833, when two of Fox Cooper's plays appeared at the Victoria, followed by the disagreement over the *Deserted Village*. The two other London theatres are dealt with in this chapter. In addition to these theatres there were others outside London of equal importance to the story.

Mention should be made of the two clues provided by the *London Gazette*, and Harwood Cooper's notes, namely Paris and Caernarvon. For the former, research is likely to prove difficult and costly but I hope one day to examine the news-papers and contemporary theatrical literature in Paris covering the years 1830–31. For the latter the British Museum have a number of playbills dated 1831–32, from which it is clear that the Caernarvon Theatre was then quite active. But the name Cooper does not appear either as manager or actor.

Fox Cooper's management of the Marylebone Theatre, supported by his residence for a period in Lisson Grove, is well authenticated. An excellent booklet by Malcolm Morley (*The Old Marylebone Theatre*) describes how Fox Cooper, with two others named Gordon and T. P. Taylor, consorted for the purpose of management in the year 1839, commencing their operations on Whit Monday, 20 May. A few random extracts from a printed announcement may be amusing. (That this was written by Fox Cooper is evidenced by the prose, and the use of a favourite word in the sentence: The Lessees beg to observe that it is their intention to bring forward a description and style of Dramatic Entertainment that shall equal the best exertions of other Metropolitan Theatres.)

"Patrons are advised that the lessees have entirely re-organ-ized the Stage, and the embellishments of the proscenium are unequalled for chasteness and splendour. A looking-glass curtain will be introduced, enabling everyone in the theatre to see, inter alia, a reflection of the gorgeous paraphernalia of the boxes. Private family boxes are two guineas; the dress boxes, seats two shillings, are exclusive and select, and bonnets will be rigidly excluded. Not less respectable, though not quite so exclusive, is the pit, price one shilling. [Upon the gallery, price sixpence, no comment was made.] The carpeted saloon will be thrown open at the commencement of the performance for those who may wait until half-price: for fathers of families, and others, this arrangement will prove invaluable."

Fox Cooper was acting manager, Gordon, the treasurer, and T. P. Taylor, the stage manager. Malcolm Morley, who said Fox Cooper had a wealthy background, could not know that he had been so frequently in gaol for debt, and had left the Fleet Prison within a month of the opening date: he was presumably met by the other two when he emerged. But it is difficult to imagine who was really in charge at the Marylebone, and who decided upon the productions. As might have been expected, the arrangement did not last for very long, possibly because the trinity was a bit unwieldy for a small theatre. Not, however, before two pieces by Fox Cooper had been performed: the first was *The Spare Bed*, in which he took the part of Captain Ardent, and according to Malcolm Morley (with some justification as has been noted elsewhere) testified to his small ability as a comedian. The other was a burlesque called *The Triumph of Venus, or Cupid and Capers*. This play is included in Harwood Cooper's list but I had no evidence of its public performance before reading Morley's work. He states that a rotund actor, described as the Archer Boy, came on as Cupid.

Many pertinent references to the Marylebone Theatre at this period are contained in *Figaro*. The earliest describes a benefit performance for Fox Cooper in December 1838, a few months before his period of management; I have a small playbill, headed 'The Author's Night'. That journal, remarking that the entertainments were for the benefit of the author, waxed sarcastic and questioned whether this meant the author of the Royal Marylebone Theatre. After a performance of T. P. Taylor's *Nicholas Nickleby*, the celebrated American comic singer, Mr Harper, brought down the uproarious thunder of the "gods", who were (according to *Figaro*) charged by the worthy author the trifling sum of four-and-sixpence each. The author then produced a most elaborate sketch, that it seems had been discovered in a deed box between the ceiling and the flooring of Whitehall some time back, the enacting of which excited from its originality a perfect paralysis in the audience. This is evidently a reference to a performance of a scene from *Cromwell*, in which Fox Cooper took the name part.

Figaro went on to say that the author was eminently successful, T. P. Taylor's imitations were peculiarly original, Mr
Atwood was inexpressibly funny, and the representation of the
Coronation of Queen Elizabeth was a most gorgeous spectacle
in which 375 supers were rapturously encored. The performance concluded with *The Spare Bed*. Eventually the author
was called for, and after some minutes he appeared, placed his
hand on his heart and bowed most gratefully to the audience
who seemed highly delighted with the great treat they had
witnessed. "Really, we passed a pleasant evening and must
say the theatre is well conducted and deserves support." On
14 January 1839, *Figaro* said that the author's benefit at the
Marylebone had been a serious loss, in spite of his extraordinary
talents as an actor. The boys in the neighbourhood were not
enlightened enough to appreciate the sterling worth of the
entertainment but they admired the flowing locks of Mr T. P.
Taylor. In *Figaro's* opinion, baked 'taturs and leg-of-beef soup
were more to their liking, although Johnson and Lee were
quietly pocketing a thousand pounds a week! The last named
were the lessors.

In due course *Figaro* reported that the Marylebone had opened
under the new management with about the best company
it could ever boast of. The programme went off well, and an
address was given by Mr Gordon, apologizing for the absence
of the glass curtain which had been heavily advertised. Fox
Cooper also addressed the audience, and *Figaro* thought it
was in rather bad taste to tell them that there were faults but
that they could not find them out. On 3 June, the Marylebone
was playing the very devil with the unwashed of the district.
The management was strong in quality but weak in power.
"Fox Cooper writes plays in his best style, but the sooner the
theatre is turned into a Methodist Chapel the better." Next
week the heading was Royal Marrowbone, and a line is
unfortunately missing from the printed paragraph. But, to
paraphrase the comments, after the theatre had been open
for twelve nights Gordon, whose real name was Brookman,
disappeared in company with someone else and the cash, leaving the half-starved actors to dine off a red herring and a stale
potato. Mr Fox Cooper had made a hit in *The Spare Bed*,
and retired nightly in ecstasy to a more downy one at home,

while Mr T. P. Taylor, the Lord of everything, bewailed in accents positive the bitter fate of the theatre in Marylebone. In the following issue it was alleged that the actors had shared only fifteen shillings each the previous week, and one shilling each the week before. Furthermore, the firm of Cooper, Gordon (alias Brookman) and Taylor was infirm, and could not stand, but the theatre still held on, resorting to any means to keep going: even the rats and mice were not expected to pass unmolested.

On 29 June, *Figaro* announced that a benefit was expected for Fox Cooper, the gifted author of so many dramatic pieces: "To one possessed of so much poetry in his soul and to whom the public are under so many literary obligations, it can need no excitement of ours to induce a four-mile promenade in the genial month of July." A fortnight later *Figaro* reported that the Marylebone was again closed, and feared it had been a disastrous season for all concerned. "We were to have had a glass curtain costing at least a thousand guineas in a place called a theatre which never cost two. But alas, it never appeared. There has been some talent, after all, during the season: Mr Cooper (or, as he is jocularly called 'Careful John'), and Mr T. P. Taylor, an uncommonly promising young man."

While these notices contain much more sarcasm than praise, and while much of it was obviously pure invention, it is curious that *Figaro* took such a persistent interest in the happenings at the Marylebone. One possibility is that Fox Cooper had been dramatic critic of that paper, and his successor was having fun at his expense. *Figaro* itself closed down in August 1839, after a lifetime of about seven years. It is remarkable that as in the case of the *Crim. Con. Gazette*, the last issue contains references to the Sovereign in terms which are both impudent and indelicate. One of the least offensive mentions the Queen's love at first sight disclosed in an imaginary conversation with Lord Melbourne. Some of the others may have gone too far.

Management at the Marylebone was unprofitable, and Fox Cooper was no doubt earning more from his "*journal des amours*". The next theatrical venture, already foreshadowed, took place at Dover in Kent, obviously in consequence of Fox Cooper's residence in the castle. My first clue to this episode had come from a small leaflet preserved by Harwood Cooper about the re-modelling of the Theatre Royal by "Mr Cooper, the lessee". From thence I searched in the Enthoven Collection, finding the Davy manuscript which provided sundry references to the period during which Fox Cooper was in charge. Subsequent research at Colindale disclosed quite an appropriate sequel to the story of the *Nelson Examiner*.

Various announcements appeared in the *Dover Chronicle* in December 1841, followed by an advertisement stating that the Theatre Royal would open for a winter season on Boxing Day under new management, with decorations after the model of the San Carlos at Naples, regardless of expense. There was also a proposal to use the saloon as a gallery for the sale and exhibition of works of Art and Science. Eight (or sometimes ten) new boxes had been provided for the exclusive convenience of private parties and heads of families. On the opening night an occasional, original, and impromptu address would be given by the spirited new lessee followed by the National Anthem. And the programme would include two of his works: *Master Humphrey's Clock*, or *The Old Curiosity Shop*, and *The Black Sentinel*. There was also to be a pantomime entitled *Harlequin and the Men of Kent, or The Fairy of the Magic Rose*, written by the lessee, in conjunction with Mr Walbourn who would undertake the part of the Clown. In that pantomime my grandfather, Harwood, made his first appearance on the stage, as a youth of fifteen playing the Lover, an alternative description for Harlequin. Early in the New Year ten patent calorifere gas stoves were installed for the greater comfort of the audience, not forgetting the players, since two stoves were placed on the stage. On 25 January the performance was free to the public in honour of the christening of the Prince of Wales, but the theatre was criticized for giving too frequent performances of the same plays. Brief references continued to appear in the press until March, when in an advertisement for a benefit to be taken by Fox Cooper, there was a note about losses sustained by the lessee, and his hope to do better in the ensuing season.

Easter was spent in London at Paris Street, Lambeth, where the rest of the family may have been living while Fox Cooper and Harwood were in Dover. They both duly returned for the summer season, and the theatre reopened with the assistance of Messrs Fitzjames and Tyrrell as stage manager and acting manager respectively. On 1 August there was a special performance of *Hamlet* with Henry Betty in the title part, Gladstone as Horatio, Tyrrell as Laertes, and Fitzjames as Osric. It was announced also that Fox Cooper had entered into engagements with Mr and Mrs Charles Kean, Mr Farren, Mrs Nisbett, and Mrs Honner. And thus the season continued until one evening towards the end of August, when some of the company, just before the performance, said they would not go on unless Fox Cooper paid up their arrears of salary. This he was unable to do, so he went before the curtain and explained the situation to the audience. Two of the cast did the same thing. There was then a commotion, followed by a dismissal, with the result that some people got their money back, and others were given tickets for a future performance. It was afterwards made known that Fox Cooper was also in arrear with the rent of the theatre. A couple of days later, Fitzjames and Gladstone, formerly Osric and Horatio, but now both described as comedians, were charged by Fox Cooper with assault. According to one account, he was knocked down (for which Fitzjames was fined ten shillings) and threatened with his life. In view of the latter both actors were ordered to keep the peace, and to find two sureties of ten pounds each. This event was to have interesting consequences.

During the time that these gentlemen were waiting for bail they were treated as ordinary felons with the result that, after examination by a surgeon, orders were given for their hair to be cut off. This was obviously no treatment for members of a calling usually associated with flowing locks, and they protested in vain to the turnkey that want of hair would be detrimental to their profession. The turnkey replied, in jest, that he would just as soon cut off their heads if the gaoler bid him. So they amused themselves by singing "All's Lost" until the gaoler came, whereupon he informed them that they would have no dinner but bread and water and pick oakum if they did not stop the song. Bail duly arrived in three or four hours, and Fitzjames, gaining his liberty, brought the gaoler into Court next day for exceeding his duty and acting as a barber. After the matter was heard by the local bench the Mayor gave a decision that the gaoler was quite within his rights in doing what he did. But this was not the end of the tale.

The circumstances excited the interest of the London and provincial press, and the story spread throughout the country, thanks to accounts of the episode given in the *Dover Chronicle*, and the *Kentish Observer*. A London evening paper called *The Sun* was quite indignant, and this was followed by a leader in the next issue of the *Sunday Times*. Many newspapers, under the heading of "A Pair of Comedians in Trouble" or "Doings at Dover" were highly critical of the action of the local authorities, and prison rules were quoted to support their contention that a grave injustice had been done. The *Sunday Times* stated that they were certain Mr Fitzjames was a gentleman by birth, and it was new to them that he should be treated as a felon while waiting for bail on a common assault; such procedure might be approved at Dover but it would not find advocates elsewhere. Even the *Dover Chronicle* joined in the criticism and, in a leader on the cropping question, asserted that the barbarous act had called forth almost universal condemnation. The same journal took umbrage because the *Morning Chronicle* had copied their report, attributed it to the *Kentish Observer* (which emanated from Canterbury) and had added that in Dover, abounding in some of the finest specimens of rascality, it was easy to get involved in a quarrel with one of them.

This widespread perturbation gained the attention of the Home Office, and the Minister, Sir James Graham, sent down Mr Whitworth Russell to investigate the matter and report. Mr Russell, after a patient investigation, concluded that the gaoler (Coulthard) had not legally overstepped the mark but had, perhaps, been too hasty; following this conculsion he expressed his regret to Fitzjames and Gladstone, but said that singing and uproarious conduct in gaol could not be tolerated. When they had departed Mr Russell had some pretty sharp things to say to the unfortunate gaoler, and the turnkey. Moreover, the local justices were further humiliated by a request from higher authority to convey to the gaoler their marked disapprobation of his conduct. Later press comments suggest that prison rules were to be amended or at any rate clarified: misdemeanants of the first division should be bathed, cleansed, and have their hair cut, only when necessary for health.

Thus the end of Fox Cooper's tenancy at Dover came about

rather abruptly, if not violently, with a blaze of publicity in which he was almost forgotten to the extent of being described as *a* Mr Fox Cooper. And to rub salt into the wound, the theatre was shortly reopened by the performers under the management of the same ill-used Fitzjames. Subsequently it was stated that the theatre was being well patronized by visitors to the town, including the Prince Esterhazy; but the *Kent Herald* reported that the theatre closed on 31 December 1842 after a brief and unsuccessful season.

Failure at Dover left Fox Cooper with an appetite for theatrical management unsatisfied, and he became lessee of the City of London Theatre for a short season which commenced in April 1844. As we have seen, he was labouring under a load of debt incurred by the publication of *Cerberus* in 1843, and he had failed to obtain the protection of the Court. This was one of the occasions on which he justified the sobriquet "never-say-die", but not "careful John". The *Era* said that the new management under Fox Cooper, the well-known dramatic author, raised the curtain on 8 April 1844 to a very numerous audience; an excellent company* had been engaged and they formed the most favourable presages of a long and prosperous career. The career could not have been very long, for reasons other than theatrical, and my only playbill is dated 18 May when a performance was given for the benefit of F. H. Cooper, Treasurer: in this office my grandfather, still under the age of eighteen years. An item of interest in the programme was a military spectacle called The Flight of Tekeli, obviously based on the melodrama by Theodore Hook† with whom Fox Cooper's father had a nodding acquaintance. This season also witnessed the production of T. P. Taylor's play, *The Destruction of the Bastille*. The manuscript shows that when

---

* The company included principal actors from the Adelphi, among whom were George Weiland and Herbert.

† This highly successful play was produced before Hook was twenty years old. In the course of the melodrama, Tekeli (concealed in a barrel) is nearly shot when three Dragoons threaten to put bullets through the bunghole at thirty paces. Byron, a contemporary at Harrow, thought little of it; and so in *English Bards and Scotch Reviewers* we have:

> Gods! O'er those boards shall folly rear her head,
> Whom Garrick trod, and Kemble lives to tread?
> On those shall Farce display buffoonery's mask,
> And Hook conceal his heroes in a cask?

submitted for licensing by Fox Cooper the intended date of representation was 29 April. Production may have been delayed until June, in which event it must have been near the end of the season which terminated, like that at Dover, abruptly with an incident.

The records of the Lord Chamberlain appertaining to the licensing of theatres, now housed in the Public Record Office, contain in some years a flood of effusive letters from Fox Cooper. In 1844 there are several, the first of which was dated 16 April (a week after he had taken over the City of London Theatre), applying for a licence, giving the names of his sureties, and concluding: "it will be my pride and study to carry on this establishment with every regard to respectability and character." By June, however, a disagreement about the rent had arisen with the proprietor, Mr Cockerton, who proceeded to eject his tenant. So Fox Cooper poured out his heart and his complaints to the Office of the Lord Chamberlain. (See Appendix I(b).) Letters to that official were also written on Fox Cooper's behalf by some of the company, and by his solicitor, a John Beart, who besought the Lord Chamberlain to delay the issue of a licence to any other person. But there was little sympathy in that quarter, and a note by Mr E. M. Browell, who was in charge of the Office, indicates that the lease from Cockerton to Fox Cooper was cancelled, and that he was ejected at the end of June. His last letter, dated 29 June 1844, bewails the fact that he was no longer the actual and responsible manager, and expresses regret at having caused any trouble. Within three weeks Fox Cooper was in the Queen's Prison as already related, probably as the result of the failure of *Cerberus*, with a little bit of bad luck in the City thrown in.

In October 1844 *Oxberry's Weekly Budget* reported that Fox Cooper, who had made such a failure at the City of London, was negotiating for the Olympic Theatre; nothing had been done, however, and the theatre would be let to the highest bidder. This piece of gossip could scarcely justify Fox Cooper's claim to have been the lessee of the Olympic, but there may have been some kind of subtenancy.

Between two spells at the City of London, a short period of management commenced on 6 January 1845 at the Royal

G

Kent Theatre on the north side of High Street, Kensington. A playbill for the opening night, treasured by my father, contains the following ambitious announcement which left Fox Cooper short of syntax if not short of breath: "It is the intention of the Lessee to endeavour by the engagement of Actors of Established Talent, Authors of Celebrity, and Artists of known Ability, to place this Establishment upon an equal footing with other Metropolitan Theatres. Due regard will be paid to the 'Getting up' of every Drama submitted to the Public, and it is presumed that by Good Acting, New and Superb Scenery, Costly Decoration, Appropriate Music, and Magnificent Costumes, the inattention displayed by previous Managements, will, by these powerful and necessary adjuncts, be surmounted, and by unwearied exertions, secure patronage and success." In the programme were *The Blood Red Knight, or The Fatal Bridge; Jenny Jones, or The Valley of Llangollen,* described as a new, laughable interlude produced for the first time; and Harwood Cooper's pantomime, *Harlequin and the Valley of Diamonds, or Sinbad the Sailor.* Was it Fox Cooper, or the printer, who forgot that *Jenny Jones* had been produced at the St James's Theatre in 1838?

The proprietor of the theatre was a Mrs Marland (or Morland), the lessee is printed ambiguously as Mr Cooper of Walcot Place, Lambeth, and Mr Harwood Cooper is billed as taking the part of the clown in the pantomime.

It was also announced that the theatre was under the direction of Mr Cooper, of the principal London theatres. T. P. Taylor was the stage manager. Although the *Theatrical Journal* said that the son of Fox Cooper had opened this theatre early in January 1845, I am inclined to think father was really in charge; Harwood was now eighteen, but had only played in Town at the City of London Theatre. Such reticence on the part of Fox Cooper, who was usually only too delighted to place his name before the public, may have been due to past or impending insolvency proceedings with which this period of his life was so frequently embroidered. Whatever the arrangement, I expect it terminated when Fox Cooper returned to the City of London Theatre on 24 March.

This further season at the City of London Theatre lasted for about five months. Again it is interesting that on the playbills, of which I have over a dozen, Fox Cooper was described as director (or as sole manager) of the theatre, and not as the lessee, a situation that may have been occasioned by legal proceedings in which he claimed not to be a trader. Otherwise it may have been a precautionary measure, in consequence of the previous quarrel, on the part of Cockerton, who still held the licence.

The opening week, full of promise, included *As You Like It*, *The Fortress of Guntsbourg* (from the French of Scribe), *Adventures of Whittington and his Cat*, and *The Wet Nurse*. Next week came *The Stranger*, and then *The Hunchback*, by Sheridan Knowles, both with Vandenhoff who also played Shylock. Other strong features were *Antigone*, and *Robert the Devil*. Among the company during this season were John Dunn, W. H. Harvey, Hudspeth, George Wieland, and E. F. Saville who acted Hamlet. Specially advertised was a danseuse, Floretta Camille. Fox Cooper's own plays are described in the next chapter; but it may throw some light on his tactics to observe from a string of playbills how he went about the business of running a theatre, and to note *en passant* that he was not unacquainted with the wiles of propaganda, or the art of showmanship. For example, on 3 April the production of *As You Like It* was to be repeated with Mr and Miss Vandenhoff, whose opening performance had been highly successful, and the playbill states: "In consequence of the enthusiastic reception and the unbounded plaudits which have nightly been bestowed upon its representation, the lessee thinks he would ill appreciate the taste of his patrons if he withdrew it from the bills."

In May, Fox Cooper announced a farewell benefit although he continued to run the theatre, at least until the middle of August. In the programme for this benefit performance there was a play "founded on fact and embracing Events most extraordinary and startling" called *Bush Rangers, or The Horrors of Transportation*. No author is given and it does not appear in any of the reference books I have been able to consult, but it is clearly based on *Van Dieman's Land, or Tasmania in 1818*, by W. T. Moncrieff. The list of characters is almost identical, and many of the situations are similar. I wonder if it was put together by Fox Cooper in the vivid recollection of the New

Zealand episode, which accompanied the death of G. R.
Richardson? Depicted in one of the scenes were the Aborigines
of Van Dieman's Land swearing an oath of vengeance on the
white man, but apart from the deaths of the convict Pirate,
and the Captain of the gang of Bush Rangers, a happy ending
is contrived.

The production of *Wellington* (one of Fox Cooper's own
pieces) also in May was heralded with the announcement:
"To the veterans of Waterloo! The lessee begs to notify to
those noble and gallant men who so bravely distinguished them
selves on 18 June 1815, that the production of the medal bestowed upon them for their bravery on the plains of Waterloo,
will be a passport to any part of the theatre free of all expense."
After thirty years from the date of that conflict it would seem
that Fox Cooper was not giving very much away, except a
good piece of advertisement. It was also claimed that a treble
company would be introduced, and that upwards of one hundred supernumeraries were to be engaged from the Tower
of London: there may not have been "standing room only"
in the auditorium, but this must have been the order on the
other side of the curtain.

In the same programme was Mr Canfield, a muscular
American, who undertook to break a new rope of two inches in
circumference. Any gentleman in the audience was invited to
mount the stage and examine the rope before it was broken to
prove that the task was completely free from trickery, a
physical effort never before attempted. "This miraculous feat
was beyond the power of the imagination of the mind to
conceive." The modern Samsom would also bear on his chest
a cannon weighing 600 lb. which would be fired while in this
position. Such an adventuresome act was not free from risk
as on one occasion Mr Canfield was badly injured and one of
his assistants was crushed by a cannon ball. Early in June
there was a revival of *The Destruction of the Bastille*, the playbill
stating that it would convey all the reality of the horrors of
the French Revolution.

On 23 June the lessee (whether or not Fox Cooper)
announced that no charge whatever could be demanded for
seats in this theatre. All gratuities were voluntary, and any
incivility on the part of the servants of the establishment

would be visited with Instant Dismissal.* A small handbill for 7 July advised parties to be early in their attendance, as 9,800 persons had paid at the doors during the previous week: the attraction was *Jack Sheppard* with E. F. Saville, and the number of admissions was evidence of the popularity of that piece. Fox Cooper also cashed in on *Oliver Twist*, a production equally popular, but equally distasteful to the authorities. On 18 August, near the end of the season, there was a benefit for Harwood Cooper, for which he produced "a splendid oriental spectacle" entitled *The Death of Tippoo Sahib, or The Storming of Seringapatam*; to give effect to this National Military Pageant, it was once again necessary to engaged supers from the Tower of London. The playbill is of interest because it contains a rough illustration, in faded red, of troops with bayonets fixed, scaling a steep wall under the shadow of the Union Jack. Preceding *Tippoo* was *Richard III*, with E. F. Saville, and the evening concluded with a comedy, *The Phantom Corporal*.

Notwithstanding all these efforts Fox Cooper once again failed to make money out of running a theatre, as later on he was to say in Court that this period at the City of London completed his ruin.

The Lord Chamberlain's records again provide a few intimate glimpses of Fox Cooper at work and play during this 1845 season. In July, following various letters of criticism, some of them anonymous, police investigations were made at several of the minor theatres. The City of London earned the worst report. On the night of the inspection the gallery was reported to be crammed to suffocation with 462 people, mainly young folk between the ages of eleven and eighteen years. Some were from honest families such as tradespeople, but others were of doubtful character and of recognizable occupations.

A further abuse disclosed by the inspection consisted of the admission of two or even three persons for the price of one, by means of a free order,† which effectively reduced the prices

---

* Prices of admission, e.g. to the Pit, evidently just gave access to that part of the house. One can imagine a system of tipping for the better positions.

† Also the subject of a derogatory notice in *Lloyd's Weekly Newspaper*, 20 July 1845, which includes a facsimile of a free ticket for the City of London Theatre, admitting two to the gallery on paying for one. Such a ticket was obtainable gratis at the doors by the purchase of a galvanic ring for a

below the levels authorized by the Lord Chamberlain: Boxes two shillings; Pit, one shilling; Gallery, sixpence. Objection was also taken to the representation of *Jack Sheppard* and *Oliver Twist*, both of which were known to be favourite pieces with the denizens of the City of London Theatre. Strangely, the report that reached the Lord Chamberlain, while referring to the free orders, and the objectionable *Jack Sheppard*, stated that the theatre was well behaved and conducted, from which one concludes that the police were powerless at that time to prevent the use of theatres as meeting places for undesirables.

In consequence, the Office requested the pleasure on 28 July 1845 of representatives from the City of London Theatre, and the minute reads that a son of Fox Cooper, and the Treasurer attended. My great-grandfather was not a man to be dictated to.* The complaints were cited and undertakings were given; evidently these were honoured as somewhat later in the season Cockerton himself attended the Office, and confirmed that as the proprietor he found the conduct of the theatre quite satisfactory. But Fox Cooper afterwards said that the action of the authorities on the question of prices of admission had compelled him to give up the theatre.

Early in April 1845, just after the City of London season had commenced, Fox Cooper made an arrangement with a Mr Van Sandam (one of the proprietors) to take a short tenancy of the New Strand Theatre. That gentleman supported the application by Fox Cooper to the Lord Chamberlain for a licence, in the submission of which he stated that he wished to come to a more fashionable part of the Town. Rather surprisingly, Cockerton agreed to be one of the sureties. The licence, to run from 12 April to 29 September, was duly sealed, but never delivered. And from one of Fox Cooper's typical effusions to the Office it would appear that Van Sandam had suddenly changed his mind, wrongfully cancelled the lease, and let the theatre to a Mr Hodges at a higher rental: the deposed lessee would thus incur a huge loss as the result of

penny. The notice regretted the association of Mr Saville with the theatre, and the consequent damage to his reputation; as for the manager [Mr Cooper] to be rid of his reputation would be the most beneficial thing that could happen to him.

* Cf. Appendix I(d) where Fox Cooper implies that he had attended in person.

forming a company, and the only course would be a "hideous" lawsuit, a remedy that was clearly distasteful to him.

Not surprisingly the Office referred the complaint to the owners, which elicited a reply from Van Sandam disclosing that in the first instance he had obtained from Fox Cooper an undated letter of renunciation, as a safeguard against bad faith. He had put that letter into effect (and indeed sent it to the Office) because of Fox Cooper's character as evidenced by a cutting from the *Sunday Times* of 13 April 1845 which he also submitted for the perusal of the Lord Chamberlain, who, sagely from my point of view, filed both documents.

The cutting related to a case at Worship Street Police Court before Mr Combe, the Magistrate. A clown named Gomersal* had brought an accusation of assault against Mr Levy, who had engaged him for the City of London Theatre, and a constable named Russel, who had used his truncheon. Levy (or Levi) had referred the question of Gomersal's unpaid salary to Fox Cooper, here described as the Lessee and Manager, who said that it was none of his business. Giving evidence in Court, the latter admitted that there was little money in the treasury *et hinc illae lacrimae*. He also stated that Gomersal and Levy had laid hands on each other. The Magistrate wisely did no more than order the two parties to keep the peace, and the three withdrew. But later on, according to the report, all concerned re-entered the Court, and Fox Cooper made a complaint about Levy's language in the passage outside: he had said that he did not know whether Gomersal or Cooper was the greater rogue. Levy told the Magistrate that the words did not apply to Cooper "personally", which was accepted. Once again they were all dismissed with caution; friendship remained nevertheless and Gomersal was in the cast at the City of London on 5 May.

The action of Van Sandam was naturally upheld by the Lord Chamberlain, and Fox Cooper threatened to commence proceedings; but I have no evidence that they were pursued, and he did not succeed until two years later in taking over the Strand Theatre, in a more fashionable part of the Town.

Another clue to a season of management lies buried within a

---

* Edward Gomersal: also in partnership with B. O. Conquest at the Garrick Theatre, and renowned as Napoleon in *The Battle of Waterloo*.

London Gazette of March 1846, in the text of an advertisement relative to certain proceedings the nature of which will come as no surprise. There it is stated that Fox Cooper, after being at the City of London, was lessee and manager of the theatre at Deptford. Not much seems to be on record about this place, but in more prosperous days it had enjoyed the company of Edmund Kean, Henry Neville, and Miss Lydia Foote. By 1840 degeneration had set in, as a private box could he had for sixpence, and a seat in the pit for twopence. Things were looking up in 1845 because stalls were then two shillings, the pit one shilling, and the gallery sixpence. Fox Cooper's tenure must have been between August 1845 after leaving the City of London Theatre, and May 1846, by which time he was again in gaol.

The Davy manuscript in the Enthoven Collection throws no light on this venture, and the West Kent newspapers—at that period Deptford was related more to the County of Kent than to London for news items—carry no advertisements or inspired paragraphs. I have, however three playbills. Two of these are dated 29 September and 26 December 1845 respectively, when the theatre was under the management of Mr W. Lawrence. Fox Cooper does not appear at all, but Harwood Cooper is in the cast as an actor. The September bill, for the opening of the season, commenced with *The Steed of the Disinherited, or The Conquests of Ivanhoe*. This may well have been a version by Fox Cooper and possibly, under another title, *The Lists of Ashby, or The Conquests of Ivanhoe*, produced at Astley's in 1837; there are only slight differences between the names of the characters in the print of the play published in Dicks', and those in the Deptford playbill. Moreover, two of the principal actors at Deptford (G. H. Lawrence and W. H. C. West) were in the bill at the City of London Theatre in August 1845 under Fox Cooper. The programme also includes the *Caudle Curtain Lectures*, probably the same piece as the *Singularly Domestic Conjugal Comedy, Mr and Mrs Caudle*, by T. P. Taylor, which had been given at the City of London in July. The Boxing Night programme features *Harlequin and Don Quixote, or The Enchanted Knight of the Woeful Countenance*, a pantomime stated to have been written and produced by Harwood Cooper, who played Sancho Panza, and the clown,

My third playbill is dated simply, Monday, March 9, from which it is deduced that the year was 1846. Harwood Cooper is still in the cast, but the theatre is now called Prince of Wales, licensed to Mr Cockrell, and under the joint management of Miss Fielding and Mr J. Mould.

From this evidence alone it is impossible to confirm that Fox Cooper had a hand in the management of Deptford, but the indications are that he was there during part of the winter of 1845–46, and for some good reason, perhaps connected with debts unpaid, did not publicly disclose the fact.

In November 1846, Fox Cooper made an unsuccessful approach to the Lord Chamberlain to obtain a licence for a building known as the National Baths in the Westminster Bridge Road, where he proposed to stage dramatic pieces (see Appendix I(b)). In support of his application he claimed that he had been treated unfairly by the withdrawal of his licence for the City of London Theatre in 1844. This had been the consequence of his making unauthorized reductions in the prices of admission, in view of the poverty in the neighbourhood and the competition of unlicensed saloons. He added that Mrs Honner was then doing the same thing and making a fortune. A minute by E. M. Browell corrected these inaccuracies: the loss of the licence in 1844 was due to the quarrel with Cockerton, and the remark about Mrs Honner was pure imagination! Sir William Martins, the deputy licensor, wrote from Ramsgate to the effect that Fox Cooper had a glib tongue and a facility in writing, and unless he was mistaken Fox Cooper was a specious and dangerous character. The answer was obvious, but the Office was perhaps wrong in ascribing their refusal to the fact that September was the proper month for such applications.

Chapter 6

Dramatic Productions—1840–46; Financial and other Affairs

THE output and production of plays during this period, 1840 to 1846, was probably not stimulated by the insolvency and bankruptcy proceedings, by Fox Cooper's absence from London during part of the time, or by preoccupation with the *Cerberus* newspaper in 1843.

To commence with 1840. This year saw *Master Humphrey's Clock* produced at the Victoria Theatre on 26 May, and *Black Sentinel* at the Grecian Theatre in August.

Master Humphrey's Clock was Fox Cooper's first adaptation from Dickens, and it was produced within two months of the first number of that weekly publication. S. J. Adair Fitz-Gerald, in *Dickens and the Drama* (1910) prints the characters and cast together with the spoken prologue. For him Fox Cooper was "a notorious annexer of other men's brains", but he said little about the play. Malcolm Morley wrote about it in *The Dickensian* (Autumn 1947) and took a modicum of innocent pleasure in pulling it to pieces, chiefly on the ground that it bore little or no relationship to the work from which the name was taken. ". . . . a play where the spirit of Dickens is nowhere present and where not even a distorted echo of his writing reaches the stage." However, according to the same authority this "balderdashery hung on a Dickens peg" enjoyed the advantage of a strong cast, including a much better playwright than Fox

Cooper. But the latter, like W. S. Gilbert, preferred to call himself a dramatic author.

As this adaptation was not licensed by the Lord Chamberlain, and thus no manuscript deposited, twentieth-century critics are fortunate that it was published first by Duncombe (who printed the prologue), and then in Dicks'. But the *Era* in 1840 described it as a very successful, very powerful and interesting piece; while the *Theatrical Journal* said that the play struck the audience with surprise and gratification. The *Penny Satirist*, with the claim to be a "cheap substitute for a weekly newspaper", allowed that the production was more attractive than they should have imagined. It ran until after the end of June, when it was transferred to the Queen's Theatre as the main attraction.

There were some voices even then bold (or rash) enough to offer criticism of Dickens rather than rapturous praise. Thus *Kidd's London Journal* reviewed the programme at the Victoria Theatre which concluded with *Master Humphrey's Clock*. "The last is a boon for it contains much food for laughter. The original from whence it is taken is as bad as a dose of opium. To laugh at that is impossible; to go to sleep over it is a matter of weekly occurrence." This same paper said early in July that it was still the standing dish at the Victoria, and asked why Fox Cooper did not introduce Mr Quilp. And so from the prologue to *Master Humphrey's Clock* I cull the following:

> And now one word about our play tonight
> The why and wherefore that has made us write,
> 'Tis Boz composes with such railroad speed
> He leaves unfinished half of what we read.
> We beg a hearing—perhaps he'll make no quail—
> He gives a head—we furnish forth a tail.
> He the Colossus great—we side by side,
> The pigmy men that 'neath his legs must stride.
> We have no monstrous puff to aid our cause
> But trust to your good sense for your applause.

My view is that the above exordium is a disarming reply to a great deal of the criticism that has been levelled against this piece. It claimed to be of little importance as compared with the original, and some may find it difficult to understand how an author with a commercial flair could be entirely displeased at the publicity which must have resulted from the use of his titles in the naming of plays. The absence of copyright could sometimes be an advantage, and Dickens is known to have assisted at rehearsals of plays adapted from his works without prior permission.

The characters are roughly sketched without much depth of motive, but there is plenty of action and suspense. At the climax in Dicks' version, Master Humphrey takes the attesting papers from an old trunk, but in Duncombe's print they were produced from the long case of the clock. I wonder why Harwood Cooper altered this significant detail when editing Dicks'; it was the only change he made. I shall defend it no further against the formidable adversaries who have mounted their striking attacks: it was probably commissioned by the Victoria Theatre and put together hurriedly. All in all I feel that Fox Cooper's concoction from *Master Humphrey's Clock* was more suitable to the taste of the public in 1840, than to a captious critic in the present age.

About the *Black Sentinel* I have little information. A.N. has recorded the play as produced at the Grecian Theatre in August 1840, author unknown. I am inclined to attribute this vaudeville entertainment at the Grecian to Fox Cooper—he certainly included an item with such a title in the programme at Dover in December 1841 and it was contained in Harwood Cooper's list. *Modern English Biography* (1892) gives this title among Fox Cooper's plays, an attribution copied no doubt from the *Theatrical Times* (1847). There is also an earlier advertisement, unattributed, for a performance of the *Black Sentinel* at the City of London Theatre in February 1839 in which Mr Dunn was to appear as Jim Crow with the songs: "Such a Getting Upstairs" and "Clear de Kitchen". A play entitled *Jim Crow*, by T. P. Taylor, had been produced at Sadler's Wells Theatre in 1836 with Mr Dunn in the title part. James Pattie published it, and Philo-Dramaticus (probably Fox Cooper) wrote the very favourable introductory remarks. The original coloured Jim Crow was T. D. Rice.

Black Sentinel inspired a farce entitled *The Black Guard*, or *Love and War*, at the Royal Pavilion, Whitechapel, on Easter Monday, 8 April 1844. Leading the cast were William Rogers (as Tommy Popps, rather a spoiled child, on a courting expedition), and John Dunn (the Black Guard) with the songs "Jump Jim Crow" and "Such a Getting Up-stairs". The playbill acknowledges the authorship of Fox Cooper, and states that to place the piece before the public in a superior manner, a perfectly original scene had been arranged, giving an idea of a town residence with cross-roads.

In 1841 there was one play by Fox Cooper: *Old St Paul's*, based on Harrison Ainsworth, and produced at the Queen's Theatre in February of that year. This little theatre was situated near the Tottenham Court Road, where the Scala has taken its place, and it had one of the smallest stages in London, about the size of that of the Garrick, the proscenium width being eighteen feet. For a review of this production I was obliged to resort to *The Town*, an amusing but scandalous weekly paper with moral values somewhere between *Figaro in London*, and the *Crim. Con. Gazette*. That journal said the play bore little resemblance to Harrison Ainsworth's novel. It contained of mystery a vast deal, of murder much, a trifling sprinkle of love and adventure, a little cowardice, a small collection of old proverbs, a patient with a plague, and a wizard. Fortunately the play was saved by the acting. One can scarcely complain that no text of this piece has survived.

Apart from the pantomime at Dover for Christmas 1841, there is a break in dramatic output until 1844 when, after *Black Guard*, a play entitled *Burnt at Sea* was produced in June at the City of London Theatre, then under the management of Fox Cooper. It is attributed to him by A.N., who refers to *Oxberry's Weekly Budget*, vol. iii, No. 5. Here it does not appear to be printed, but a short paragraph states that several novel and startling effects were introduced, yet we are left guessing what they were; John Herbert was very comical as a stage-struck Middy who spouts Shakespeare to his faithful sable attendant, a device to which the author was partial, as noticed elsewhere. The reviewer expressed the hope that Fox Cooper's spirited exertions would meet the reward they so fitly merit. As on other occasions the use of the word "exertions" suggests that the author may have written his own critique.

In 1845 I have traced four plays, all presented during Fox Cooper's tenure of the City of London Theatre although one of them, *The Old Fleete Prison*, had been previously produced at the Surrey on 12 May. The author, of course, had his own experiences in the Fleet in 1832 and 1839, and it is characteristic that he used the prison as a background in the year before it was finally closed. At the beginning of the manuscript is written: "Could these walls speak, what horrors would they tell." In the early part of the eighteenth century marriages in the Fleet Prison were of common occurrence, and were performed by persons of dubious clerical qualifications. In the play they were characterized as Doctors: Fairwell, Tietight, Fondlove, and Muzzle; all prisoners in the Fleet. The opening scene discloses their respective offers, from the *exterior* of the prison gates, to perform the marriage ceremony:

> at the old original "Blazing Heart"—charge five shillings
> at the "True Nuptial Knot"—charge half-a-crown
> at "Cupid's Torch"—charge only one shilling
> at the "Pen in Hand"—pay what you please.

The sub-title of the play: *The Widow and her Suitors*, anticipates her amorous and numerous would-be-husbands, most of whom became incarcerated within the Fleet, plotting and counter-plotting against each other. The dénouement takes place within the prison where the widow is handed over by her serving man to the only honest, but spendthrift, suitor played by E. F. Saville. Included in quite a strong cast were also Waldron, Dunn, and Hudspeth, with C. Smith as the Warden of the Fleet.

London by Night, on 5 May, was advertised as a powerful Romantic Drama, in two acts, by Fox Cooper from an epoch in the writings of Boz. The characters in this play are taken from his *Master Humphrey's Clock* with two exceptions, and the spelling of the names is slightly altered. It was produced for Fox Cooper's benefit performance, and likely enough concocted for the occasion, by cutting down his full-length play. In the same programme was *Hercules, King of Clubs*, and the author made another of his rare appearances as Capain Darling, in which character he delivered Shakespeare's *Seven Ages of Man*.

Next comes *Wellington, Nelson and Napoleon*. This grand historical, equestrian, military and naval spectacle was in three epochs: Nelson—Trafalgar; Wellington—Spain; Napoleon—Waterloo. The first part ended with the death of Nelson, the second found its climax with the "dames" of Madrid. The third part led finally to the total rout of the French Army, and the flight of Napoleon. Harwood Cooper who played the parts of Sam Surf (a seaman), Perrara (a guerrilla), and Renac (a Prussian), confirms the date as 1845; A.N. has a similar title by an unknown author at the Standard Theatre in December 1852.

The last play I have established at the City of London in 1845 is *The Sea Wolf, or The Old Well of the Manor Lands*, on 21 July. Described as a nautical melodrama, the playbill states that it was founded on one of Fox Cooper's popular works: it might thus be related to *Perils of the Main* (1837), or *Burnt at Sea* (1844), but neither of the latter could fairly be described as popular.

In 1846 the only play was another adaptation from Dickens, the full title of which is: *Dealings with the Firm of Gamp and Harris*, or simply *Mrs Gamp*. A.N. has Queen's Theatre, with the title but no author attributed; Malcolm Morley, however, gives it to Fox Cooper with the date, 16 November. After a number of dramas based on *Martin Chuzzlewit*, the rage for Mrs Gamp led to farcical treatment of which this was the second example. It dealt with the dilemma of a Mr Carroway who is to inherit a fortune if he does not marry a widow— which he has already done. Mrs Gamp was played by Manders, and Mrs Harris by Hudspeth, who had been Mrs Caudle at the City of London. It ran for only a week.

The year 1846 again witnessed a climax of financial troubles. The course of events was similar to that in 1844, except that Fox Cooper admitted by implication the jurisdiction of the Bankruptcy Court. I am told that it was possible to be the subject of proceedings both in that Court and the Insolvent Debtors' Court, more or less at the same time, until the distinction between them was abolished in 1869. Such was the position of Fox Cooper who made an appearance in the Bankruptcy Court in April, and in the Insolvent Debtors' Court in July.

The story opens with an advertisement in the *London Gazette* during March, similar to that in February 1844. This states that whereas a petition of an insolvent debtor, Fox Cooper, dramatic author and shorthand writer, having been filed in the

Court of Bankruptcy, and the interim order for protection from process having been given under the provisions of the Statutes, the said Fox Cooper is hereby required to appear before R. G. C. Fane on 23 April in the Bankruptcy Court, Basinghall Street, for a first examination, etc. On this occasion the proceedings of the Court were reported fairly extensively in the newspapers, although there are elements of confusion and contradiction throughout. Possibly the best account appears in the *Morning Post* on which this epitome is based.

The debtor applying to the Bankruptcy Court upon his own petition for an Interim Order, lives in Walcot Place (Lambeth), and is a theatrical manager, dramatic author, and a shorthand writer. He had edited *The Railway Annual** and had been connected with various minor theatres, both town and provincial, e.g. City of London, Dover, and Deptford. To the failure of these speculations was attributed his present embarrassments. His debts amounted to £1,625, and his assets (good and doubtful) to £783. The creditors were principally gentlemen and solicitors [*sic*], also the managers of the Dublin, Belfast and Bristol Theatres, the latter being Mrs Macready for appearing in *Jenny Jones* and *Black Sentinel*.† It was Fox Cooper's third appearance as an insolvent debtor since 1839, from which year he had received £1,200 as a dramatic author and for literary contributions. (This was not a negligible figure, and would have contributed to the provision of quite a decent standard of living, if it had been augmented by profits from theatrical management instead of being offset by losses.)

Mr Sturgeon 'supported' the insolvent, who was opposed by Mr Lloyd and Mr Cox. It was stated that Fox Cooper had petitioned the Insolvent Debtors' Court for relief from custody, and was bailed; a vesting order was made, but he did not

---

* I have been unable to trace *The Railway Annual*, or the *Railway Atlas*, which some newspapers mentioned. There was, however, a *Railway Argus* in the spate of literature about railways in 1845–46, and it had two columns of theatrical news. But there were only three issues, and it discloses no other obvious connexion with Fox Cooper. However, three issues would be enough for him to lose a substantial sum.

† This was apparently Sarah Desmond who became the second wife of Macready senior in 1821, and who sometime after his death in 1829 took over the lease of the Bristol Theatre. Her first season opened in 1834, and she lived until 1853.

appear at the time fixed for him to be heard,* Mr Sturgeon
said that there was no opposition to his discharge at the time
he petitioned the Court two years ago, and he had not traded
for three years. Legal argument took place about a debt of
less than twenty pounds due to a Mr Peel, and reference was
made to the Act prohibiting imprisonment for such an amount:
new debts, however, had been contracted since the former
petition. Mr Cox contended that as proceedings were pending
in the Insolvent Debtors' Court, this [Bankruptcy] Court had
no jurisdiction. The ground for objection was that the insolvent
had applied for relief and had been dismissed, it being proved
to the satisfaction of the Court that he was a trader. Mr
Commissioner Fane having heard the arguments refused to
entertain the insolvent's application, and commented with
some severity on the "harassing of his creditors". The question
was whether he was not a person against whom a fiat could
issue; in the year 1844 he was a trader, and a sufficient peti-
tioner's debt existed at that time. The petition was therefore
dismissed. Once again this led to a term of imprisonment and
back to the Insolvent Debtors' Court. There is no evidence that
Fox Cooper was made bankrupt.

On 23 May 1846, the *London Gazette* records an order of the
Insolvent Debtors' Court vesting the estate of Fox Cooper in
the Provisional Assignee. He was then in the Surrey gaol
(Horsemonger Lane). A later notice states that the prisoner,
who had applied for his discharge, was ordered to be brought
before the Court on 13 July. His attorney was now a Mr
Sheppard. Fox Cooper said that he had been connected with a
newspaper called the *Cerberus* "an ephemeral publication in
1843" as well as some unsuccessful theatrical ventures: the last
of which (as lessee of the City of London Theatre) had completed his ruin, and he was thus compelled to make his appearance again in this Court. There was some discussion about a
debt due to Mr George Hetherington, a parliamentary agent,
and about a bill of exchange upon which he had evidently
been sued by Fox Cooper. Reference was made also to certain
furniture claimed by a relative named Chappell who had
advanced money.

* It is not clear whether this refers back to 1844. But it might account
for his being incognito at Deptford in the winter of 1845–46.

Asked by the Chief Commissioner if he were connected with any newspaper, Fox Cooper replied that he wrote leading articles but did not wish to mention names. Whereupon the Commissioner (rather unnecessarily) remarked that he had no desire to probe the secrets of the prison house, and was not anxious to know in what papers Cooper enlightened the world. But Fox Cooper obtained his discharge forthwith, for reasons which are not quite clear from the press reports, although the *Morning Chronicle* stated that he had given fresh securities. The register in the Public Record Office shows that he must again have spent about two months in goal.

In the year 1846 Fox Cooper indulged himself in much correspondence with the Lord Chamberlain, during the course of which Lord de la Warr was succeeded by Lord Spencer. On 20 April a long letter to that dignitary called attention to the abuses of the law, and contained suggestions about the better regulation of the public theatres; following the City of London affair this was a straightforward case of poacher wanting to turn gamekeeper, as among the suggestions was that of a new appointment in the Lord Chamberlain's Office, which Fox Cooper clearly (or rather, misguidedly) thought he might be offered. A brief reply from Lord de la Warr thanked him for the information, but stated that there was no intention of making such an appointment as the writer alluded to. This correspondence was interrupted by the period in prison between May and July.

After his unsuccessful application in November 1846 for a licence to use the building known as the National Baths for dramatic entertainment (see Chapter 5) Fox Cooper, obviously dissatisfied with the reply and the reason given, wrote on 1 December drawing attention to the prevalence of price reductions in the minor theatres.* He added that he intended to take a benefit at the Olympic or the Strand Theatre within the next ten days, and enquired if he would be permitted to reduce the prices for that occasion. To this trial balloon the Lord Chamberlain replied that no reductions had been authorized; but he took an immediate interest in the matter by calling a

---

* There had previously been an article attacking "The Threepenny Theatres" in the *Sunday Times* dated 22 November, obviously by Fox Cooper who was then very likely the dramatic critic of that newspaper.

meeting on 4 December of the managers from seven of the minor theatres (including the City of London, and the Victoria) to explain what had led them to reduce their prices.* One manager pointed out that the practice had been started by Fox Cooper at the City of London Theatre, and several reasons were given; but the main reason was the competition of the saloons, where little or no payment for entrance was demanded, and in which the profit arose from the sale of drink.

The Lord Chamberlain then decided to ask all the theatres in question to send to him each week copies of their playbills, and Fox Cooper hearing of this at once pointed out in writing that it had been one of the suggestions made in his communication of the previous April. Having devoted so much of his time to the study of the problems involved, he asked for an interview to put forward his plans in detail. A brief acknowledgement by E. M. Browell, brought forth a further appeal from Fox Cooper on 8 December regretting that the Office had forgotten his earlier suggestions (see Appendix I(b)). But the establishment must have felt that co-operation would be unlikely to succeed, and no other answer was thought to be required.

Meanwhile on 6 December an open letter (see Appendix I(c)) to the Lord Chamberlain appeared in the *Sunday Times*, from which a cutting is preserved in the file, with an endorsement to the effect that Fox Cooper was the supposed author. This provenance was suggested by Osbaldiston, lessee of the Victoria Theatre, and the Earl Spencer to whom the letter was shown wrote: "I do not doubt it is by Fox Cooper—the style is his." I am equally sure that he was the author of this second and more trenchant attack on the "Threepenny Theatres" which forms the subject of the epistle. He was generous enough, however, to admit that the managers were not wholly without an apology for their conduct, owing to the unfair competition of the saloons.

The same subject was reported in the *Standard* on 12 December (see Appendix I(d)), and the Office file contains a cutting with the endorsement as before. Osbaldiston also informed

---

* The Victoria Theatre was described by a police Superintendent as worse than any brothel in the district, and a letter from the Earl Spencer had hinted at the possible suspension of the licence.

E. M. Browell that Fox Cooper had publicly boasted he would "do for" the managers, while Messrs Johnson and Lee, who operated the New Standard Theatre, vigorously challenged the letter in the *Sunday Times*. Other press communications either from, or on behalf of, managers appeared elsewhere. All this was obviously vexatious to the Lord Chamberlain who blandly replied to Messrs Johnson and Lee that he had not read the letter in the *Sunday Times*. There, one can say, the matter rested, and my great-grandfather's attempt to become a civil servant had failed.

Fox Cooper duly took his benefit, but it was at the Surrey Theatre on 21 December. Hudson Kirby played in *Damon and Pythias*, and *Hercules* was performed, after which Fox Cooper addressed the audience; but a comment in Thos. Marshall's *Lives of the most celebrated Actors and Actresses* states that the treatment displayed towards his friends and the public was disgraceful in the extreme. His action in trying to enlist the sympathy of the Lord Chamberlain at the expense of his colleagues in the theatrical profession must have alienated a lot of support.

It now remains to comment on the rest of the biographical information from the *Theatrical Times* in June 1847, which was the foundation of so much of my research. It is claimed herein, that the newspaper *Cerberus* was eminently successful at first, but was discontinued when Fox Cooper became the lessee of the City of London Theatre. This has been shown to be misleading because he gave notice of his intention to present a petition to the Bankruptcy Court in December 1843, only one month after the paper closed down, and the report of the proceedings in the *Morning Chronicle* was headed "The *Cerberus* (late newspaper)". But perhaps the operative words were "at first".

Another remark concerns the *Nelson Examiner*, the origins of which were described in Chapter 4. In June 1847, Fox Cooper still maintained that he owned the paper, so it will not be out of place here to relate the sequel to the sailing of the *Mary-Ann*. On the voyage out Charles Elliott, the printer, met the young lawyer named George Rycroft Richardson, who came of a good family from Blackheath. Until then he had lived a desultory life, with interests in farming and literature.

As printer without editor, Elliott was naturally attracted by this amiable and talented young man, and invited him to become editor of the pending newspaper, to which proposal Richardson agreed. *Mary-Ann* duly arrived in February 1842, and the *Nelson Examiner* was launched within six weeks. It was the only organ of public opinion in the South Island for over a decade, and served a most useful purpose. Its subsequent decline, and eventual demise, in 1874, was the result of a too close adherence to the interests of the larger landed proprietors. Elliott was the sole owner of the paper for a considerable time, and he became a Member of the New Zealand parliament.

The comment in the *Theatrical Times* that Fox Cooper sent over his friend Richardson as editor, is thus untrue, although they may have met. But a remark that Richardson was shot in a *rencontre* with the natives is unfortunately correct;* so also is the written statement of E. L. Blanchard, after Fox Cooper's death in 1879, that the latter was engaged to accompany the vessel to New Zealand, but came ashore when the ship reached Dover. Evidently the reason for leaving the ship was unknown to E. L. Blanchard, or charitably forgotten. Whether Fox Cooper, in view of his defection, retained any interest in the paper seems very doubtful, although he may have had a claim in equity against Elliott. Nevertheless the end of Fox Cooper's story in the *Theatrical Times* was that this speculation was likely to turn out very profitably, and he had been offered a large sum for it by a gentleman proceeding to the colony. Yet it could scarcely have been one of the assets disclosed in the course of his insolvency proceedings in 1846, when the good and doubtful ones amounted only to £783.

The last section of the article in the *Theatrical Times* contains one of the few personal glimpses of Fox Cooper I have been able to obtain: "in private life Mr Cooper is the staunch friend, the kind parent, and one of the most companionable men of

---

* This took place in the summer of 1843 at the massacre of Wairau. A special supplement of the *Nelson Examiner* published in December of that year contains a long account of this ghastly event. A number of brave civilians were killed in an expedition designed to put an end to local incidents and rivalry between the emigrants and the natives. Notwithstanding this outrage the *Nelson Examiner* could still claim that there should be one law for all, and the leader in the first issue after the loss of Richardson, dated 8 July 1843 was simply signed "J" who alluded briefly to the memory of his lamented chief.

the day. He possesses a vast fund of anecdotal conversation upon every conceivable topic, and is well known to love fun for its own sake, and to be eminently the cause of it in others.'' This *penchant* for harmless pleasantry was illustrated by the story (which I abbreviate) of a wealthy resident in the east end of the City of London who requested the pleasure of Fox Cooper's company to dinner. His invitation was accepted, and on the appointed day, three cabs, heavily laden, deposited their living cargo at the door of the host, much to his astonishment. The lessee of the Strand—it was an 1847 story—leading the group of strangers congregated round the dwelling, met the enquiring gaze of his friend, and dissipated his surprise by remarking that as he had signified a wish for the pleasure of his company he (Fox Cooper) had taken him at his word. In consequence every individual connected with his establishment had arrived to do honour to the proffered hospitality. The end of the tale is that the joke was taken as it was intended, and the day was pleasantly spent.

Having enlarged, in the interest of historical accuracy, upon the summary of Fox Cooper's personal career from the *Theatrical Times* in June 1847 we can now turn to his management of the Strand Theatre in 1847–48.

Chapter 7

Management of the Strand Theatre 1847–48
(including own plays)

FOX COOPER'S Association with the Strand* formed the
longest period of theatrical management I have been able to
trace, as it commenced in March 1847 and continued until
February 1848. It is also well documented with the aid of
many playbills that have been preserved, the *Era* newspaper,
the *Theatrical Times*, and a number of other sources including
The Times itself.

The opening under Fox Cooper's management (a Mr B.
Hurwitz was still the lessee) was advertised for Monday, 22
March. In the programme were no less than five items, including the author's *Hercules* (claimed as the first time for seven
years) and his burlesque: *Ion, Travestie*. Although this latter
was described as new, it had been produced in 1836, but from
the tone of the announcement it would receive a new lease
of life. The playbill gave *Ion* a tremendous blurb: it was
described as an entirely new shriek-creating, boisterous,
glorious, mysterious, uproarious, and anything but seriously
affecting, pathetically heartbreaking, agonizing and subduing,
terrific, heroic, ridiculous, extravaganzical Burletta written
by Fox Cooper and not by Sergeant Talfourd. A number of
important musicians would appear in person, including Sir

---

* Sometimes called the New Strand because of the rebuilding in 1831.
It stood on the site which later housed the Aldwych tube station.

Henry Bishop. To prevent any ill-effects the manager had
provided antidotes for hysterical fits and faints; any lady who
intended to swoon for more than half an hour was requested
to acquaint the management so they might bespeak the attendance of proper physicians.

The *Theatrical Times* said that when the Strand Theatre
opened, the house was full, and praised the performance of
Bertram in which the chief part was played by J. R. Scott.*
The *Illustrated London News* said that the house was tolerably
well filled, but that the tedium of *Bertram* was only relieved
at the end of the fourth act by an unrehearsed effect when St
Aldobrand died in the way of the act-drop roller. Amidst
applause he was rescued by the hero of the play. That journal
feared, however, that this was another of those hopeless speculations which would only terminate in lowering the prestige
of all engaged in it. The *Era* (perhaps in ignorance) said that
Ion concluded the performance, but that it was unequivocally
damned and had since been withdrawn; a further paragraph
in the *Illustrated London News* suggests it was not actually
performed, and I have an untraced press cutting saying that
it was withdrawn by order of the Lord Chamberlain, who did
not condescend to assign a reason. Consequently the programme was altered and replaced with as much novelty as
was compatible with the time allowed. The advertisement
for *Ion* certainly showed Fox Cooper making a tremendous
effort, but really failing by overdoing it. I do not know on
what grounds the play was banned unless, as suggested elsewhere, it was because the male parts were to be played by
females, and vice versa.

As a result of the withdrawal of this play, and the interven-
tion of Passion Week, there was a gap in Fox Cooper's management, shown by the absence in the *Era* dated 4 April, of any
advertisement for the Strand Theatre, while in the following
issue there was a paragraph stating that "this pretty but
neglected little theatre" was giving a new series of musical
entertainments by Mr H. Russell.

But at this point Fox Cooper took a lease of the theatre for
the curious period of forty-five weeks from 26 April 1847,

* This actor featured in the next number of the paper, which is adorned
with a picture of a short, stout man as Bertram in *Bertram*.

with possession a week before to assist his preparations. He obtained a licence from the Lord Chamberlain from 21 April to 29 Spetember, when it was renewed for a year. And the *Era*, from an advertisement in *The Times* (see below), discovered that Fox Cooper intended to provide entertainment similar to that produced by Madame Vestris at the Olympic. Remarking that Mr Cooper was certainly ingenious, a bold man, and a sort of Caleb Quotem* in his way, the *Era* questioned whether he possessed the exquisite taste of that discerning lady. "We do not wish to damp the ardour of Mr Cooper but we should be glad to know where he is to select a company to carry out his lofty ideas. Not at the City of London or any of the three-penny theatres. . . . The West-Enders look for something more recherché." The *Era's* interest continued: "Mr. Fox Cooper's startling advertisement re the Strand Theatre has been reduced from a mountain to a molehill by the announcement of the prices of admission. We hinted last week that threepenny prices would not suit the West-Enders; Fox Cooper has become more humorous: a joey, or fourpence, being for the gallery, and one shilling for the boxes. We are convinced this is not the way to conduct the Strand Theatre, and that charges should be not less than those at the Lyceum and at the Adelphi." In point of fact boxes were advertised at eighteenpence.†

In support of his price policy Fox Cooper said that whilst daily communications from kin to kin were whirled in safety with lightning speed throughout the entire kingdom for the incredible sum of a single penny, and kin itself for the same sum per mile on the railroad, the stage, which should reflect the manners living as they arise, clung to monopoly with the conventional charges of: boxes four shillings, pit two shillings, gallery one shilling. At nearly all the minor theatres these had remained unchanged since the days of Garrick, and although they had, shamefully, reduced the salaries of the working many to enable them to pay the extortionate demands of the starring few, they had never condescended to open their doors at charges commensurate with the times.

* Parish clerk and Jack-of-all-trades, a character in a play by George Colman the Younger: *The Review, or Wags of Windsor*. The sub-title was borrowed by Fox Cooper (see Chapter 9).

† I believe this represented the charge for a seat in a box, and not the price of a "private box".

It was, therefore, left to the little Strand to effect this desirable end. And all persons paying for admission to any part of the theatre would receive gratuitously from the money-takers a perfect Bill of the night's entertainment. This suggests that Fox Cooper, although obviously himself an individualist, was on the side of the under-dog, an attribute that is discernible in some of the columns of *Cerberus* in 1843. I should judge that he was at all times willing to receive from the rich to give to the poor.

The *Era* announced that an experiment in low prices was to be tried also at the Olympic Theatre, under the same management as that of the Strand, which might mean that Fox Cooper attempted to take over—as we should say today— the management of that theatre also. There had been a rumour to this effect in October 1844 (see Chapter 4). But on 4 April 1847, Mr George Bolton was advertised as lessee and manager; the programme, however, included *The Spare Bed.*

A series of advertisements in *The Times* is worthy of separate record. This was an outstanding piece of advance publicity, and in *The Times* of all papers, even then the most Olympian of dailies. What is more, they were contained among the usual sober, matter-of-fact theatrical announcements (e.g. for Covent Garden and Drury Lane) on the same page as the leading articles. If only the performances had lived up to their promise, or if publicity alone had been the criterion of success, Fox Cooper could, I believe, have become the C. B. Cochran of his day:

> 16 April, New Strand Theatre. "Mr Fox Cooper having become the lessee of this elegant place of amusement for a term, begs to announce that he intends to commence his season on Monday, April 26, with dramatic performances after the style of the Olympic, when under the management of Madame Vestris. Letters and applications for engagement to be addressed to the theatre only. Walcot Place, April 12."

> 17 April. "The ladies and gentlemen engaged for the ensuing season are requested to meet the lessee on the stage at the theatre at one o'clock on Tuesday, April 20, preparatory to the distribution of parts.
> Signed, J. Williams, Stage Manager; late of the Lyceum Theatre." [This advertisement was repeated on 19 April.]

22 April. "In consequence of the numerous applications which have been made for engagements, Mr Fox Cooper finds its quite impossible to answer all the letters he has had the honour to receive. He takes the opportunity of thanking the writers, and expressing his deep regret that the size of the Little Strand does not permit him to avail himself of more than one-twentieth part of the talent which has expressed itself ready to rally round him. The theatre will open on Monday, the 26th, when he flatters himself that the public will approve and support his selection."

26 April, New Strand Theatre. "Open for the season at prices commensurate with the time. One and sixpence, Boxes; one shilling, Pit; fourpence, Gallery."

(The programme was *Hogarth's Mirror*, *Capers and Crushers*, *Are you coming to bed?*, and a ballet. Unfortunately, this opening conflicted with a production of *The Hunchback*, by Sheridan Knowles, with Miss Kemble.)

27 April. "In consequence of the immense applause bestowed upon the whole of the performance last evening, Mr Cooper begs to announce that *Hogarth's Mirror* will be repeated every night until further notice. The public are requested to be early as the house overflows nightly." [This advertisement was repeated the next day.]

29 April. A similar advertisement with the addition of the comment that Mr Cooper refers the public to the published opinions of the Press as regards the splendour and brilliancy of *Hogarth's Mirror* and the Ballet.

30 April. Another similar advertisement, with a lengthy addition about the engagement of some female Ethiopian Serenaders. There would also be a series of morning concerts at 2.30 on 3 May and the following days. The Editors of the Press were invited to attend, and "Mr Cooper feels assured that the Town will be taken by surprise with this most chaste and truly fascinating performance." The Galley would not be open for the morning concerts.

In spite of this lengthy, persistent, and presumably expensive outlay in *The Times*, no review of a performance at the Strand Theatre appeared in the columns of that august journal.

But some lively notices were given from time to time in the

short-lived *Dramatic Mirror*.* On 26 April: "Fox Cooper, 'never-say-die' Cooper, reopens the Strand Theatre tonight. He is going to attempt the establishment of a vaudeville theatre which is right, and the production of ballets which is wrong. Drury Lane is the place for dancers and beasts; let the Strand be consecrated to the lively interpretation of the small follies of life. Mr Cooper's bill is rich in promise; we shall go and see if the cookery is up to the carte."

Next week this paper was somewhat critical, especially in comparing the productions with those of Madame Vestris. There were no good pieces, and no good actors except Mr Lee. The reviewer was not incensed, only sorrowful; he could not contemplate a prolonged successful season. On 17 May, Fox Cooper had introduced some female Ethiopians, and Carter's Mammoth Horse (an animal of twenty-five cwt. and twenty hands) just arrived from France, and on view exclusively at the Strand prior to its departure for St Petersburg. What next, they asked, would he do in imitation of the Olympic in the time of Madame Vestris?

On 14 July a more favourable notice: the lessee was a brave man struggling with the frowns of Fate. Fox Cooper had begun under a multitude of disadvantages, with neither capital nor company. He had seemed inclined to trust to every expedient, but the legitimate one, for bringing an audience together: mammoth horses and women, nigger dancers, and all sorts of extras. There was no objection to this, but it was not English vaudeville as had been advertised. Since then changes had been made. "He is now keeping faith with the public, and the programmes contain good farces, vaudeville, and light entertainment. The lessee has dropped the fat women, turned the horse out to grass, dispensed with the foreign caperers, refurbished the theatre and properties, and improved the company. We wish Mr Cooper every success." But the last notice I found was on 10 November, drawing attention to the fact that any person could obtain admission anywhere at the Strand Theatre during the performance for one-and-ninepence. This cheap tour was effected by paying one shilling for a box, sixpence for the pit, and threepence

* E. L. Blanchard mentions that this was published by Barth, also a publisher of plays.

for the gallery. The paper asked why did not the Lord Chamberlain interfere to prevent this degradation of the theatre. On this note we can revert to comments in the regular weeklies as the season progressed.

A review in the *Theatrical Times* of the opening night admitted (with adequate reason) that the lessee had previously made a very fair statement of his intentions, and felt bound to say from the entertainment presented that abundant promise for the future might be anticipated. The success of this venture could hardly be doubted if the present persevering system of novelty were pursued: the costumes were in strict keeping, and most of the scenery seemed entirely new. The *Era*, however, pointed out that the drama called *Hogarth's Mirror* was nothing more that a piece known as *The Curse of Mammon* which had been produced some years previously at the Surrey Theatre.

That paper also commented that in the programme was an interlude, written by Fox Cooper, entitled *Are you coming to bed?*, "a title more novel than delicate for the neighbourhood of the Strand". Described elsewhere as a "screamer", this was probably one of the earliest bedroom farces but the details of the plot have been lost to posterity. Also on the opening night many patrons had complained of a "swindle" in the playbill in which some very small type was introduced making the price of admission more than it looked at a general glance. The *Era* hoped that such a disgraceful subterfuge would not again be used. I have seen this bill in the British Museum. The subterfuge consisted in printing the so-called half-prices (which operated after a certain hour) in large print, with the ordinary prices in small print; a similar device is used even to this day for expensive commodities such as mushrooms, where a small *quarter* is inserted before a large *pound*. The ordinary prices were practically what the *Era* wanted, and in the next week's playbill the size of the printing was reversed. Subsequent bills showed stalls at three shillings, family boxes at ten-and-sixpence, and omnibus boxes (for eight) at one guinea.

In the ensuing weeks the *Era* continued to be mildly critical of Fox Cooper's productions, and asserted that old pieces were still being foisted on the audience under new names. So it was perhaps to provide some novelty that the morning performances were inaugurated on 3 May, with a company of 'Bayadère female Ethiopian serenaders', enjoying the euphonious names of Jonia, Orinthia, Cleopatra, Alathea, and Bona. On 22 May the *Theatrical Times* again had a very complimentary paragraph about the Strand Theatre:

> The spirited lessee,* Mr Fox Cooper, seems determined to persevere in his efforts to secure the patronage of the public, and we hope that his exertions receive in golden opinions the reward they so well merit. The theatre is well attended each night. We know of no place of amusement in the Metropolis where an evening can be more pleasantly spent than at this house. The Company is talented, the pieces are put upon the stage with artistical care and skill, and the public are sure to meet with civility and attention.

This composition supports my impression that Fox Cooper had some influence with that journal, and the use of the word "exertions" implies a direct participation. His own personal feature came in the following month.

On 30 May the theatre announced a performance by female American serenaders, and the following week a new set of Ethiopian ones. Serenaders were rather in the fashion, first set at the St James's,† but the *Era* was unkind enough to suggest that the Americans engaged by Mr Cooper, who were stated to have come over in the *Margaret of Anjou*, were in reality attached to the Britannia saloon. They were billed as Cora, Woski, Yerico, Rosa, Miami, Womba, and Jumba: a suggestion of polygenesis that leaves their nationality a matter of doubt.

In June evidently the long evenings forced a closure as the *Theatrical Times* early in July stated that the Strand Theatre had reopened after a short vacation. "From the nature and variety of the entertainment provided the establishment is really worthy of the public support. The Company is a talented one, and several additions have been recently made." But the *Era* reported that the Strand was miserably attended, and they were really sorry for Mr Fox Cooper as he has attempted a

---

* Lessees were often described as spirited: the words go together like pius Aeneas. Other quite serious examples only too frequently met in Victorian newspapers are: frightful occurrence, and awfully sudden death. But the most macabre of those I found referred to the execution of a criminal: turned off.

† This followed a trial appearance at the Hanover Square rooms.

little of everything. A fortnight later the *Theatrical Times* said that the hot weather was acting very detrimentally to the interest of theatres then open in London; nevertheless there was a good audience at the Strand on Monday evening to witness a piece called *The Destruction of the Bastille* in which the principal characters were sustained with great effect by Mr Reeves and Miss Love. This play was probably the version produced by Fox Cooper at the City of London Theatre in June 1844.

By August it is clear that business had improved, and the house was nearly full for the production of *Dombey and Son*, by T. P. Taylor. On this occasion Fox Cooper expressed the hope that he had selected no premature or offensive adaptation of a very popular tale, which was in fact only a little more than half way through its long period of gestation. With some effort to mitigate his action, he claimed that the drama was superior to every other form of amusement: it at once expands the heart and refines the intellect. But it would be rash to judge the truth of that statement from the partiality of the review in the *Theatrical Times*, which I reproduce:

The prestige attached to this house, in connexion with the works of Charles Dickens, dramatically illustrated, is of very long standing. Hammond's Sam Weller is still fresh in the recollection of the town, and *Martin Chuzzlewit* had a run which, for many weeks, sustained the falling fortunes of the establishment, when under the management of Roberts. We were not, therefore, surprised at the announcement made by the present indefatigable lessee, that *Dombey and Son*, the latest serial production of Boz, was about to be presented, albeit a more difficult story for the purposes of the playwright could scarcely have been selected. The most we can expect in a dramatized novel is to see some of the best and most stirring scenes taken out, and the engravings realized in the shape of tableaux: and Dickens owes no little portion of his success as an author to the skill of the adaptors of his works. *Dombey and Son* was produced here on Monday. The original work not being yet concluded by the author, Mr T. P. Taylor, the adaptor, has had to exercise his ingenuity for the catastrophe. We will not say that he has anticipated Mr Dickens, but his concluding scenes are highly creditable; though we shall not trespass upon the time of our readers by describing the plot, advising them to witness and judge for themselves.

A few remarks occur to us as to the principal characters: Mr C. Williams made an efficient Mr Dombey, and Mr Reeves showed, by his representation of Carker, that he was well studied in the character of the wily manager of the house of Dombey and Son. Mr Tyrrel was rather stickish, and a great deal too plausible as Walter Gay; Mr Huntly is a low comedian of merit, but Major Bagstock is above his grasp; Mr Rogerson made the most of Captain Cuttle; Solomon Gills is a part well suited for Mr Ayliffe; Mr Richardson was created for Rob the Grinder. The ladies follow, and here we must pay a tribute to the artistic acting of Mr Harwood Cooper as Good Mrs Brown; it was the best sustained character in the piece. Miss Marian Atkins looked and played the haughty beauty, Edith Granger, remarkably well. Mrs H. Hearne made an amusing Susan Nipper; and Florence Dombey found an efficient representation in Miss Coleman. The whole of the performers seemed to exert themselves to the utmost; and it is due to the efficient management of Mr Cooper, to state that the piece is put upon the stage with the greatest taste and care. The theatre is well attended. An amusing ballet, in which Stilt (from Sadler's Wells) appears, has filled the house at half-price.

This struck Adair Fitz-Gerald as a very good theatrical picture of the period, but he vehemently rejected the statement about the indebtedness of Dickens to the adaptors of his works. Attempting to be impartial, one might suggest that their value as media for publicity was greater than their literary or their dramatic merit.

On 6 September the house was still open and crowded every evening for a troup known as the Bosjesmans, or Wild Bush People, whose performance at the Egyptian Hall had created considerable sensation among the nobility, and the scientific gentlemen of the Metropolis. Performance is perhaps an exaggeration, as these pygmies from a country bordering the Great Orange River, some 1,200 miles from Cape Town, were little more than an exhibition. They consisted of two men and two women, with a child born at sea on the way to Europe in the brig *Fanny*.

The *Era* likened them to the baboon for their absence of

intellectual or higher faculties, and said that their dancing was characteristic of wild beasts, although the women exhibited a great deal of natural grace. *The Times* said they were little above the monkey tribe. *John Bull*, however, thought that, though far removed from the pale of their fellow creatures and made fierce by persecution, these forlorn beings were not

No match for the dog. From the *Theatrical Times*, 30 October 1847

destitute of kindly and gentle emotions. Appearances also took place in the provinces. On an occasion at Totnes, one of them stepped off the stage while the keeper was not looking, and went to his caravan from which dreadful shrieks emerged. He was found severely beating his wife, with whom he had quarrelled, and both of them obstinately refused to appear before the audience.

The master of these ceremonies was Mr James Saunders Tyler who, according to the *Theatrical Times*, "came from the West country where he played the organ in Worcester Cathedral, but his prominence in the Metropolis was peculiarly as custodian and cicerone of that almost intractable bevy of human beings the Bosjesmans. By curbing their passions, soothing their resentments, and stimulating their better tendencies, he had inspired affection and attachment, where fear and ferocity had place; and by example and familiarity he had weakened some of the most ill-favoured and unamiable points of their barbarous dispositions." Mr Tyler also possessed a remarkable Newfoundland dog named Talma. This animal performed various feats, alleged to be novel, in relieving his imprisoned and fettered master in a drama by T. P. Taylor entitled *Avalanche, or Dog of the Desert*. After the Bosjesmans it must have been a comparatively simple matter to train "the beautiful, colossal dog of the Newfoundland species to a high state of culture where instinct ceases and intelligence begins". Both master and dog are depicted in the journal mentioned; the master, although a heavy, thick-set individual, looks no match for the dog.

Mr Oxberry made his first appearance at the Strand early in September in the farce: *A Day well Spent*. The *Theatrical Times* said they had witnessed an "amusing drama" called *The Magic Glass*; the burlesque of *Grizelle*, with the dancing of Mademoiselle Blanche, and the laughable contortions of Oxberry, had filled the house at half price. In the same week the *Era* went so far as to say that few managers excelled the lessee of this theatre in catering for the amusement of the public. *The Days of Oliver Cromwell*, or *Cavaliers and Roundheads*, was produced on 4 October. This may well have been Fox Cooper's version of *Oliver Cromwell* (see Chapter 3).

On 11 October the Strand produced a version of a currently

popular theme, *The Bottle*. And although a playbill of this date gives no indication of the authorship, the *Theatrical Times* later in the month, and subsequent playbills leave no doubt that it was by Fox Cooper, and not by T. P. Taylor whose play bearing the same title came out at the City of London Theatre on 18 October. As stated elsewhere, Fox Cooper and T. P. Taylor were good friends and probably engaged in amicable rivalry: on this occasion in point of time the former won by a short head. The Strand production was described as the most decided hit yet made by Mr Cooper. "The horrible evils of intemperance, the crimes and miseries it produces, are faithfully depicted in the plates which attract the passer-by, but how truthfully and vividly they are presented in dramatic form, a visit to this establishment alone can tell. Painfully life-like are the tableaux, and the skilful blending of the pathetic with the broadly humorous, redounds highly to the lessee's reputation as a dramatist." The *Colored Acting Drama*, No. 2 (but advertised elsewhere as No. 1), contains a print of the text with a hand-coloured picture on the front, reproduced in outline opposite page 184.

The play is a straightforward and brief sermon on the bottle, with the familiar device of a dream to provide a happy ending after the tragedy. Quite a lot of comedy is interspersed in the drama, and it would not be difficult to play the whole thing in burlesque. One of the characters, Dick, talks almost entirely in Shakespearean language, a device that Fox Cooper repeated more than once. He asks the housemaid: "Ain't I a walking wolume of his most wonderful work? Don't I see him before my eyes every blessed hour of my life?" (He is selling beer and sandwiches.) "Look here," (holding tray) "don't I give measure for measure? And when Missus catches me kissing of you up in a corner, don't she make much ado about nothing? And when master whops missus ain't that the taming of the shrew? And if you was to refuse to have me, wouldn't that be love's labour lost? But it you do marry me, shan't I have to coddle you, and that will be as you like it?" A poor tribute, one might say, but an honest one.

At the end of October the *Illustrated London News* said that *The Bottle* was still the favourite piece at the minor houses, but the City of London version was reputed the best; there were at least four. "To advertise another version of the play a troop of men gravely marched along the pavement dressed to represent large bottles, their hats forming the cork, which afforded great sport to the boys who are ever amateurs of gratuitous pageants."

On 30 October the Manager's Night was announced: Fox Cooper was taking a personal benefit, although the financial outcome could hardly be different from the result of any performance during the season, excepting perhaps benefits for other members of the company. The programme included *The Bottle*, *The Spare Bed*, with Fox Cooper as Captain Ardent (his first and only appearance during the season), and a new farce from the pen of the lessee. This might have been *Shooting the Moon*, which had been advertised in a playbill as in rehearsal on 18 October, and was licensed by the Lord Chamberlain on 21 October; but I can find no evidence of its performance on the benefit night, and the production of this farce seems to have been delayed until the following year.

Kenilworth, author unnamed, was produced on 1 November under the able superintendence of Mr Broadfoot, with great taste and splendour. On 7 November the *Era* stated that Fox Cooper really deserved for his perseverance more patronage than he received: "the houses are very good, but they must be crowded at the present cheap charges to ensure a remunerative return; the performances are well worth double the cost of admission." Later in that month the *Era* carried a paragraph stating that the American actor, Harry St Cyr Percy, making his first appearance in England, had taken the part of Ben the Boatswain, and added that reduced prices had attracted large audiences; once again this journal thought that the perseverance of Mr Cooper deserved a larger patronage than he was enjoying.

In the Enthoven Collection is a playbill containing a proclamation on 29 November anent the Christmas pantomime. This was to be the work of the Lord Chief Joker, Mr Frederick Foxy Copero, the sole lessee of our dominion called the Strand, whose duty it was to collect by the 27th night, Boxing Night (from Box, to knock down or astonish) all his best jests, bons mots, etc., etc., etc. This purported to come from the Treasury of Wit, dated 22 November 1847, the first year of our reign there. On it was printed "Vivat Everybody", and it was signed Momus Broadgrin. Not a bad idea, but perhaps too artificial, or should one say, naïve, for Victorian teenagers.

The playbill for 27 December 1847 stated that the pantomime, *The Man in the Moon*, had been written by a Mr Vandeightone, and that it was produced under the superintendence of Fox Cooper. But in view of the first announcement I assume that the latter was a part author. A Mr V. Deightone acted at the City of London Theatre in 1845 under Fox Cooper's management, and at Deptford in 1845–46 when, as suggested, he was probably associated with the theatre. There seems to have been at this period a small company of players whose names appear under the management of Fox Cooper at several theatres: apart from T. P. Taylor and Deightone, there were Broadfoot, Hamilton, Lawrence, Manley, and others. The *Theatrical Journal* reported that the pantomime gave the most unlimited satisfaction to all except some of the noisy denizens of the gallery whose over-anxiety tended repeatedly to injure the very fun so anxiously expected, and upon one occasion Fox Cooper was obliged to entreat that order might be better preserved. The scenery was truly superb, the dresses new and splendid, and the whole performance highly calculated to satisfy the "grown children" for whose especial entertainment it had been provided on so liberal a scale.

The *Theatrical Times* stated that Mr Cooper had not been behind his neighbours in catering for holiday amusements, and the house had been full on the opening day. The *Era* reported that they were really surprised at the effective way the pantomime was produced but added that Harwood Cooper's Clown was not all that could be wished, though considerably above mediocrity, and this was his first attempt. He was only twenty-one years old, seemingly young for a clown, yet elsewhere it was suggested that he bade fair to be the genuine successor of Grimaldi and Bradbury. But what was one among so many? Also in this pantomime was George Huntley in the part of Young England. Huntley was also only twenty-one years old, but he had played at Maidstone, Rochester, Dover, and Liverpool before joining Fox Cooper at the Strand. He features with a contemporary memoir and portrait in the *Theatrical Times*.

Despite the favourable tone of these notices funds must have been running low as on 13 February 1848 the *Era* made this announcement:

> Mr Fox Cooper, who by some persons has been thought to have achieved managerial immortality, has at length been compelled to bow to the will of Fate, and after many vain struggles to avert his doom has receded from the management of this house, little Oxberry taking the reins of government in his stead.

According to a note in the records of the Lord Chamberlain, Fox Cooper's lease of the theatre (as distinct from his licence) expired on 10 March. So he was unable to hold on to the end of his tenancy. But he continued to figure in the playbills as the lessee even down to 10 May, when there was a benefit for Mr E. Laws. On this occasion Fox Cooper took the part of the Advocate of Mantua in *The Wife* by Sheridan Knowles.

The *Theatrical Times* remarked on 19 February that under the judicious management of Oxberry the Strand Theatre was rapidly rising from its fallen state into public estimation. Such implied criticism of Fox Cooper contrasts somewhat strangely with the complimentary notices which that same journal had printed during his period of association. On one occasion it even went to the rescue of Fox Cooper, unless the following incident was merely the manifestation of a private vendetta.

The *Pictorial Times* (1843–48) was one of the earliest papers to use the art of the engraver to lay before its readers the events of the week, and in the issue of 1 May 1847 there was an attack on the management of the Strand Theatre. "Everything indicated poverty and wretchedness. Not a single ingredient of success was to be found in the new enterprise. The pieces are bad, the scenery, properties and costumes, daubs and rags. Mr Collier mistakes his line: he is a good mimic but the moment he opens his mouth, the absence of all comic humour is discovered." On 15 May, under the heading: "Pen and Ink Slanderers", the *Theatrical Times* said that someone had lately opened the fire of his weak artillery against the Strand Theatre in a pictorial paper that professed to act impartially and whose proprietor, they were assured, would regret that their columns should be defiled with falsehood. This individual was evidently at one time the editor of the *Cicerone*, a paper produced in 1843–44 by W. W. Barth.

The lambasting of a fellow journalist, although irrelevant to my story, is good enough to record. "There has floated upon the surface of society for some time past a fungus— hermaphrodite, half-playwright, half-scribbler, who, backed up in his abortive efforts to traduce a respectable profession, has attained to an unenviable notoriety. In the hebdomadal production which owns him first scribbler he has run riot in the extravagance of mendacity. The bold face of impudence, even if adorned with the vulgar accompaniments of mustachios, will ever fail to gain public approbation save with the few who lack the sense of common humanity, and the scoundrel who lies in print, is with the weak creature giving it existence, consigned by general approbation to the quietude of oblivion". It is no wonder that the profession was said to be paid at a penny a line.

The direction of Oxberry was not to last very long, and the *Era* stated on 5 March that the little Strand Theatre had really passed into other hands. As the previous lease had come to an end, a fresh one had been granted by the owner to a Mr Barnett. I have looked forward through the *Era*, but can find no further reference to Fox Cooper, or to any financial consequences resulting from his gallant adventure in the Strand. There must have been some unpaid creditors, however, as will be seen in the next chapter.

During this period of management Fox Cooper produced only two or three of his own plays, apart from a pantomime of which he was the joint author. It is not improbable that the duties of an entrepreneur and the gradual onset of financial stringency took his mind away from effort of a more creative kind, or even works of adaptation. His publicity was enterprising, he had a definite price policy, but his old enemy, the financial bogey, won again.

Having closely scanned many issues of the *Theatrical Times* in 1847–48 I have grown to like this little paper, because in its short life a lot of light was thrown on events at the minor theatres, and particularly on Fox Cooper's policy during his tenure of the Strand. The element of praise usually contained in the notices, apart from their frequency, suggests that the lessee of the Strand was his own critic. But this is not proved despite the interesting fact that Harwood Cooper possessed the three volumes, which he sold for thirty shillings in 1891. I was glad to pay five pounds for the year 1847 and part of 1848, unbound. Each week's issue presented a portrait of which that of Fox Cooper is an example, and even if the heads are sometimes too big for the rest of their anatomy—thus producing the impression of grown-up children—they are not without their charm. The gossip columns also repay perusal although a magnifying glass is helpful: they abound with the "on-dit", and with little glimpses into the trivial which convey an intimacy with the period, so difficult to acquire except by personal contact with someone who has made it a special study. I conclude with a choice example from the issue of 4 March 1848:

> American Criticism. The following is a Yankee notion of *Macbeth* after having witnessed a representation: "From what I could make out of the play, I don't think Macbeth was a good moral character; and his lady appeared to me to possess a dictatorial temper and have very loose notions of hospitality, which, together with an unpleasant habit of talking to herself and walking about *en chemise* must render her a decidedly unpleasant companion."

Chapter 8

A Bid for Drury Lane; Gravesend, and other Events: 1848–53

A FEW months after the end of the Strand tenancy, Fox Cooper made an attempt to land a bigger fish altogether. In June 1848, as a reflection of certain current anti-Gallic feeling, Drury Lane Theatre had been the scene of violent and riotous protests against a company of French players, and after they departed it was advertised to be let. Later in the month the *Theatrical Times* in some inspired paragraphs heralded the opening of Drury Lane under the direction of "one of the most persevering Managers in the metropolis, backed by some of the most extensive capitalists in the Kingdom." The intention was to represent the "fast-going" portion of the legitimate drama, until the public could be worked up to a just appreciation of Shakespeare. An attempt would also be made towards more fairly balancing the salary list. The price of stalls would be five shillings, with four shillings for the dress circle, and among the company were to be Mr and Miss Vandenhoff, Messrs Brooke, Ryder, G. Bennett, and Vining.

It was therefore with no surprise that, shortly afterwards, the *Sunday Times* and a few dailies formally announced that Drury Lane Theatre would be reopened for the restoration of British Drama and the employment of native talent on 17 July. Communications from ladies and gentlemen of acknowledged celebrity who wished to treat with the management were to be addressed to the lessee, care of E. T. Smith, the acting manager, 92 New Bond Street. But the name of the lessee was not divulged.

Also not divulged were the reasons of the governing committee of Drury Lane for subsequently refusing to grant the lease, a situation described in a letter published in the *Era* on the day before the expected reopening:

Sir,—I perceive in the morning papers a paragraph respecting the lesseeship of the Theatre Royal, Drury-lane; allow me to inform you the full particulars of the case, as various reports have gone forward to the public respecting the management of this theatre.

True it is that Mr Cooper entered into an agreement with Mr Chappell, on behalf of Mr Beale, for the theatre, for the next ten weeks, commencing the 17th July, and, after the 6th of December, for the winter season. True it is, that Mr Cooper gave a bond for the due performance of his agreement, by two approved parties, in £2,000. True it is, I paid down for Mr Cooper £150, the rent in advance for the week for the theatre. Mr Cooper employed me as acting manager. Mr Chappell was so satisfied that Mr Cooper had engaged the first available talent in the metropolis, together with ladies and gentlemen of acknowledged celebrity in the provinces, that he stated in my presence it would be a mere matter of form to ask the sanction of the Committee, and further, that he was happy to congratulate Mr Cooper and myself for the spirit in which we appeared determined to aid the fallen cause of the drama on the boards of Old Drury.

On Tuesday, Mr Cooper waited for the reply of the Committee, and he was then peremptorily refused as a tenant. At this stage of the proceedings, and knowing that the next morning a call of the whole company engaged was to take place for a rehearsal, the refusal of Mr Cooper as lessee would, as a matter of course, throw a large number of families, who had given up their engagements at other theatres in town and country, totally out of employ, I then undertook to accept the original proposition of Mr Chappell (but which I had previously refused in consequence of the heavy responsibility), that I should be the lessee on the same terms as entered into by Mr Cooper. You may judge, then, of my surprise, when I was also refused, on the ground that it would be merely "changing the name". The principal objection (which subject was settled previously with Mr Chappell) was the reduction of prices as announced by Mr Cooper. It must obviously be impossible for me to penetrate into the true cause which has led to the singular decision of the sub-committee. If it be as they urged, the reduction of prices, surely I may be at liberty to inquire why the dictum should be directed against an "English company", when a "foreign entertainment" (for the preparation of which "the national establishment" was almost rendered a perfect wreck) was tolerated for many weeks at the prices I proposed?

It would be uncourteous on my part, ere I conclude, I fear, this long epistle, if I did not take advantage of this public opportunity to return my grateful thanks to the large body of the profession who so kindly assisted me with their advice, more particularly to Mr Vandenhoff and his talented daughter, who came forward spontaneously to aid the cause of the "legitimate drama," without reference to pecuniary motives. In conclusion, I beg to state that myself and Mr Cooper have done all in our power to reopen Drury-lane Theatre for the British drama, and it will be something worse than an absurdity, nay, an insult to common sense, if the sub-committee, in the face of this statement and my engagements, attempt to repeat a recent observation of theirs, viz., an English company could not be found for Drury-lane Theatre.

I have the honour to be, Sir,
Your most obedient servant,
E. T. SMITH.

92, New Bond-street, July, 13, 1848.

Lloyd's Weekly London Newspaper described the incident in the following terms:

ATTEMPT TO REOPEN DRURY-LANE THEATRE. —Within the last few days considerable sensation has been excited in theatrical circles, in consequence of a rumour, followed by placards and advertisements, announcing the opening of Drury-lane on the 17th. inst., under the patronage of Her Majesty, the company to be composed exclusively of British artists, and the object the restoration of the legitimate drama. Upon inquiry it appears that in consequence of a negotiation pending between Mr E. Smith, auctioneer,

New Bond-street, Messrs Chappell and Beale were induced to enter into an agreement with Mr Fox Cooper, to let him Drury-lane Theatre for a summer season of ten weeks, to commence on the 17th of July, at a weekly rent of £150, one week to be paid in advance, and a bond for £2,000 to be given for the fulfilment of all engagements; this agreement having been duly signed on the 3rd instant, and the rent paid in advance, it was settled that Mr Cooper should enter upon the lesseeship on the 11th instant, and on the 10th a bond was given to the Messrs Chappell and Beale for two thousand pounds, and the securities having been accepted, arrangements were entered into, and engagements in many instances made.

On Monday, however, Mr Cooper was informed that the committee objected to the low prices of admission, which was met by the observation that they were the same as charged by the French riding company (Franconi's); and he was further informed that he must await a meeting of the committee, which was fixed for the next day (Tuesday). The result of this meeting was a formal rejection of Mr Cooper as a tenant. Mr Smith then presented himself, producing a correspondence which had passed between him and Colonel Anson, from which it appeared that Her Majesty would patronize the undertaking, and offered himself to give sufficient security, and become lessee. He was, however, it is stated, rejected.

The *Illustrated London News* reported disdainfully that the "intended opening of Drury Lane by a Mr Fox Cooper has fallen to the ground. This is a matter for congratulation, since, if the national drama is to be revived it must not be by unknown hands, aided by such stray members of the profession as may be wandering about without engagements." It was also rumoured that Macready might remain in England and take over the management, instead of paying a projected visit to the United States.

Probably on account of his unenviable notoriety Fox Cooper was unacceptable as the lessee of a major theatre, and the committee may have doubted his ability to shoulder the "heavy responsibility", which E. T. Smith had at first declined. But it is pertinent to recall that in 1852 the latter became the lessee of Drury Lane Theatre for several years. He was also the lessee of Cremorne Gardens from 1861 to 1869; Fox Cooper's reputed association with Cremorne (unverified) might have been during that period.

By way of a *douceur* it seems, according to a note in the *Sunday Times*, that a performance of *Don Carlos* (by Lord John Russell) was given at Drury Lane on 31 July for the benefit of Fox Cooper. That play had been produced at the Surrey Theatre in June, but little notice was taken of the single performance at Drury Lane.

Following the Drury Lane bid, Fox Cooper not unnaturally gave theatrical management a rest, and became editor of the *Theatrical Chronicle*, which he revived after a lapse of five years. Volumes I to IV had been published in 1841–43, and the editor is recorded as C. T. Fowler. But volume V,* appearing between September 1848 and March 1849, strongly supports the *London Gazette* notice (see later) from which my clue was obtained. Apart from the style of many articles, the frequent references to Fox Cooper and his activities point to his editorial influence. In the early numbers the Drury Lane affair is often introduced even when "answers to correspondents" is used as a pretext, and from time to time Fox Cooper would ride a number of his hobby-horses: neglect of Shakespeare, lower prices of admission, over-payment of stars, under-payment of authors. He was also able to make sallies against his pet opponents: Osbaldiston of the Victoria Theatre, and Johnson and Lee of the Standard.

His self-description included "an eccentric manager", "a fellow of infinite wit", and even "the Immortal Fox". But he sometimes published jokes at his own expense: thus although the name of Mr Hooper (who had succeeded him as the manager of the Strand Theatre) had only one letter different, he was a man of principle whereas his predecessor was full of self-interest. Perhaps his best leg-pull was an advertisement, answers to which were to be sent to F.F.C., c/o Kennington Post Office:

> A Professional Gentleman who has much time to dispose of, would devote it to the service of managers; from his universal knowledge of obsolete and foreign drama, and his rapidity and richness of fancy, he would be able to undertake the

* Copies of the sixteen numbers were kindly furnished to me by Harvard University Library.

practical business of one or two theatres in all its branches, according to the present system, upon reasonable terms and with the strictest secrecy. He has already metamorphosed several pieces which have succeeded far beyond Shakespeare. He will undertake to turn tragedy into comedy, and comedy into opera, without the slightest fear of detection; and to make or alter characters so as to fit exactly the particular excellence or defect of any popular actor or actress. Novels, ballads, pamphlets, and public occurrences, dramatized with the greatest dispatch.

The advertiser begs to say he will make it his particular study to conform to the present taste and policy of managers, that his pieces shall abound in metaphors, allegories, screams, rantings, faintings, processions, battles, choruses, statues, red hot swords, boiling hot poison, drawbridges, dungeons, castles, conflagrations, and explosures [*sic*], the whole producing the most splendid *coup de théâtre* and effect; and that nothing whatever like legitimate drama shall expose the incapacity of the performers or manager to the invasion of ambitious genius.

N.B. The advertiser can at all times command a number of well-dressed persons to attend as clappers on the first nights of representation: he is particularly skilled in Scotch dialect and vulgarisms so much in request by managers.

A case in the Queen's Bench: Wigan *v.* Gadderer, was reported in December 1848. The former, an actor, brought an action against the latter, manager of the Lyceum Theatre, for twenty pounds (or two weeks' pay). The dispute arose because the actor had declined to play a small part which he considered unworthy of his talents, and more suitable to a "walking gentleman". He had consequently been fined by the manager, and sought to recover his due. Fox Cooper seems to have been introduced as an expert witness, and his evidence testified that in his opinion the plaintiff was the only man who could have made a part out of the trifling character, "Alfred Jumble" in *Gun Cotton*. Lord Denham in his summing up said he accepted this view, but pointed out that the part was not so made to the plaintiff's hand, and judgment was given in his favour.

On more than one occasion the circulation of the *Theatrical Chronicle* was claimed to be over 15,000 a week, while editorials overflowed with confidence and success. But at twopence a copy, this was not enough, and the end came suddenly with the issue dated 3 March 1849; unheralded and unexplained. The fact that Fox Cooper had changed his printer several times during the six months suggests that he found it difficult to make ends meet.

During the above events the family continued to live at Walcot Place, Lambeth, where they had been since 1843: easily the longest period at one address.

Failure in journalism invited a return to theatrical management, and later in 1849 Fox Cooper took over two enterprises in Gravesend: the theatre in May, and the Terrace Pier Gardens in July. His partner in this venture was a Mr Frank Durrell Pratt, who under the name of Durrell was described by the *Era* in July as joint manager of the theatre with Harwood Cooper. The latter played a part in Fox Cooper's *Hercules*. Although the theatre had been redecorated "regardless of expense", business was not good. But a little colour is added by a report in the *Theatrical Programme and Entr'acte* that a short day's excursion had been made to Gravesend by the new North Kent line on 23 August: the Rosherville Gardens were under the direction of Baron Nathan, and the theatre under the leadership of Fox Cooper, with a well selected company.

The opening of the Royal Terrace Pier and Harmerville Gardens took place on 25 August with Henry Lee as acting manager. J. H. Tully, the composer, was in charge of the musical department. Fox Cooper must have thought that he had at last brought off a successful deal, as this event is recorded in a press cutting containing a piece of gossip by a journalist drawing on sixty years' experience, probably about forty years after the event:

> Speaking of the Terrace Pier Gardens at Gravesend, brings a well-known journalist and newspaper proprietor into my mind, one Mr Fox Cooper, who started a paper in London called the *Cerebus* [*sic*] or the dog with three heads. He struggled on as long as he could with it, but at last he got into difficulties with the Stamp-office people in the days of the newspaper stamp* and the advertisement duty, and so he

* There is no evidence in the reports of the insolvency proceedings in 1844 (following the failure of *Cerberus*) that the Stamp-office was a creditor, but this comment may relate back to the prosecution in 1831–32.

had to give it up. One day at a grand gala at the Terrace
Pier Gardens, after the newspaper failure, Cooper whom I
knew well, came to me in high glee and told me he had got a
good chance at last of making his fortune. I replied, "Well,
if you have, Cooper, hold it fast, for you have had a good
many chances during the time I have known you, but they
have all slipped away from you." He said he had got a lease
of the Terrace Pier Gardens, from the Corporation of
Gravesend, and if he did not make a precious good thing of
the "spec" it would be no fault of his. He was very sanguine
about it, and laughingly told me as we parted that he would
not take less than £10,000 for this chance. I met him some
few years after this, when he was in rather depressed circumstances, and when I asked him how about his £10,000
chance with the lease of the Terrace Pier Gardens, he threw
up both his hands in dismay and said, "I was robbed and
done out of it all." So poor Cooper never got his £10,000,
I am afraid. He left two sons, both clever men and one of
them is now, or was a few years ago, an actor at one of the
London theatres. Mr Fox Cooper was a prolific and clever
journalist; he wrote several dramas, and when I first knew
him earned a great deal of money, but I do not believe he
was ever a rich man. As he used to say, he could make any
man's fortune but his own.

I do not think that Fox Cooper was actually robbed, but
the goose failed to lay the golden egg, or in other words the
ghost failed to walk.

The *Kentish Independent* on 1 September 1849 announced
that for three days a week galas would be held in the Terrace
Gardens, with two performances a day. Of the opening gala
it was remarked that the management knew how to do the
thing first rate, and there were nearly 4,000 visitors, while the
Era said that the Gravesend gardens had been arranged rather
like Vauxhall, and that it was equivalent to the restoration of
old Ranelagh. It is clear that Fox Cooper was endeavouring
to attract metropolitan patronage, as advertisements pointed
out that the train to London was at 10.20 p.m.

On 20 September the *Era* correspondent reported from Maidstone that there was still no tenant for "our pretty little establishment". Overtures had been made to Fox Cooper the
spirited manager of the Terrace Gardens and theatre at

Gravesend to pay that town a visit. Whether or not this invitation was accepted, Fox Cooper's journey to Maidstone in the
following year was the consequence of overtures in quite a
different key as will be seen later in this story.

Although some success was achieved at the Terrace Gardens,
the summer season at the Theatre Royal had been a failure.
A playbill for Monday, 24 September 1849, shows Fox Cooper
organizing a benefit after what he describes as the most
disastrous season ever known in Gravesend. He got together
a lot of friends from theatres in London and elsewhere to put
on a mixed programme, including *The Merchant of Venice*,
and selections from *Richard III*. Among the guest artists were
Stuart of the Theatre Royal, Haymarket; Rafter of Covent
Garden; Mortimer of Her Majesty's Theatre; Mrs Desmond
from York, and Miss Desmond from Bath.* The company was
completed by T. P. Taylor, with imitations of other actors,
Harwood Cooper taking the lead in a ballet called *Hob in the
Well*, and by Fox Cooper, making his first and only appearance
as the Duke of Gloucester in *Richard III*. Musical arrangements
were under the direction of J. H. Tully, described as of Drury
Lane and Covent Garden. This performance marked the end
of Fox Cooper's association with the Gravesend Theatre,
as distinct from the Terrace Gardens.

Despite that most disastrous season, one week in the summer
was a complete success according to John Coleman,† who had
been tempted by an offer to be starred in his pet parts, and to
"divide the plunder" each night. Fox Cooper's object in
securing his services was to stage an experienced actor opposite
a lovely young red-headed pupil of Jack Ryder's, accomplished
and wealthy, who had paid valuable consideration for the
privilege of appearing as Juliet, Ophelia, Desdemona, Lady
Teazle, Letitia Hardy, and Pauline. And so enthusiastically
did she portray the youthful affection of Juliet on the first
night that the lady who was keeping company with John
Coleman was seized with fury until assuaged on the Saturday
by the strangulation of Desdemona. So perhaps the lessee's
claim that the season had been disastrous was made with at

---

* Miss Desmond was quite possibly the Sara Desmond mentioned in the
footnote about the insolvency in 1846.

† *Fifty years of an Actor's Life* (1904).

K

least one eye upon his benefit night, and without reckoning the receipts from any extraneous source.

After September 1849, advertisements peter out rather suddenly, and except by inference I have not been able to obtain further details about the progress of this season. But I happened to notice in the *Kentish Independent* for 13 October 1849, a report of proceedings in the Gravesend County Court under the heading: Judgment Summons, Bradford *v.* Cooper. As the defendant had incurred the debt while lessee of the Strand Theatre, evidently in 1847–48, he could have been none other than Fox Cooper. Upon examination he said that, after the original order, execution was levied against his goods, which were sold at a ruinous sacrifice not sufficient to meet the liability. Defendant then made further payments under a revised order by the Judge of the Lambeth Court, but in May 1849, in conjunction with Frank Durrell Pratt, a person of some property, he unfortunately speculated with the Gravesend Theatre. In July he also became lessee of the Terrace Gardens, and Mr Pratt (the Treasurer) fell a victim to cholera*: he had thereafter been unable to continue payments under the court order. His Honour J. Espinasse, reviewing the evidence, animadverted very severely on the conduct of the defendant in meddling with such large speculations while in financial difficulties, but observed that having examined the defendant he could not see that he had made away with any property, and could not find reason for a committal. He therefore made a fresh order for payment.

Mr Gibson for the defendant rose and, while not presuming to reply to the observations of His Honour, thought it his duty to his client to remark that as respected persons in his profession, their only means of living was by such speculation. If, after one unfortunate speculation, they were prevented from entering upon another they would become ruined men. He further remarked that if a man made a fortunate speculation he was looked upon as everything that was good and honest, but if the speculation was unfortunate he was looked upon as a rogue and everything that was bad. The spirit of Mr Gibson must be admired in making the best of what reads like a chapter of misfortune.

* This is confirmed at Somerset House.

How long Fox Cooper remained in Gravesend I do not know, but Harwood Cooper's notebook shows that he, and presumably the rest of the family, spent Christmas 1849 at Fountain Place, City Road. Harwood was back in Gravesend at Easter (31 March), and the *Kentish Independent* said that Mr Levy had become lessee of the Terrace Gardens while Mr J. F. Cooper [*sic*] would be the manager. A similar reference in the *Era* stated more anonymously that Levy would be aided by a gentleman of great practical experience. E. L. Blanchard relates that he met Fox Cooper in Gravesend on 19 May 1850, a lovely day.* He went with a friend named Sola (possibly Sala) to Gravesend, visited the ship *Parland*, then returned to the town and slept there.

In the course of the day he went to Baines's Lounge, Terrace Gardens, where he met Tom Matthews, Fox Cooper, Rafter, Lawrence and Levy. At night all the voyagers met at The Falcon, and the parting glass was taken. This was one of the only two references to Fox Cooper I have found in the memoirs of E. L. Blanchard, who wrote such an informative obituary about him in the *Glasgow News*, and a possible explanation is that there was an initial friendship which was broken off. Tom Matthews had become manager of the theatre, and was also Chef de Bal for the Terrace Gardens; Lawrence was connected with the Deptford Theatre. Other advertisements for the Terrace Gardens in May and June include Harwood Cooper as a vocalist but make no mention of Fox Cooper, the reason being that he had gone to Maidstone: in the prison for debt. Possibly Mr Bradford, who had taken Fox Cooper to court in the previous October, was still unsatisfied.

On 4 June 1850 the *London Gazette* reported that the Court for the Relief of Insolvent Debtors had vested the Estates and Effects of Frederick Fox Cooper (late Superintendent of the Royal Terrace Pier Gardens, Gravesend, and then in the gaol of Maidstone) in the Provisional Assignee, who must have grown weary of receiving so little under that compendious formula. A subsequent notice indicated that the prisoner would be brought before the Judge of the Maidstone County Court on 9 July. Fox Cooper was therein described as formerly of 17 Walcot Road, Lessee and Manager of the Strand Theatre,

* *Life and Reminiscences*, vol. I, p. 72.

then of Commercial Road, Lambeth, Editor of the *Theatrical Chronicle*, then of 59 New Road, Gravesend, Lessee of the Gravesend Theatre and the Royal Terrace Pier Gardens, carrying on the said theatre with Francis Durrell Pratt under the style of Cooper and Durrell, then of 7 Fountain Place, City Road, London, Editor of the *Pictorial Plays*, and late of 3 Milton Road, Gravesend . . . and during the whole time Dramatic Author. The *Maidstone Journal* briefly reported on 16 July that Mr Cooper was discharged, there being no opposition.

The *Pictorial Plays* were a series entitled *Penny Pictorial Play* of which there is a bound volume in the B.M. Each contains an illustration probably coloured by hand. Many of the series are versions of plays with which I have found Fox Cooper's name directly or indirectly associated: *Oliver Twist, Dombey and Son, Jack Sheppard, The Blood Red Night, The Dumb Man of Manchester, A Miller and his Men, The Vicar of Wakefield, Black-Eyed Susan, The Corsican Brothers, Uncle Tom's Cabin, The Bottle, Little Dorrit, Herne the Hunter, Ivanhoe.* Other titles make up thirty-two in all, but identification of any particular version would be difficult: for example, the opening lines of *The Bottle* are slightly different from those in the versions of T. P. Taylor and Fox Cooper. None of the plays is attributed to a definite author. They are described as: adaptation, translation, founded on, based on, or simply as performed at. . . . . But *The Corsican Brothers* (No. 16) shows marked similarities to Fox Cooper's version (Dicks' 752). Although the order of the first two acts is reversed, some of the wording and a lot of the stage directions are almost identical.

Many of the numbers contain a note to country managers saying that the Acting Copyright is vested in the Proprietor (i.e. of the series of plays), and offering to give written permission, pursuant to the Dramatic Authors' Act, upon moderate terms. Towards the end of the series it is indicated that they were printed by G. Purkess (the publisher of a *Library of Romance*), whose name is faintly discernible at the fold of the paper in the earlier numbers. I should imagine that Fox Cooper edited some of them, or perhaps most of them, but we are given no precise dates to indicate when the series was completed.

The *Theatrical Journal* in December 1856 advertised the publication of No. 26 (*Dred*), based on a novel by Harriet

Beecher Stowe about the slave trade. Family association is once again suggested by the fact that a version by Harwood Cooper was performed at Sandwich in the same month. In January 1858, and again the next year, the *Theatrical Journal* advertised the series down to No. 29 (*Herne the Hunter*): it was added that as the plays were "stereotyped" they were never out of print. On the above evidence the *Pictorial Plays* provided Fox Cooper with occasional occupation and remuneration over a decade or more. It seems probable that the object of the whole edition was to collect royalties or fees from provincial theatres.

When the subject of this biography was released from Maidstone in July, Harwood Cooper was still at the Terrace Gardens, assisting Tom Matthews. It is obvious, however, that Fox Cooper returned there because on 4 September the *Kentish Independent* reported that a benefit had been held for "F. F. Cooper, the gentleman who first opened these gardens, and who this year [1850] has been acting as director of the amusements". The benefit had been a bumper attended by nearly 2,000 persons. There was to have been a balloon ascent with horse and rider, but it all failed to lift, which was probably just as well. To the general entertainment were added extra vocalists, fireworks, a ballet on the pier, with supper in the wine-room at midnight. Dancing continued to the early hours, and as the journal said, no doubt all to the satisfaction of Mr Cooper.

The use of the word "gentleman" in the above account, together with a report of the proceedings of the Corporation in May 1850, suggests that Mr Levy, the new lessee of the gardens, was not entirely acceptable to all parties concerned. But it is probable that Fox Cooper forfeited his tenancy because of his insolvency, and it may well have been due to some kindness on Levy's part that he was retained as manager. Other references in this biography show that they were well acquainted; perhaps too well in 1839, when Levy helped to put Fox Cooper in gaol. But it might have been another member of that family.

On 21 September, Tom Matthews, still the lessee of the Gravesend Theatre, produced the *Vicar of Wakefield* from the pen of "F. F. Cooper, late of Terrace Gardens". The local paper formed the opinion that it was written to introduce the low comedy of Harwood Cooper. No other mention of this play has come to my notice, and it was not one of the three versions with the same title that were licensed by the Lord Chamberlain in the early months of 1850.

Fox Cooper's association with Gravesend which ended in September 1850 may have been connected with his brother, Henry Octavius William, who was also insolvent in 1850, and in the gaol of Maidstone. His name appeares in a *London Gazette* notice announcing that a vesting order had been made, and that the prisoner was to be brought before the Judge at Maidstone on 3 September. The two brothers could well have been guests of the Queen at the same time, and it is not unlikely that their financial fortunes, or lack of them, were in some way interwoven. Henry Cooper, as he was commonly known, formerly lived in Bloomsbury Square, and then in Kensington Square. At one time he was clerk to C. J. Coates, a stockbroker, and afterwards carried on business with John Bailey, under the style of Bailey & Co., as stock and share brokers dealing in railway shares on commission. He later resided in Baker Street, Portman Square, and occasionally lived at Gravesend. Henry was discharged on 10 September, but no report of the proceedings was given. He was not a full member of the London Stock Exchange, but probably what is termed an outside broker. I have discovered little else, but there was a further term of imprisonment in Norwich, also for debt, in 1857. In May 1874 he died at the age of sixty-nine in the Old Palace, Richmond, and he was described as a Land Proprietor; yet there is no trace of his will at Somerset House, so that land was probably a *mot d'estime*.

The next venture of Fox Cooper was the briefest period of theatrical management, again at the Strand Theatre, in the autumn of 1850. A playbill in the British Museum shows that the theatre was under the joint management of Bolton (the lessee) and Fox Cooper. The lessee, whose licence had started to run from 2 September, had been unable to pay the cast later that month, and the *Theatrical Journal* went so far as to say that the partnership was calculated greatly to increase the prosperity of the theatre, but gave no reason why. Bolton produced Fox Cooper's farce, *Shooting the Moon*, on 29 October, and in the same month the Strand Theatre had played *The Deserted Village, Hercules,* and *The Spare Bed.*

The characters in *Shooting the Moon, or The Cove of Cork,* are principally Irish, and the main title was a current expression for leaving one's apartment by night without paying the rent. One critic said it proved to be anything but moonshine in its wit, and another that it was full of practical blunders, which kept the audience in a roar of laughter during the whole of its performance. For a brief period it was quite a success. But *The Cove of Cork* did not prevent Fox Cooper's joint occupation of the Strand Theatre coming to a sudden end, since only one week after its hopeful sentiments, the *Theatrical Journal* had to announce the closing of the theatre by order of the Lord Chamberlain. Various statements were afloat, some not creditable to the late lessee, and while that reputable but tantalizing journal forbore to give them publicity the remark was made, *en passant,* that parties almost entirely destitute of capital were hardly suitable to become lessees of theatres. The point of this comment was that Bolton's brother, one of his sureties, was a tailor in Pall Mall.

A note in the records of the Lord Chamberlain states that Mr Barford declined to grant any further use of his theatre to Mr Bolton after 16 November, apparently because he had not paid the rent. So Fox Cooper wrote one of his typical letters to the Lord Chamberlain in defence of his partner. He explained that he had been retained to assist from 21 September, and in view of the financial position he had devised a curtailment of the company. This had engendered some animosity among the players, who took advantage of the situation to make trouble for Bolton. There had been much argument as to whether the rent and the actors had been paid, but Fox Cooper would only admit that trifling sums were due. He complained that at one point Bolton had been locked in the theatre, and that eventually he had been locked out. The actors themselves had since been allowed to put on the show without permission from Bolton. But the Lord Chamberlain was not impressed, and let well alone.

Indications from Harwood Cooper's notebook are that his mother and young brother did not leave London to live in Gravesend, which even in 1850 represented a journey by a

fast train of no more than forty-five minutes for the twenty-four
miles from London Bridge. They were still in Fountain Place,
City Road, at Easter 1850. But a removal took place that year,
and by reason of the address for Christmas 1850 and Easter
1851 the notebook provides a valuable clue to the composition
of the family on the date of the 1851 census, at the end of
March. They were then in Britannia Street, City Road, near
the Grecian Theatre, and the census return shows:

Name	Age	Occupation	Born
Frederick Fox Cooper	45	Author	Westminster
Ann Cooper	45	Wife	South Wales
Frederick Harwood		Professor of	
Cooper	24	Elocution	Lambeth
Alfred Edgar Cooper	11	—	,,
also resident in the house:			
Thomas Pool Taylor	36	Dramatic author	Walworth

My researches into the life of Fox Cooper had frequently
led to a fellow dramatist and actor, Thomas Proclus Taylor,
so I was not surprised to find him with the Cooper family
at the time of the census. His middle name was evidently
beyond the capacity of the returning officer, who resorted
to simplification.

I have mentioned the coincidence over the production of
plays called *The Bottle* in October 1847; the similarity was not
confined to the title. The opening sentence in T. P. Taylor's
reads: "Come wife, one glass, only one, now; just take a glass."
In Fox Cooper's version, shorter all the way through: "Come,
Mary, just one glass." A catch-phrase in T. P. Taylor's runs:
"I like to make everybody happy", while in Fox Cooper's
we have: "I love to make everybody comfortable." Even the
illustrations on the prints of the plays are strikingly alike. But
T. P. Taylor's was thought the better piece, as it obtained a
number of first-class provincial bookings in the autumn of 1847.

There are many occasions when both names appear in the
same playbill. That they were close friends, is apparent from
the dedication of T. P. Taylor's play, *Fair Rosamund* in
Duncombe's edition.

To Fox Cooper, Esq.:—

Upon the dedication of a piece, it is generally subscribed to the best friend; and therefore, I dedicate this to you.

In this busy world of trouble and anxiety, it is difficult to find a friend; and it is with some pride I publicly acknowledge, that, in the real acceptance of the word, such I have found you.

From the many kindnesses, from the gentlemanly and generous conduct that, I am happy to say, I have always received from you, I subscribe this trifle; with a regret that it is not more worthy of being dedicated to you.

I am, Dear Sir,

Yours faithfully,

T. P. Taylor.

The above was written from Rose Cottage, Lambeth, on 13 May 1838. How different would it be if written today: but it could not be more sincere.

According to A.N. the last play by T. P. Taylor was produced in 1849. This suggested to me that he did not survive for very long, and I then discovered that his death took place in June 1852 from consumption, twelve months certified. He was unmarried and was living with the Coopers in Singleton Street, Hoxton New Town; so Fox Cooper deserves some credit for having provided a home, even a humble one, for his consumptive friend. It must have entailed an element of risk, at close quarters, for the twelve-year-old Alfred Edgar. The *Era* said that T. P. Taylor was the son of Dr Taylor, the celebrated professor of Greek and Latin. He had been intended for a learned profession, but was attracted by the stage, and about fifteen years before had been for a short period the lessee of Sadler's Wells. For some time he had suffered from declining health, and his death was a happy release from his sufferings. He was highly respected in the profession, but apart from that he left no one to deplore his loss. According to the *Theatrical Journal* he had barely attained the age of thirty-eight, which tallies closely with the census, but on the death certificate his age is entered as forty years.

The parentage of T. P. Taylor is a matter of some interest, and there is additionally an element of mystery about his birth. Thomas Taylor, his father, (1758–1835) was not *de facto* a Doctor or Professor, but he was a most learned and unusual man, often described as a Platonist, or Neo-Platonician. His portrait by Richard Evans, after Lawrence, is in the National Portrait Gallery, or rather in an inside apartment to which I gained access on application. It shows a man of about forty-five years of age, seated at a table, with some Greek ruins in the background, and his right hand resting upon a book. His father was Joseph Taylor, staymaker of St Martin's-le-Grand, who sent him to St Paul's School at the tender age of eight. (In his term two entrants were only seven.) But he was removed after three years during which he suffered more by the cane than he profited by the classics. After leaving school he developed an interest in mathematics, and tried to square the circle; this was followed by an attempt at chemistry, when he invented a perpetual lamp ending in an explosion. The metaphysical side of mathematics led him to the works of Aristotle and Plato: thus he met Plotinus, and studied the commentaries of Proclus which he read three times, a task perhaps never performed by any other man. Hence the name of the reputed youngest child of his first marriage, but herein lies the problem.

Thomas Proclus Taylor from the evidence of the census return, and at his death, must have been born in about 1812 or 1814. According to the *D.N.B.* the first wife of Thomas Taylor, named Mary, died in 1809, having given birth to four sons and two daughters. *Notes and Queries* in March 1890 gave the dates of birth of four sons and one daughter of Thomas and Mary between 1779 and 1787, including the son, Thomas born in 1785. If the latter were eventually called Thomas Proclus, and if he were the dramatist, he would have been about sixty-seven years of age, when he died (in 1852) and not thirty-eight or forty. It is possible that Thomas Proclus was a son of the Thomas Taylor born in 1785. But it seems to me more likely that he was a son of the second wife of Thomas Taylor, the Platonist, who is reputed to have had issue, although the date of the second marriage is not on record. This second wife died in 1823 at the early age of thirty, through preternatural enlargement of the liver. She was evidently talented, and the *Gentlemen's Magazine* described her as a woman of the rarest occurrence.

Despite the above uncertainty T. P. Taylor had an intellectual background far superior to that of his contemporary, Tom Taylor, a more renowned dramatist, which whom he is liable to be confused. But if T. P. Taylor had enjoyed better health or a longer life, there might have been less to choose between their merits. Fox Cooper's capacity for friendship seems to have extended to all sorts and conditions of men, and in this case he found a good companion. Sometimes, alas, the good die young.

We now move on to the summer of the census year 1851, the year of the Great Exhibition. In that season Fox Cooper assumed the management of a place of entertainment known as the Royal Chinese Junk, which (by permission of the conservators of the River Thames) was firmly established on the mud-bank at the end of Essex Street, Strand, close to the out-fall of the sewer of St Clement's parish.* Performances commenced in about the middle of June and continued until the early part of October, when the company departed for France.

The *Illustrated London News* for 2 August shows a picture of an assault of arms between two Chinamen taking place on a boat illuminated with Chinese lanterns. In the foreground is a mother with two children, and there are a lot of top-hatted men witnessing the display, accompanied by exotic musical instruments and a drum. According to the report the leader of the band ("a sort of Costa and Mario rolled into one") beat time with a stick upon a kind of saucepan-lid supported upon three legs. The reviewer thought that the singing was somewhat harrowing and ludicrous, but it was relieved by sword dances and war demonstrations.

A press cutting in Harwood Cooper's book states that the Chinese Junk was nightly filled with a highly respectable company. The orchestral department was under the management of Mr Harroway† of the Grecian saloon (or theatre) while the general arrangements were entrusted to Fox Cooper: "a gentleman whose spirit as a caterer for the public is

* The vessel had left China waters in 1846, and had been exhibited in America.

† This is probably the Harroway mentioned as the joint composer of the music for *Jenny Jones* (Chapter 3).

deserving the highest commendations: for many years he was the successful lessee of many of our metropolitan theatres and his experience consequently well fits him for his present appointment. The appearance of the place when lighted up with innumerable pagoda lamps, banners, and decorations, the Chinese in their singular costumes, the strains of music, the movements of the dancers, and the ripple of the waters upon the bosom of Old Father Thames, altogether make up a scene that for novelty cannot be equalled in the three kingdoms."

After this effort Fox Cooper disappears from the public eye, and from October 1851 until July 1854, I have little to relate in spite of a close study of the *Era* and other likely journals. It is possible that some of this period was occupied in the writing of plays, as at least six were produced in the second half of 1854. But Fox Cooper's dramatic efforts do not normally give the impression of having taken long to compose; it is more likely that he was engaged as a reporter (parliamentary or otherwise), or as a journalist whose work, then as now, was often unsigned, and thus anonymous.

To this period probably belong two minor efforts to widen still further the scope of Fox Cooper's activities. The first was a theatrical agency from 13 Wellington Street, Strand, the former office of *Paul Pry*. Ladies and gentlemen wishing to adopt the stage professionally, or for pleasure, were invited to ascertain the terms upon which they could be accommodated. And parties who had written serious or comic dramas could have them produced at a first-class metropolitan theatre.

The second was a literary agency from 416 Strand, where Messrs Cooper and Sons, pending negotiations for an extension of the lease, had opened temporary offices. Authors seeking a new medium for publicity were invited to send in their manuscripts at once for the Spring trade. Cooper and Sons (young Alfred Edgar was presumably employed) were disposed to deal liberally.

The family continued to reside at different addresses in Lambeth, after leaving Singleton Street in 1852; and although Harwood Cooper had been in Norwich to play the clown at Christmas 1851, there is no evidence that his father was there. But in April 1852, Fox Cooper is mentioned by E. L. Blanchard who met him at Bushell's with the brothers Sala and William

Beverley, and after his name is printed an exclamation mark in brackets. This may be an indication that Fox Cooper had again been in hot water. Bushell's* was the Coach and Horses, a public house kept by Thomas of that ilk at 324 Strand, opposite Somerset House.

For 1852 I have only one other reference: a play entitled *Trip to Paris*, entered in Harwood Cooper's list. A.N. records this title, but the date was forty years on and the author unnamed; no doubt a different piece altogether.

In December 1853 instead of being a debtor Fox Cooper was a creditor, or rather a would-be creditor, appearing as a complainant in the Insolvent Debtors' Court when a Richard Pridmore applied to be discharged from prison. This gentleman was the lessee of Saville House in Leicester Square, which contained the Linwood Gallery. He had converted it into a theatre at which there were performances with marionettes, and was about £1,000 in debt. Fox Cooper said in Court that he was a creditor for £100, for theatrical dresses and manuscripts, because he had been unable to gain admittance to recover this property. He felt strongly (perhaps from personal experience) for the poor children, as they might be considered orphans. The Chief Commissioner said he could not regard Mr Cooper as a creditor, for reasons which are not clear from the account in the *Era* except that his agreement was with Mr B. Rolt, who rented the theatre from Pridmore. Fox Cooper was told that there was another place to obtain redress, and one can only hope that he succeeded.

* Featured in the *Theatrical Chronicle*, 18 November 1848, and evidently a rendezvous of authors and journalists.

Chapter 9

Management of the Strand Theatre again, 1854–55; and the Garrick Theatre, 1856 (including own plays)

FOX COOPER had his third and last period of management at the Strand Theatre in 1854–55. For a part of the time, at least, he was acting manager under J. H. Tully who had previously been his musical director, and with whom he was associated on other occasions, e.g. in 1860 as librettist and composer respectively of the opera *Garibaldi*. J. H. Tully had assumed the management of this theatre in July 1854, and it is probable that Fox Cooper joined him for the purpose of producing a number of his own plays, including some for which J. H. Tully would contribute the music, or share the authorship.

Thus the adaptation of *Hard Times* was produced on 14 August, only two days after the appearance of the last instalment of the serial in *Household Words*. Malcolm Morley wrote about it in *The Dickensian* for March 1954, and included a few appropriate remarks concerning Fox Cooper, but he repeated a number of statements which I have since shown to be inaccuate. For his own part he describes Fox Cooper as "an old offender. His distortions from Dickens began with *Master Humphrey's Clock* and were to continue intermittently

HARD TIMES.

A DOMESTIC DRAMA, IN THREE ACTS.

FOUNDED UPON THE POPULAR NOVEL BY CHARLES DICKENS.

BY FOX COOPER.

First Performed at the Strand Theatre, Monday, August 14th, 1854.

Dramatis Personæ.

[*See page 20.*

THOMAS GRADGRIND, ESQ. (M.P. for the Borough of Coketown—"Inflexible, dry, and dictatorial; whose head had scarcely warehouse room for the hard facts stored inside") ... ... Mr. R. Romer.

MR. JOSIAH BOUNDERBY ("A man who was always proclaiming, through a brassy speaking-trumpet sort of voice, his old ignorance and his old poverty") ... ... Mr. Barrett.

JAMES HARTHOUSE, ESQ. ("A thorough gentleman, made to the model of the time—weary of everything, and putting no more faith in anything than Lucifer") ... ... Mr. Belford.

STEPHEN BLACKPOOL ("A good Power-loom Weaver, and a man of perfect integrity—one of the hands who has known a peck of troubles") ... ... Mr. Herbert.

No. 785. Dicks' Standard Plays.

Design from Dicks' *Standard Plays*, No. 785, published 1886

until *A Tale of Two Cities*". Actually there were no less than
ten adaptations from Dickens, including *Under the Earth*, as
will be seen from the list of plays in Appendix II.*

Malcolm Morley remarks that naturally enough when Fox
Cooper was managing a theatre he used his managerial pre-
rogative to produce his own plays and adaptations. This was
true of the 1854–55 period at the Strand, but it was not strikingly evident in 1847–48. He also states that Fox Cooper,
like Dickens, served for a time as a parliamentary reporter;
unlike Dickens he lacked inspiration and imagination; his
literary efforts never exceeded the commonplace: in fact, they
rarely reached it. He admits, however, that Fox Cooper was
an enterprising individual and a man of multifarious occupations. This at least will have been gathered from what I have
already related.

To return to his comments on *Hard Times*:

> . . . it contained a modicum of Dickens served on a platter
> of stale clichés from stereotyped melodrama. Not always
> coherent, the story in the play revolved round the names
> in the book and wound up with Bounderby bestowing boun-
> ties all round amid general rejoicings as the final curtain
> fell. Tom Gradgrind, the weakling who stole from the bank
> where he was employed, restored the money, giving the
> simple explanation that it was no robbery at all, merely
> that he had removed the cash from one place to another
> for safety. His sister, Louisa, after leaving her husband,
> Bounderby, conveniently returned to their home, making
> it a condition that the discarded Mrs Pegler, Bounderby's
> mother, be established there as well. Honest Stephen Black-
> pool falsely accused of stealing the missing money, did not
> lose his life in the colliery accident but was rescued by Sissy
> Jupe and Rachel. And the smiling Stephen, at Bounderby's
> instigation, plus a gift of £150, took Rachel for wife, curiously
> forgetful of the existence of the first Mrs Blackpool.

This almost too bald account of the action must be corrected,
as Bounderby said to Stephen that he would give him Rachel
for wife, and £150. The obvious inference is that he intended
to bring about the divorce which they had discussed in the first

---

* It is not without interest that my immediate chief for some years was
the youngest son of the youngest son of that celebrated novelist.

act. Despite all his faults, Fox Cooper would hold no brief for bigamy.

Malcolm Morley also relates that some weeks later, on 2 September, the Cooper "contraption" was seen at the Bower saloon. That this "contraption" had some audience appeal is shown by its revival at the Strand in October 1856, and by being chosen by John Neville for his benefit at the Marylebone in March 1858.

In my opinion, Malcolm Morley, with whom I have spent some interesting hours, is a little severe with Fox Cooper. What he wrote was at the time more or less what the public expected: far removed from the highest class, but entertaining at the level then demanded in minor theatres, of which the evidence of two critiques is given below.

Hard Times scarcely sustained the reputation of its author: the characters are often overdrawn, and Davenport Adams in a *Dictionary of English Literature* describes it as one of the least successful. It is a grim story. A playbill in the Enthoven Collection states that it had been necessary to arrange and condense the original and to alter the *dénouement,* a liberty admitted, but taken with deferential apologies. It was thought that the termination was too fearfully harrowing for the sensibilities and sympathies of a mixed audience. The *Era* said that no adaptation from Dickens had achieved greater success, enforcing upon the management the pleasurable duty of arranging a representation of this popular original, and pathetic [*sic*] drama every evening until further notice. The adaptor had closely identified his drama with all the main points of the story.

The *Illustrated London News* said that the novel had been very cleverly dramatized: the insufficiency of education—the leading doctrine of the novel—was insisted prominently in the drama; no stage plays, closet poesies, no public vaultings, wrestlings or tumblings—all hard, dry intellectual instruction; the dialogue was as much as possible preserved in the play, but a happy *dénouement* was contrived instead of the terrible catastrophe of the original. This treatment was greatly resented by Charles Dickens the younger, and caused him to say some very bitter things. It might have been preferable for all concerned if the theatre had left this novel severely alone.

L

Relatively speaking, it has. According to F. Dubrez Fawcett (1952) there have been only three adaptations, of which two, *Hard Times* and *Under the Earth* (see Chapter 12) must be attributed to Fox Cooper; but Malcolm Morley has disinterred three other minor efforts (see *The Dickensian*).

A very timely and topical farce, *New Wags of Windsor*, described as by the spirits of Beaumont and Fletcher, was produced on 18 September 1854. In fact Fox Cooper was a joint author, and possibly on the strength of one playbill in the British Museum, the co-author has been described as J. Howard, an actor who took the leading part. Several later bills and a reference in the *Era*, however, show the joint author as J. H. Tully, who is credited with the music. I have little doubt that the play was the joint effort of Cooper and Tully, which is pertinent because the same joint authorship is ascribed to two other topical plays produced in October and November at this theatre.

The *New Wags of Windsor* was about two young officers of the 146th Regiment who paid their attentions to a couple of milliner's apprentices at Windsor. For this offence they were arrested by order of the Colonel, but succeeded in making an escape. In order to avoid detection they found it necessary to take the place of show-dummies at the side of the milliner's shop. Eventually there was a full discovery, and the officers were condemned to trial by a jury of milliners, in a court where the officials were all female characters. The *Illustrated London News* said that if the merits of the piece were judged by the laughter, never was one more successful. Possibly owing to the continuing publicity given to the actual source of the burlesque the play remained in the bill until nearly Christmas.

The Courts Martial (factually) of Lieutenant Perry of the 46th. were liberally reported in *The Times* from August until November 1854. It was disclosed in evidence that junior officers of the day behaved rather like older boys at a boarding school where "ragging" is, or used to be, accepted as normal practice; for reasons not disclosed the young lieutenant had objected. Furthermore, the whole conduct of the Court was ridiculed in a leader on 25 August, which demonstrated that amidst the complex and complicated procedure the prisoner himself was treated as no more than a cypher. On the next day a letter followed from "Fair Sex": after the disclosures in the Court Martial the writer suggested that the social inferiority of the civilian would come to an end, and men of literature or commerce need no longer fear their epauletted rivals. To return to the trial, although Perry was found guilty of assault upon a superior officer, mercy was recommended on grounds of provocation. But the army fought back, and at a second trial Perry was found guilty on three charges, the gravest of which was that he had asserted that his complaint against the commanding officer had been ignored. He was dismissed, and *The Times* had some more hard things to say about the conduct of the Court. It was fairly quick work to get the *New Wags of Windsor* on the boards by 18 September, although the subject was a gift for Fox Cooper.*

On 30 October another farce was produced by the same authors. This was called *Who's a Traveller?*, and it owed its origin to a current controversy between the law-givers and the licensed victuallers. The scene was in the Somerset House Hotel, while the plot turned on the difficulties of obtaining rooms on a Sunday, and the various annoyances with which travellers of the day had to contend. One of the characters was policeman, X49, or Shakespeare Bob, who had a heavy sense of humour and a vivid yet inaccurate recollection of the author's works; thus one quotation became: "O God! that men should put an enemy in their mouths to steal away their trousers." He was obviously not unrelated to a corresponding type in *The Bottle*. It is interesting to speculate when the stage or music-hall policeman was first linked with the number 49: in recent years it has been a feature of a successful radio programme.

A third *pièce de circonstance* by the joint authors, entitled

* Subsequently a fund of some £1,700 was raised to purchase the promotion of Lieut. Perry if the verdict of the court were set aside, otherwise to be placed at his disposal as a civilian. Perry went off to Paris, and was reported to have drawn a cheque on the fund prematurely for his own investment. In a letter to *The Times* he said it was to purchase shares in a certain railway, the existence or even projection of which was contested in the city column on the following day. Eventually Perry indicated that he did not wish to rejoin the army, or to enter the public service, as he had met in Paris "a wealthy American who had given him one-half of all he possessed". It would seem that the paltry sum of £1,700 was no longer of interest to the gallant lieutenant.

Where's Cruvelli? was produced on 6 November. The background of this farce was the sudden disappearance of a celebrated singer Sophia Cruvelli* from the Paris Opera House, when an expectant crowd was waiting at boiling point, and where the management had turned three parts of the pit into stalls. So the authors contrived that at the shortest possible notice an English actor and actress should take the parts of Amina and Elvino in *La Sonnambula* by Bellini. The last scene of this opera was burlesqued in the play; Senora Onizetti, alias George Honey, and Senor Beaumont, alias Fanny Beaumont, enacting the respective characters. According to a note in the *Era* of 12 November, Mme. Cruvelli had in fact disappeared just previously from the Opera House, in most Lola Montez-like† fashion, possibly in the cause of matrimony, but had later returned. So it was again quite rapid work on the part of the joint authors to produce the burlesque when the news was red hot.

On 18 November the Strand produced an original domestic drama in two acts entitled *The Soldier's Wife, or The Heights of Alma*, by Fox Cooper alone. It was obviously very topical, but little is recorded about this piece because theatrical reviews at that time were sacrificed to provide for the cover given to the Crimean War. However, it does not require a great deal of imagination to think out the sort of play Fox Cooper would construct around this theme. The *Era* said that new scenery and the stage mechanist contributed to the success of the production, and added this comment: "When gallant spirits and faithful hearts are taking their share in the frightful havoc of the Crimea, such demonstrations at home are but the due

* Her real name was Johanne Sophie Charlotte Crüwell. She was born in Germany in 1826, and Italianized her name in 1848 for the purpose of an appearance in London. Her contralto voice was ill-trained, but she had a fine face and a good figure, and scored an enormous success upon her appearance in Paris in 1851, receiving a contract with the Opera worth 100,000 francs a year. In 1854 she appeared at Covent Garden, when her Desdemona was ranked with that of Malibran. In 1856 she married the Comte Vigier and left the stage. From occasional references in the *Era* her health and movements were always of interest; for over fifty years she was a Comtesse, and she died in 1907—quite appropriately at Monte Carlo.

† Maria Dolores Porris y Montès, a dancer known as Lola Montez (1820–62). She was a Bohemian adventuress, much travelled, and was made Countess of Landsfeld by the King of Bavaria. This led to his abdication.

tenders of homage to united bravery and honour." On 4 December the last four plays produced here were all together in the same programme. What a feast of Fox!

Another adaptation from Dickens by Fox Cooper, the *Christmas Carol*, was produced at the Strand on 11 December. As the story had been dramatized over ten years previously, Fox Cooper's version was somewhat belated; but it may have been played in the provinces before the London presentation. The Crimean War being still much in the news, it was claimed in the playbill that this production was opportune:

> When the best sympathies of the human heart were awakened on behalf of human suffering, no apology was required for realizing a story from the exquisite pen of Dickens which called in its operation the heaven-born virtues of love, charity and forgiveness. The Adaptor is no ghostly innovator, but he feels assured that the spirit which will haunt the audience will prove of such agreeable description that no visitor will wish to lay it.

But the press took no notice of it, and the run was short.

The work of Charles Dickens again inspired a Strand Theatre advertisement in the *Era* on Christmas eve for a play to be entitled *The Seven Poor Travellers, or Heart Strings and Purse Strings*, in preparation by the author of *Hard Times*: it was clearly a version by Fox Cooper. On this occasion he had taken the story from the current Christmas number of *Household Words*. A playbill for 8 January 1855 (with Fox Cooper shown as acting manager) indicates that rehearsals of *The Seven Poor Travellers* were continuing. On that date the theatre produced the last play by Fox Cooper under the Tully-Cooper combination entitled, *Who'll Serve the Queen?*, a "New Local Drama", elsewhere described as a comedietta, altered from O'Keefe.* *Taffy was a Welshman*, the Christmas pantomime by Peter Parley, commenced its last week on 22 January, after which a new company under the direction of Miss Isaacs took over the Strand Theatre.

So *The Seven Poor Travellers* had to go elsewhere, as Fox Cooper ceased to be acting manager when the change in direction was made. Incidentally, Malcolm Morley informs

* Possibly from a play entitled: *The Poor Soldier* (*circa* 1798), reprinted in Dicks'.

me that the title "acting manager" at that time referred to the
management of the front of the house, as distinct from the stage
manager who managed the affairs behind the curtain. I am
somewhat at a loss from my knowledge of my great-grandsire
to decide for which side of the curtain his particular talents
were the more suitable; on either side he could be very successful, or quite dangerous. I believe that publicity was his forte,
although he was apt to exaggerate. But it would be difficult
to maintain that there is no exaggeration in the advertising
world today, even when truth in advertising has become
axiomatic.

Unlike so many of Fox Cooper's adventures in theatrical
management, and in the absence of contrary indications,
the 1854–55 season at the Strand Theatre appears to have been
a financial success. But in this case it was evidently Mr Tully
who held the purse-strings; the heart-strings were not so
important. Perhaps the order was changed when Miss Isaacs
took over, as it is on record that the Strand reassumed the
character to which it was so well adapted, of a drawing-room
theatre. Such was never Fox Cooper's cup of tea.

On many occasions the Garrick Theatre had been the
scene of productions or revivals of plays by Fox Cooper. He
must have known the theatre intimately and—presumably
with his eyes well open—took a lease from the owner, (Lawrence Levy) early in 1856 for a season which endured for only
seven weeks. Possibly owing to the expense of renovating the
exterior and interior, once again there was financial failure.
But economy was exercised in other directions as only two
advertisements were placed in the *Era*. In one of these the
lessee asked the "artistes" to meet him at the theatre, a tech-
nique similar to that adopted on the opening of the Strand
in 1847, and subsequently for his benefit performances at the
Charing Cross Theatre in 1873.

E. B. Gaston (a previous lessee) was Acting Manager, and
John Neville was Stage Manager. On the opening night,
Easter Monday, the programme consisted of *William Tell*,
Paris Life, or the Day of Dupes, and *Sister of Mercy, or the Ruined
Cloister*. W. H. Simpson appeared as Tell, Miss Prescott Warde
(niece of the tragedian) played five different characters in
the second piece, while the strong cast for the last play included

John Hudspeth, John Neville, and Rose Edouin. During the course of the second week the ambitious programmes included Sheridan's *Pizarro*, the *Beggar's Opera*, *Guy Mannering*, with the *Sister of Mercy*. The latter was now described as by the author of *Hard Times*, and thus clearly Fox Cooper's own contribution: a drama in two acts, taken from the life of Fénelon, Archbishop of Cambray.

In the third week there was a revival of the lessee's *London by Night*, with the sub-title, the *Fatal Fire*. Next week saw the ominous announcement of splendid free gift distributions of pictures, books, tickets, and *bon-bons* from the lessee. Later programmes included Fox Cooper's version of *The Bottle*, and an anonymous version of *Napoleon*. *Hard Times*, with the author in the cast, was given for his benefit performance on 5 May.

Despite the claim that the free gifts (probably a theatrical S.O.S.) had created a furore, another manager took over on Whit Monday. But, Fox Cooper was not alone in his failure. The compiler of a volume of playbills in the B.M. records that various attempts had been made by penniless managers to keep open this wretched place: few bills were printed, and sometimes an outside poster was the only indication of the holding of a performance.

Chapter 10

General Events: 1855–65

AFTER leaving the Strand, Fox Cooper found a lodging for *The Seven Poor Travellers* at the Grecian Theatre. This theatre was one of lesser importance but it enjoyed a delightful address: Shepherdess Walk, Britannia Fields. The other name for it was the Eagle saloon, and it was on the corner of the City Road in the locality of Hoxton. It is remembered from the song, "Pop goes the weasel", which my father said was incapable of translation into French.

There were at least four current dramatic versions of *Seven Poor Travellers*, of which three appeared respectively at the Surrey, Victoria, and Pavilion Theatres, before Fox Cooper's was produced on 12 March 1855; it is identified by the signed manuscript licensed two days later. Richard Watt's charity at Rochester provides the background. It will be remembered that six poor travellers were to have "gratis for one night, lodging, entertainment, and fourpence each". The seventh traveller was Dickens himself, who had visited Rochester in May 1854. At the Grecian *The Seven Poor Travellers* stayed no more than three weeks, but they may have made subsequent appearances on occasional nights.

A close association with B. O. Conquest existed during the winter season at the Grecian Theatre, as in December 1854 the patrons had been introduced to *Who's a Traveller?*, and *Where's Cruvelli?* This was followed by a production of *Hercules* in January 1855. Plays by Fox Cooper continued to make their appearances at the Grecian at least until the end of April, but from such a small theatre the royalties or fees cannot have been very substantial.

A few months later Harwood Cooper, my grandfather, was married to Emma Barrett, daughter of a deceased builder, on 9 August 1855, at St Mary's, Lambeth. The groom, then aged 28, was described as a comedian; his father, a witness, was described as an editor. Previously in 1853 Harwood had joined the company at the Olympic Theatre where he remained until 1869. I expect he felt secure. From the parental home in Hercules Place, Lambeth, he went to live not far away in Tenison Street. It would be interesting to know what view Fox Cooper took of his son's marriage; he can scarcely have disapproved. He was left with his wife, Ann, probably ailing already from heart disease, and his fifteen-year-old son, Alfred. But as Harwood was such a very different person from his father, as I shall show in a later chapter, it was high time the younger bird built his own nest.

The above description of Fox Cooper as an editor in 1855 links with the brief flicker of an imaginative journalistic effort, which took some pains to trace. In the year 1879 E. L. Blanchard wrote that, shortly after the *Cerberus* publication (i.e. in 1843), Fox Cooper had brought out a cheap illustrated weekly paper, the engravings being all roughly coloured by hand. He added that it was thought a wonderful undertaking in those days; it would, of course, be an impossibility today. For this I naturally made a thorough search in the B.M. index for the 1840's, but without success. Eventually the Cambridge Bibliography provided me with the correct clue, namely the *Colored News* in 1855. There were only nine issues, and one is missing from the bound volume at Colindale. The first four numbers, which came out in August, betray no obvious connexion with Fox Cooper, but at the end of the fifth it is added "published by Frederick Harwood at the office, 183 Fleet Street". It is a matter of conjecture why only the first two names of my grandfather were used as the publisher, and why that of Fox Cooper was suppressed. The disguise of the former was surely too faint to be effective.

Among the advertisements was one for *The Bottle, or The*

Drunkard's Doom, to which was later added *The Seven Poor Travellers*, but no other dramatic works. Those two plays were stated to form Nos. 1 and 2 of the *Colored Acting Drama*, thus providing the link with Fox Cooper, the author of this version of *The Bottle*. (See Chapter 7); probably No. 2 was his version of the Dickens story. Advertisements in the *Colored News* also appeared for the *Colored Almanack for 1856*, the *Colored Songster*, and a new work entitled the *Colored Novelist*, which was to comprise *The Buccaneer* from the German of Van der Velde. I doubt if these were ever published. The seventh issue of the *Colored News* dated 15 September contains the following announcement:

> On and after next Saturday the *Colored News* will be increased in size and altered in appearance. Arrangements have been effected for the most artistical attention to its embellishment and general contents. It is hoped that the improvement will be satisfactory to the public, and evince the gratitude of the proprietors for the unexampled support and patronage they have received at the hands of their subscribers.

The publisher was now given as F. Mitchell, whose name appears on the print of *The Bottle*, but in this format there were only two issues; the unexampled support could be read either way.

Each copy of the *Colored News* was partly illustrated in colour. The first issue contained two large and three small coloured illustrations, but the number in colour gradually decreased until the last two issues had only one large illustration apiece. Roughly outlined, the colours are not without effect, and some-one must have worked at a furious rate for little money. The price of the paper was only two pence (reduced to one penny for the last two issues), which took advantage of the abolition of the penny stamp duty as from 1 July 1855. But according to Andrews' *History of British Journalism* the paper was an insane attempt which, of course, failed! It was probably too cheap, whether at the price of one or two pennies. Nevertheless, if Fox Cooper had been possessed of greater persistence, or per-haps a longer purse, he might have brought the paper through to success. It was a good idea, although dependent upon cheap labour which probably was imported from France,

Fox Cooper's tenancy of the Garrick Theatre in the Spring of 1856 produced an echo in the Court of Exchequer on 9 December of the same year, reported in the *Era* under the heading: "Sheriff's Officer too kind to an Actor". The plaintiff, for whom Fox Cooper appeared as a witness, was one Howe, a Yorkshire printer, who did some work for a gentleman by the name of Sheridan Smith, the lessee of two theatres in that county. The latter left Yorkshire without paying his printing bill, came to London and appeared under his real name, (which was Swanborough) at the Strand Theatre, where he was due to take a benefit on 19 February 1856. The defendants were Aldermen Kennedy and Rose, late Sheriffs of London and Middlesex, against whom Howe brought an action for not executing a judgment against his debtor. Now it happened that the Sheriff's officer was Lawrence Levy, a solicitor and the proprietor of the Garrick Theatre, and into his hands the warrant for the arrest of Swanborough, alias Smith, was placed. Levy asked Barry, one of his henchmen, to take the writ of *capias ad satisfaciendum*, but he did not take Swanborough into custody for reasons which came to light in court. The defendants pleaded that as Swanborough was destitute, and had been in the Insolvent Debtors' Court, the plaintiff did not suffer as the result of the failure of their officer to take the proper action. In that court Swanborough said that he kept out of the way of his benefit because he feared arrest: Mr Frederick Cooper had informed him that the Sheriff's officer was on his track.

Mr Hawkins for the defendants said that those who knew Mr Cooper best called him "Fox", he believed. (Laughter in Court.)

Fox Cooper was then examined by Mr Joyce for the plaintiff. He was at the time resident in Ramsgate; and he was a dramatic author. Levy was known to him, and was with him at the Garrick on 19 February, when unfortunately he became the lessee of that theatre. He went to see Barry, who asked him a lot of questions about Swanborough, which induced him to think that Barry meant mischief; and when pressed he admitted he had an execution against the person of Swanborough. Upon this admission the witness said: "Oh! you must not take him— it is his benefit-night." Barry said that if he did not take

Swanborough he would want ten shillings, so witness made an appointment to meet him at The Norfolk Arms opposite the Strand Theatre. From a mistaken feeling of friendship he most regretted he jumped into a cab, and told Swanborough of the danger he was in. Swanborough said: "Impossible, I do not owe anything." Witness then borrowed the warrant from the officer and showed it to Swanborough, who mustered his friends and raised the ten shillings, which witness gave to Barry at The Spotted Dog* in the Strand. After that Swanborough proceeded to regale himself in the saloon of the theatre; Barry went in and looked at him, but did not speak.

Cross-examined by Mr Hawkins, witness said he was not an actor, but a dramatic author. After the events related, Levy asked him about Swanborough's wife, and witness told him that her mother lived near the Tottenham Court Road. Barry also came to him and said, "Mr Cooper, do not betray me, my head is in your hands." Asked whether he received money from Levy for informing him about Swanborough's wife, witness in a towering passion, demanded: "How dare you ask such a question!" Reply: "I want an answer." "No, I did not. Now you have your answer." Witness continued that Levy had the audacity to say he would indict him with Barry and others for conspiracy, but that did not make him angry. (The highly excited state of Fox Cooper while giving this portion of the evidence convulsed the court with laughter.) Witness believed he had unfortunately told Levy that his officer (Barry) had not received anything for allowing Swanborough to escape; he had lent Swanborough half-a-crown to make up the ten shillings for Barry; he saw Swanborough and Barry in the saloon between pieces; and there were eight or nine entrances to the theatre. Like a rabbit warren, suggested Counsel. Was this not natural for John Doe and Richard Roe† said witness; all doors were guarded by Cerberuses, one a female Cerberus who received a small salary for guarding four doors, North, South, East and West. The Lord Chief Baron commented, amid laughter, "a female Cerberus with four

---

* A few doors away from The Norfolk Arms.

† Alias: "Goodtitle" and "Troublesome", legal fictions formerly introduced into ejection cases for the recovery of possession of land. Their services had been dispensed with in 1852 by the Common Law Procedure Act. The allusion does not now appear very apposite.

heads".* Witness went on to describe how any Sheriff's officer might be trapped in the theatre: he might go down below, or up with a spring—Heaven knew how high. (Roars of laughter.) He did not know if Swanborough performed on his benefit night: he could not sit it out, it was so shocking bad. (Laughter.)

MR JOYCE (re-examining): You did this for Swanborough in a friendly sort of way?

FOX COOPER: Yes—just as I would do it for you, Sir, or for any other gentleman. (Roars.)

Levy, giving evidence, said Barry had been discharged for defalcation, and could not be produced as a witness; also that Fox Cooper had asked for a guinea for a clue to Swan-borough. This was once again denied emphatically by the former from the body of the Court.

In his summing up the Lord Chief Baron said that insolvency was no defence—it was for the Sheriffs to prove that every effort had been made to effect an arrest. The Jury did not trouble Mr Joyce to reply, and judgment was given for the Plaintiff for some twenty pounds. There is no doubt that on this occasion Fox Cooper stole the show. Although there was an attempt to impugn his evidence on the ground of its alleged improbability, it is this very quality that rings so true.

The year 1856 saw the foundation of the Actors' Acre at Brookwood Cemetery. That area of ground was devised in perpetuity to the trustees of the Dramatic, Equestrian and Musical Sick Fund Association as a burial place for its members. With the 200 representatives of the theatrical profession who travelled for the ceremony in a special train from the West-minster Road Station were: Benjamin Webster, the president, Mr W. Cooke, Messrs Johnson and Lee, Mr Johnson Towers, Mr George Cooke, Mr Anson, the secretary, Mr Phillips, Mr Fox Cooper, Mr Churchill, the company's secretary, and a considerable number of others unnamed. Among a dozen ladies mentioned by name as honouring the occasion by their presence were Mrs Fox Cooper and Mrs Harwood Cooper. Before the ceremony of handing over the assignment of the

* It is tempting to conjecture whether the Lord Chief Baron recollected Fox Cooper's short-lived publication about twelve years before, and the ensuing insolvency proceedings.

land, the company heard a most impressive address in the cemetery church on St John XI, 23: "thy brother shall rise again".
So Fox Cooper was one of the leading spirits in the Brookwood
project, and his body was duly interred in that place. To my
knowledge, there are buried in the Actors' Acre at least fifteen
members of the Cooper family, the earliest being Fox Cooper's
first wife, in 1860.

Shortly before the Swanborough case, *Little Dorrit* had been
produced at the Strand Theatre, on 10 November 1856, and
quickly ran into rough water, although the *Theatrical Journal*
said it was a drama of considerable interest, that it was well
received, and should have a long run. In the event it did not
last quite three weeks. E. L. Blanchard said the performance
was very slow. The *Era* was unusually pungent in remarking
that Dickens was not much more than halfway through his
novel, but this slight drawback had proved no barrier to the
anticipating gentleman who had provided the theatre with his
version of the story. But the notice was quite lengthy.

> With that easy recklessness of adaptors generally, and with
> sublime indifference to the author's original design, which
> has before now called forth the severest sarcasms from the
> writer of *Nicholas Nickleby*, we have the plot capriciously
> twisted, turned and terminated to suit this stage, and forestall
> the others, and the unfortunate victim is mutilated on the
> same principle as that adopted by the classical robber of
> antiquity and cut down Procrastes fashion to fit the place, the
> lopping off of a head or limb producing no remorse with the
> operator.
>
> The story as we have it in the drama is limited to the
> incarceration of the "Father of Marshalsea", and the piece
> ends with the restoration of Mr Dorrit to his property.
> As the novelist especially contrived to render his earlier
> chapters as undramatic as possible, it will be easily imagined
> that the adaptation of them to the stage has not imparted
> to the plot the spirit that is infused into the description rather
> than the incidents.
>
> The first act hangs fire very much, and the humour of the
> Circumlocution-office requires to be read, rather than repre-
> sented, to make it intelligible, so that with the absence of
> strong dramatic situations and the retention of long
> undramatic speeches, there is a dearth of that excitement

which is the means of sustaining, as well as creating, an interest in the progress of the plot. The circumscribed range of the story, as here told, even seems to have necessitated the constant reproduction of the same scenes, and thus the monotony is not even relieved by the variety of objects presented to the eye, which, on the special authority of Mr Lindley Murray, is to be considered pleasing. The piece, however, has the recommendation of being well acted.

Miss Emma Wilton, who plays Little Dorrit, exhibits no inconsiderable amount of talent, and her earnestness and pathos showed a power of delineation that induces a belief in a longer professional career than her apparent youthfulness would suggest. Miss Cuthbert, with an utter abrogation of feminine attractions that of itself is creditable to the judgement of the actress, makes up an admirable Maggie, whose devotion to her "little mawther" has been so well portrayed by the novelist. The nearest realization of the portraits drawn by the author is given by Mr Neville, whose very mannerism enables him to give a closer embodiment of Mr Dorrit's peculiarities, whilst his dress is so exact that Mr Hablot K. Browne might have performed himself the office of costumier. The Tite Barnacle of Mr Kinlock is another happy personation, from its being peculiarly suited to the actor's style. Mr G. Lee caricatures honest John Chivery with the red nose, long-tailed coat, and limp hair, that have been the recognized properties of the "comic lover" from time immemorial, and which have all the mouldiness of provincial antiquity about them, while Mr J. Clarke stands prominently forth as rendering the steaming, snorting Pancks a vivid, life-like character. The rest present no claims to remark, and when it is added that each tableau is marked by melodramatic music to enable the audience to remember that the respective positions of the dramatis personae are copied from the monthly illustrations, and that a well-painted scene of Southwark Bridge is the only novelty of embellishment, we have said all that the public will care to know of the "new and original" (!) drama of *Little Dorrit* (*vide* playbill *passim*) produced on Monday night at the Strand.

Because of my personal view that *Little Dorrit* has no peer among the novels of Dickens, this was one occasion when I felt just a bit ashamed to read a review of Fox Cooper's work: and the strength of my pleading must be limited to the claim that it was written at the behest of the Strand Theatre, that it was the first adaptation, and that there have been few successors.

A version of *Little Dorrit* is printed in Purkess's *Library of Romance*, otherwise the *Penny Pictorial Play*, No. 28, and a previous researcher in the Enthoven Collection has marked their copy: "Strand 13 Oct. 1856". This endorsement was possibly made on the strength of an advertisement in the *Era* of 5 October 1856 for a production of *Little Dorrit*, but I could find no review of the performance in that month. I have compared this print with the details on the playbill for 10 November, and the layout of the respective versions differs considerably. The playbill shows the drama in three parts: Night, Twilight and Sunrise; the print contains two acts. The Iron Bridge is featured both in parts one and two, while there is no mention of this in the print. The latter, however, commences with a scene in a prison cell in Marseilles which does not appear in the playbill. The cast is sometimes the same, but the print gives Miss Ternan as Little Dorrit instead of Miss Wilton. In view of these differences I examined the manuscript and took a note of the scenes. A comparison with the print shows a close similarity, the main difference being that the second act of the print omits two short scenes which are in the manuscript. There are also verbal alterations.

My opinion is that for the production on 10 November it was found necessary to make eliminations from the manuscript, which was submitted for licensing on that date, and to redesign the scenes possibly for better stage effect. When Purkess came to publish *Little Dorrit*, the version by Fox Cooper was used and amended, a notional cast being printed in accordance with a not infrequent but irritating practice. As Fox Cooper edited at least some of the *Penny Pictorial Plays*, it seems a fair conclusion. This was the only serious piece written by Fox Cooper in 1856, and I can find none in 1857.

Towards the end of 1856, Fox Cooper was once again running a theatre in Kent, this time (as already hinted in the Swanborough case) at Ramsgate. There is a little information about this venture in some of the Kent newspapers, but it extends only over a period of two or three months. It is clear that the theatre opened on 17 November 1856, under the management of Fox Cooper, described as a London manager,

late lessee of the Strand Theatre. The *Kent Herald* stated that
the theatre had been improved by the erection of a gallery
above the heads of the people in the pit and boxes, but failed to
give any of the actual programmes.

There was a pantomime at Christmas called *Harlequin and
the Magic Needle*. I have also a small printed handbill which
shows that on two occasions near the New Year the theatre was
used for a carnival in plain and fancy dress organized by Fox
Cooper. For these events the auditorium was specially fitted
up and illuminated with dazzling lights "so that the votaries
of Terpsichore could enjoy the fascinations of the mazy dance".
A costumier from London would be in attendance for hiring
Fancy-dresses. Later the newspapers reported a series of four
meetings held at the theatre on Sunday afternoons, with the
agreement of Mr Cooper, and under the guidance of a Rev.
Copeland Etheridge. Followers and friends of this cleric
assembled to hear a discourse between one o'clock and four
o'clock on "Sin and its Consequences", and many who went
to scoff remained to pray; the theatre was thronged on each
occasion. It was also related that some of Cooper's friends
wished him to disallow the sermon, stating that its influence
would be injurious to his pocket, but Mr Cooper answered
that he would not dare to enter his fiat against the promulgation of the Gospel if demanded at any time. By this action in
this and other matters Mr Cooper had gained golden opinions
for his urbane conduct.

I can find no further references to the management of the
Ramsgate Theatre, and the *Era* is silent—presumably because
they had no correspondent in that town. But the *Era* occasionally reported from Sandwich, where on 22 December 1856
a special session was held at the Guildhall before the Mayor
and Corporation resulting in the issue of a dramatic licence
to Mr Cooper of the Ramsgate Theatre. So on the next night,
Tuesday, a representation took place in the old theatre of
this most ancient of theatrical towns. The programme comprised Harwood Cooper's adaptation of *Dred*, *The Lass that
loves a Sailor*, and *Bobbing Around*. So successful was this performance that the manager and company stayed an extra
night, and played on Wednesday. On 18 January 1857 the
Era said that this unusually quiet town of Sandwich had been

M

exceedingly gay. Various performances had taken place including a pantomime: *Harlequin and the Magic Needle*, which was
well got up.

On 25 January the *Era* reported that the manager of the
Ramsgate and Sandwich Theatres had opened the theatre at
Margate for a week. The pantomime was *Harlequin and the
Magic Needle*, which pleased the gods and quite superseded
the efforts of the tragedians who performed *The Stranger*, and
The Merchant of Venice, to the noisiest audience ever heard in
Margate. Tranquillity was resumed only when the overture
to the pantomime commenced. The latter was a clever composition introducing "Life of a Clown", "Hot Codlins", and
"Tippitywitchet", arranged by Mr A. E. Cooper, a young
and rising son of the eccentric lessee. Alfred Edgar was then
only on the brink of his seventeenth birthday; perhaps the
rising son rose too early for later effulgence.

A notice about the Ramsgate Theatre on 5 February omits
the name of Fox Cooper, so in spite of his urbane conduct
his period of influence at Ramsgate was, like so many other
of his ventures, very short-lived. Neither was it very profitable,
as early in May 1857 a Mr Grant brought an action in the
County Court at Ramsgate to recover a small sum of money
lent to Fox Cooper on the security of an I.O.U. The latter,
reported to be living in Margate, was ordered to pay within a
month.

We now return to London where Fox Cooper was back in
Lambeth, and move on to 15 February 1858, when the Strand
Theatre produced, according to a current reviewer: a clever
adaptation of the Christmas tale in *Household Words* by Charles
Dickens, entitled *Silver Store Island, or Perils of Certain English
Prisoners*. This was the sub-title given in the critiques and on
the playbill, following no doubt earlier advertisements stating
that the play was founded on the story by that name. But Fox
Cooper's manuscript gives as the sub-title *The British Flag
of the South American Pirate*, and is marked Strand Theatre,
so that one might say that both are correct. Before the end of
February 1858 there were four or five stage versions of that
story by Dickens, and the critic's job must have been confusing,
to say the least. The adaptation at the Strand was described
as effective, and well placed upon the stage.

Mr Swanborough, the manager,* sustains the part of the effeminate pirate chief (Pedro Mendez) with ability, while the noble conception of Gil Davis, the unlettered soldier, is well-embodied by Mr George Bolton. Miss Portman infuses much pathos into the part of Marion and Miss Victor is comic as Beltot, her waiting-maid. But by far the best sustained character in the drama is that of Mr Commissioner Pordage, who is always aiming at routine, sticking at etiquette, enforcing new regulations, but really doing nothing. This character is committed to the care of Mr H. J. Turner, who keeps the audience in a continuous flow of spirits from the rising to the fall of the curtain. The scenery by Mr Broadfoot is effective.

The part of Captain Carton was taken by a Mr Cooper, who might have been the author.

Little else has come to light for 1858, except that Fox Cooper began an association with Astley's Theatre (or amphitheatre) which continued for a number of years. He became manager for the opening in October, and his influence was marked by a reduction in the prices of admission. On 1 November he was given a benefit at the St James's Theatre, "under fashionable and distinguished patronage": this special performance was provided by a company composed chiefly of amateurs, and starring Miss Bessie Willingham, whose friends nearly filled the house. An infant violinist also displayed his talent.

Although equestrian entertainment was still a speciality of Astley's, a farce was usually included, and *Shooting the Moon* was revived by Fox Cooper in November. Early in December he wrote a letter to *The Times* in good style about an accident during the rehearsal of a new drama as the result of a horse named Tempest falling on young Mr Cooke, and badly damaging his leg. The object of the letter was to point out that a lot of current rumours had been exaggerated, that no amputation would be necessary, and that the actor was expected to make a complete recovery in a short space of time. The impresario, Mr Cooke senior, wrote to the *Era* to the effect that a messenger from the Palace had made enquiries about his

* This is presumably the gentleman whom Fox Cooper endeavoured, with some success, to shield from the operation of the law in 1856.

son. This might have been from a Royal residence, or from another theatre. Eventually Mr Cooke junior returned to his work on 26 March 1859 in time for a piece by Fox Cooper.

The production of *Ivanhoe* at Astley's Theatre, on 25 April 1859, was reported by *Bell's Weekly Messenger* as a new dramatized version of Sir Walter Scott's novel, with all that attention to stage and scenic effects which characterizes the management of Mr Cooke. The contest between the Normans and the then newly-conquered Saxons, so admirably described by the great novelist, and the opportunities for display afforded by the story for the peculiar capabilities of this establishment, were all seized upon and reproduced in a very effective manner by Mr Fox Cooper, the author of the drama. A cutting from the *Post* said that Easter was a most appropriate season for this drama, and implied that no better choice could be made than a background of Walter Scott.

"When we consider the dramatic incidents which crowd the productions of our great novelist, we are not surprised to find that the ingenious author of the transpontine version (Fox Cooper) should have largely availed himself, and with scarcely any alteration, of the rich materials thus lying ready at hand." This might well be termed a back-hander, but it must have passed by Harwood Cooper who kept the cutting. As mentioned in an earlier chapter the synopsis of this play is similar to that of the 1837 production. That year was far enough away, however, for the piece to be called new quite safely in 1859, and Fox Cooper may have made some alterations when submitting it to the Lord Chamberlain in that year. On each occasion the full title was *Lists of Ashby, or The Conquests of Ivanhoe*. Dicks' published the play as *Ivanhoe*, incorrectly recording the date of production as 1869.

According to the *Court Circular*, a publication entitled *The Theatrical Annual Register for 1859* by Fox Cooper was in the press in the early part of 1860. And there it must have remained because there is no trace of its emergence.

On 2 May 1860, Fox Cooper lost his wife, Ann, who died after years of acute suffering from disease of the heart (dropsy), at the age of fifty-five in the presence of her husband at Hercules Buildings, Lambeth. The announcement appeared in the *Court Circular*. To a highly strung disposition, and a devoted husband, the blow would be severe. It was just as well that he was engaged on two forthcoming productions, both in July: *The Tale of Two Cities*, and *Garibaldi*. Searching through his wife's keepsakes a few days later he discovered an illustration from a magazine and wrote a few words on it to the effect that his beloved wife thought it bore a marked resemblance to their son Harwood, who looks a handsome young man of about twenty-one years old at the time. So that would be back in 1847. It may be significant that in Ann's death certificate Fox Cooper is described as a news editor, another indication that when not engaged in theatrical management, he was frequently employed in some form of journalism.

The Tale of Two Cities is dealt with in the next chapter for reasons which will be explained.

The opera *Garibaldi* was produced at the Surrey Theatre on 9 July 1860; and heralded by an advertisement in *The Times* stating that every care had been bestowed to render the exploits of that illustrious hero worthy of record. One caustic critic said of the opening performance "that English opera had assumed a new tone by the production of a perfectly new opera by Mr Tully; that is, Mr Tully composed the music; Fox Cooper Esq., writes the libretto, and that is of the wildest character. To attempt to describe it would be idle. We do not not know where the scene is laid except that the Grand Square of Palermo appears at the close. At this place also, only last month, the first wife of Garibaldi, Anita, was still living, having been recently rescued by her patriotic husband from a Neapolitan dungeon. We are sorry to hear that the Liberator is a bigamist; but if it should prove to be a libel, of course General Garibaldi will have his action against Fox Cooper Esq. In other respects the libretto is good enough."

The *Morning Chronicle* said that a scene of extraordinary excitement was kept up during the progress of three very interesting acts, and the action was prettily relieved with some very charming songs and ballads. These were nightly encored, and bade fair to become immensely popular. The notice in the *Era*, still more favourable, commented that the management had brought out a new three-act opera with complete success, the music of which, apart from some additional airs, was from the pen of one of the most deservedly popular of our vocal writers, Mr J. H. Tully. "The libretto, founded on some of the exploits of the popular and renowned hero of Italian liberation, is entitled *Garibaldi, the Italian Liberator,* and is the offspring of Mr Fox Cooper's exhaustless fancy. The plot, if it can be so called, is managed with Mr Fox Cooper's never-failing taste, and the *dramatis personae* are rendered sufficiently interesting, if not particularly natural."

I am inclined to think that the author had some association with the *Court Circular** in which it was recorded that "one and all appeared to rival each other in determination to corroborate the reputation which Mr Cooper has now already established of being one of the most successful authors of operatic drama who have elevated the national taste towards such species of composition". Shortly afterwards the same journal reported that the author of the exquisite opera of *Garibaldi* had been retained by Balfe to finish the libretto of a new work for Pyne and Harrison's theatre in the following operatic season. *Bianca, the Bravo's Bride,* was produced at Covent Garden in December 1860, but Balfe's librettist was Palgrave Simpson.

I have a print of some of the songs and choruses of *Garibaldi*: mostly in a humorous or sentimental vein, they are not unsuitable for a topical theme, when Garibaldi was advancing upon Messina. His despatches were printed alongside lists of subscribers to the Garibaldi fund, and there was even a Ladies' Garibaldi benevolent association.

A playbill for the second week indicates that it would be the last week of the opera company's season, so *Garibaldi* could not have expected a long run. It is therefore strange that the *Court Circular* reported:

The sudden closing of the Surrey Theatre in the very midst of the brilliant success which has attended the production of the new and beautiful opera of *Garibaldi*, will it is said lead to law proceedings—neither the performers who sustained the characters in it nor the clever author of the libretto have received a shilling for their services; and all concerned in the management repudiate payment of any kind. In this state of affairs application will be made forthwith to the Lord Chamberlain to ascertain who is the actual and responsible

* This is also suggested by the review of *Varieties in Verse* in 1875 (Chapter 11), and other references in 1860.

manager;* and when His Lordship officially gives the information, proceedings will be taken against all parties who were privy to most scandalous and disgraceful proceedings.

This badly worded protest, possibly inspired by Fox Cooper, serves to emphasize, if emphasis is needed, that where he was involved the operation of some branch of the law was never far away. A note in the *Era* confirms the sudden closure of the theatre on Saturday, 21 July 1860, despite the success of *Garibaldi*, a success that seems to have been confined to the fortnight at the Surrey Theatre.

From the above events I have no information until 12 July 1862, when Fox Cooper married an Irishwoman named Selina Gallagher, daughter of a deceased merchant tailor of Limerick. The wedding was at St Mary's, Lambeth and the address of both parties was given as Chester Place, which suggests that Selina was Fox Cooper's housekeeper. She was in her early twenties. The witnesses to the marriage were Alfred Edgar Cooper and Caroline (a sister of Selina) who were married in 1864. Thus father and son married sisters.

Despite my feeling that the series of insolvencies between 1831 and 1850 had seen Fox Cooper through his public financial embarrassments, I continued to study *The Times* index for later years. It was not entirely a surprise, therefore, to find his name under the heading of Bankruptcies in December 1862 and early in 1863. On this occasion the operation of the law was different, inasmuch as Fox Cooper was made bankrupt, and not subjected to imprisonment. But it provides a sorry story so soon after his second marriage, and following a period of about twelve years presumably free of legal process, although not necessarily free from financial hardship.

According to the *London Gazette*, Fox Cooper (who had an office at 5 Catherine Street, Strand) was adjudged bankrupt under a petition filed on 3 December 1862, and was required to surrender to Mr Hazlitt, a registrar of the Bankruptcy Court for a first meeting of creditors on 3 January 1863. The examination was passed unopposed. At a public sitting of the court on 11 February, before Mr Commissioner Fane (whom we met

---

* The lessees were Shepherd and Creswick, the theatre being under the direction of J. Kerschner. Probably the "proceedings" never took place.

back in 1844) the bankrupt applied to pass his final examination on an account showing liabilities of £273 and assets nil. Many of the debts were due to writers who had contributed to a publication entitled *The Times of 1962*.

The short-lived *Gazette of Bankruptcy* shows that some £200 was nominally owed to Fox Cooper, his deficiency being only £38. But these debts were worthless, and it is illuminating to note from whom they were due: Davidge, late lessee of the Surrey Theatre; Flint, lessee of St Martin's Hall; Morrison, proprietor of the *Atlas* newspaper; and two bankrupts: Fletcher of Greenwich, and a publican from Ealing. At the hearing Fox Cooper attributed his failure to severe epileptic illness which prevented him from following literary pursuits, although he was to live for another sixteen years. His lawyer* said that difficulties had arisen with the *The Times of 1962*, above-mentioned, and (amidst laughter) he feared that the bankrupt had given so much attention to the future, that he had neglected the present. As the account had been filed a day too late, an adjournment was ordered, but in the following week Fox Cooper obtained his discharge.

The Times of 1962 was a title I had first seen in an advertisement for the *Boxing Night Annual 1869*, which will be mentioned in a later chapter. This earlier reference, appearing in *The Times* itself, and describing Fox Cooper as the originator, implied that the advertisement was more than a publisher's blurb. Fortunately I was able to trace that prophetic publication in the B.M., incorporated with other incompendious items between the largest binding I have ever handled. It proved to consist of two sheets of newspaper, each about thirty-six inches by twenty-eight inches, printed on both sides, and it was got up to resemble *The Times* as it might be in 1962. This "Brobdingnagian broadsheet" was advertised in the *Era* in April 1862, indicating the approximate date of its publication. Edited by the wits of the age, it claimed to show the revolution which a century produces in our morals, politics, laws, commerce, arts, science, literature, music, and drama.

---

* This was a Mr Marshall of Hatton Garden, who had advertised in the *Colored News* in 1855. He offered to conduct the business of embarrassed persons through the Insolvent Debtors' Court, without imprisonment, and at one-half the usual charges, which could be paid by instalments.

THE BOTTLE,

AN ORIGINAL DOMESTIC DRAMA,

IN TWO ACTS,

AS PERFORMED AT THE LONDON THEATRES.

By FOX COOPER, Esq.

AUTHOR OF THE " DESERTED VILLAGE," " SPARE BED," " WAPPING OLD STAIRS," " HERCULES," &c., &c.

." WRETCHED MAN! SEE !WHAT YOU HAVE DONE !"—SCENE III.—*Tableau* 3.

DRAMATIS PERSONÆ.

Mr. MORDEN	Mr. ARCHER.	SPIDERLIMB	Mr. JONES.
CHARLES COURAGE	— FITZGERALD.	MORDEN'S CHILDREN	Miss COLEMAN, &c
Capt. FLATCATCHER CHEEK	— MONTAGUE.		
DICKEY DRUDGE	— HUNTLEY.	Mrs. MORDEN	— M. ATKINS.;
WARRANT	— ROGERSON.	MARGERY MAG..........	: E. TERRY.
Mr. ALLWORTH	— YARNOLD.	EDITH.................	: KENT
POLICEMAN L 47	— OXBERRY.	GENUS OF TEMPERANCE:.	Mrs. WOOLLIDGE.
GRIMES	— SMITH.	*Policemen, Mob, &c, &c.*	

Design from the *Colored Acting Drama* published in 1855 by
F. Mitchell, Holywell Street, Strand

(5)

36 North Street
Lambeth
1 Sept 1868

Sir,

These were performed
Macbeth for 6 weeks with
the loudest demonstrations
of applause from delighted
audiences but unfortunately
with heavy pecuniary loss
to myself arising from the
great expense to which I
went in the getting up.

I am seeking to reimburse
myself a little in the way
of a Benefit and I most
respectfully desire to
learn whether you will
graciously honor me so far

Letter written to Disraeli, 1 September 1868. The reply is
shown in the top left-hand corner.

as to take a few Tickets upon
the occasion.

I do not presume
to forward any until I
know your pleasure upon
the subject but I take
the liberty of saying that
any little aid you may
feel disposed to bestow
shall now will be most
gratefully acknowledged
and thankfully received

I have the honor to be
Sir
your obedient Servant
Fredk Cooper
Lessee Astley's Theatre

The Right Hon.
B Disraeli M.P.

The Colored News.

Vol. I.—No. 8.] [ONE PENNY.

SATURDAY, SEPTEMBER 22, 1855.

INTERIOR OF A LONDON RAGGED SCHOOL.

GOD IS LOVE

I BELIEVE IN GOD THE

THOU SHALT NOT STEAL

JESUS CHRIST

MODE OF INSTRUCTING PUPILS AT THE RAGGED SCHOOL.

An illustration that appeared in "The

One of these wits was Thomas Gaspey who had given Fox Cooper a reference in 1841, and who now figured among his creditors.

The central design at the head of page 1 is a passable imitation of *The Times*, and the lettering seems to have been closely copied from the contemporary fount. Underneath appearing on the left is the number 55,567;* and on the right: price one shilling. At the end of page 4 appear the names of the printer, and of the publisher, Baynton Rolt.† The address of the latter was the same as the office address of Fox Cooper, who evidently did not wish his name to be divulged in the actual publication.

Whether by luck or uncanny premonition the first page of *The Times of 1962* is devoted to advertisements; the second contains parliamentary reports, and letters to the Editor. The third page has leading articles, and the fourth, a variety of "news". In the political sphere the outstanding development at home has been the assumption of power by the female sex in both Houses of Parliament. By the same token a leading article discusses a resolution of the Commons to record in the Journals of the House what is left undone, rather than what has been done. Looking further afield, Royalty has been in the ascendant with a Kingdom in Ireland, and a coloured monarch at Washington, now the capital of all America.

Great ingenuity is exercised in the world of science. The last meeting of the Royal Society of Arts has been held for the reason that "everything that Nature had cautiously and impertinently hidden had been found out". So rapid have communications become that visitors can be conveyed to the Ranelagh Gardens, Iceland, from London and may return the same evening after the entertainments; fare, including admission to the Gardens, one shilling. A tunnel under the sea which separates the Kingdom of Ireland from England had

---

* If that number were intended to relate to 1 January, 1962, the error in computation over the 100 years was nearly 300. But this calculation could have been defeated by the absence of issues of *The Times* on public holidays, or for other reasons.

† Probably the Mr B. Rolt mentioned in the Linwood Gallery case in December 1853 (Chapter 8). He appeared as Macbeth at the Strand Theatre in July 1847, under Fox Cooper's management. His real name was Baynton.

just been excavated and would be thrown open on 22 July. Prices for the English: one Albert; for the Irish: half an Albert; children: gratis. (Hopefully, but in vain, I sought for a definition of that new unit of currency, and a report about the adoption of the decimal system.) At the Royal Observatory can be obtained a full view of all the planets enabling visitors to see what is going on in any part of the firmament. Elsewhere a separate advertisement enquires whether anyone would care to join a select party making a family trip to the moon.

Among financial topics there seems to be some doubt whether inflation or deflation has prevailed. The national debt has all been repaid, and the Bank of England has become a centre of curiosity. But in contrast to the low cost of the evening trip to Iceland, a correspondent complains of the high cost of accommodation at the Grand Aerial Hotel where he has recently spent a night after arriving by balloon from the Pyramids. Set out in detail, the bill came to £2 8s. 0d., including fifteen shillings for breakfast with watercress.

Domestic politics are not neglected. A brilliant forecast describes the country as in danger from a short-sighted policy, which, to provide temporary gain, is converting the land into one vast city. London already contains thirty-two million people within a diameter of fifty-four miles. The great secret (so the argument proceeds) lies not in what a country can purchase from others, but in what it produces; and there will be nowhere to grow any corn. There are also traffic problems. Pedestrians, according to the suggestion of one correspondent, should be obliged to walk only in one direction on each side of the road; and in the same letter attention is drawn to the nuisance arising from the grapnels of balloons when anchoring at the aerial car stands.

The Stage, in general, and its greatest dramatist, in particular, are having a lean time. The building in Covent Garden known as the Opera House has been recently opened by the descendants of Crosse & Blackwell as a pickle warehouse, while the dramatic critic's disparagement of a performance of *Othello* is so intense that it is doubtful if anyone will think of reviving it again.

Personal services, and other items of personal interest are much in evidence. A matrimonial agency announces that applicants will be accepted without question at their own valuation, and one-thousandth part thereof will be the basis of the fee for services rendered. A narcotic syrup enables persons to sleep at will: a single spoonful for one hour, two spoonfuls for two hours, and so on in proportion. Finally, from the agony column we learn that Rodolph Hapsburg, late King of Austria, has not removed from Golden Square, but continues to give lessons on the violin.

Prognostications, except for the short term, are usually optimistic. The extension of Fox Cooper's world in *The Times of 1962* was no exception, apart from the drama in which he had his being. Possibly the latter was a projection of his own experience.

I naturally drew this discovery to the attention of *The Times*. They found it of interest in the office, where they were able to turn up a file copy of Fox Cooper's "curious production"; but it was not of sufficient general interest to justify a reference in their columns. I was mildly surprised, and a little disappointed, especially as my disclosure happened to take place just before the beginning of 1962.

In December 1864, Fox Cooper entered upon a season of theatrical management at the Bower, a little theatre in Stangate Street, Lambeth, sometimes described as an Operetta House. The *Era* carried an advertisement saying that the sole lessee and manager was Fox Cooper; the theatre would open on Boxing Night with two new dramas, and a pantomime from the pen of the lessee: *Giovanni Redivivus, or Harlequin in a Fix and Pantaloon on Horseback*. For the following week the programme would contain a farce, a drama and the pantomime. Once again there were only two advertisements, but a good review of the pantomime was given on 1 January 1865, when the critic hoped that better fortune would attend Mr Cooper than some of his predecessors at the Bower. His stage manager was Baynton Rolt.

Giovanni Redivivus was a burlesque rather than a pantomime, there were many novel effects, the comic scenes were well arranged considering the limited resources, and it was thought to augur well for the future. (It is probable that Fox Cooper prepared this play originally in 1847 during his management at the Strand Theatre. A bill for 18 October of that year had announced the rehearsals of a grand theatrical extravaganza entitled *Giovanni Returned, or the Libertine Once More*, but I do not think that it was produced.) On 4 February 1865, Fox Cooper revived his own play *London by Night*, and a fortnight later produced *The Worship of Bacchus, or Death in the Glass*. The playbill made reference to George Cruikshank, but the author of the drama was not stated. As the names of the characters are identical with those in Fox Cooper's version of *The Bottle*, it was probably the same piece (or a slight modification), with a different title. By June the theatre was in other hands.

It is of interest that the *Post Office Directory* for 1865 contains the name of Fox Cooper with the address: 4 Chester Place, Kennington, his residence at the time of his second marriage in 1862. He had evidently settled down, and instead of living in lodgings was now a householder.

Chapter 11

A Miscellany

(a) *Three problem plays*

OVINGDEAN GRANGE, founded by Fox Cooper on the popular novel by Harrison Ainsworth, is printed in Dicks' (No. 1019). Approximately the date of the publication would be 1889, i.e. somewhere near the end of the editorship of Harwood Cooper.

The mystery is that although the novel *Ovingdean Grange* was not published until it appeared in Bentley's *Miscellany* in 1859–60, Dicks' states the play was first performed at the Surrey Theatre on 29 September 1851; and the cast as printed includes Creswick and Shepherd, who were normally at that theatre, with Harwood Cooper himself in a small part as a Roundhead soldier, as might have been expected, although his only season there was in 1852. Moreover, when one searches the playbills, the *Era*, and other sources of information, there is no corroboration that this play was performed at the Surrey Theatre on the date given. In fact at that time a season of opera was in progress. I have looked at the advertisements of other theatres round about the date, but can find no mention of the title, and have examined playbills of the Surrey Theatre for later years without success. It therefore remains a mystery.

The opinion of Malcolm Morley (which I am inclined to share) is that it never was performed in London, and that when it was printed, Harwood Cooper, using up an old manuscript by Fox Cooper, simply inserted the names of actors and actresses whom he thought might reasonably have taken the parts in the play with which they are identified in the print. *Ovingdean Grange*, with the author and the date, is recorded in A.N., presumably on the authority of Dicks'.

An unsigned manuscript of a play entitled *Ovingdean Grange*, in three acts, was submitted to the Lord Chamberlain and licensed for performance at the Victoria Theatre on 5 January 1863. From a study of advertisements in the *Era*, the *Morning Advertiser*, and other journals, there is no evidence that it was performed on that date or within a reasonable period. But Dicks' version is clearly taken from this manuscript as the language is often identical, although some of the characters have been telescoped, and some of the lines filled out. Harwood Cooper when editing the text must have had a copy of the manuscript as licensed, which I conclude to have been the work of Fox Cooper. Messrs Frampton & Fenton, lessees of the Victoria, for some reason had second thoughts about the production after the piece was approved. The actual script was ill-prepared and the spelling is poor; the handwriting is not identifiable.

Ovingdean Grange is a romantic drama in three acts. It centres upon the pursuit of Charles II by the Roundheads in 1651, and his seeking refuge at Ovingdean Grange, the home of Colonel Maunsel. There is a certain amount of plot, counter-plot, subterfuge and counter-subterfuge. People are hidden in the wainscoting and are discovered, there is fighting on the stage, and a little feminine by-play. An attempt by Charles to escape by boat from somewhere near Shoreham forms the climax, but the project is discovered, and it looks as though all is lost. At the last moment, however, a party of Royalists enters and overcomes the Roundheads, the presumption being that Charles will make his way to France. In the novel the end is quite clear if less dramatic.

Another piece of evidence (which is negative) is the omission of this title, not only from the list of Fox Cooper's plays by Harwood Cooper, but also from a handwritten list of dramatic pieces in which the latter claimed to have played at various theatres, including the Surrey. As both these lists were prepared later than Harwood's retirement, or at any rate not much before 1895, it is possible that after a gap of over thirty years his memory was at fault. It is also possible that I may yet discover a record of its performance. According to Dicks', the time of representation was two hours forty minutes: corroborative detail indeed.

An adaptation from Dickens: *The Tale of Two Cities, or The Incarcerated Victim of the Bastille*, was produced at the Victoria Theatre on 9 July 1860, the same night as the opera *Garibaldi*. Described as an historical drama in a prologue and four acts, it played for over three hours, and there were forty-two speaking parts. It is printed in Dicks' (No. 780), published in 1886, and attributed to Fox Cooper, the date of producton being given as 7 July 1860. To this play also a mystery is attached. Three or four months before the production (or at least so it has been recorded) a version of *The Tale of Two Cities*, in a prologue and three acts, was issued by the publisher Davidson, and the authorship attributed to H. J. Rivers, an actor at the Olympic.

The scenes in the two versions are similar, but split up differently into acts, and the wording is identical. Only the descriptions of the characters and some of the stage directions vary slightly. Adair Fitz-Gerald asks the question whether Fox Cooper was H. J. Rivers, as the latter had written no other plays. The answer is clearly in the negative, and I am inclined to think that Davidson's version was pirated. It is suspect because it gives the cast as performed at the Lyceum, with Madame Celeste, which relates to the version by Tom Taylor. It is also curious because George Daniel in the preface makes two sallies against that author. He points out that Tom Taylor's version was set entirely in Paris, so the title was miscalled; and he claims that Davidson's version was in his hands before Tom Taylor's tale unfolded itself in January 1860. Was this evidence of some private vendetta against the renowned Tom Taylor? Cumberland, for whose edition of plays George Daniel was Director-General, published none of that author's works.

Harwood Cooper was a stock actor at the Olympic in 1860, and may have lent the manuscript of his father's play to his

THE TALE OF TWO CITIES;
OR, THE INCARCERATED VICTIM OF THE BASTILLE.
AN HISTORICAL DRAMA, IN A PROLOGUE AND FOUR ACTS.
ADAPTED FROM CHARLES DICKENS'S STORY, BY FOX COOPER.
First Performed at the Victoria Theatre, July 7th, 1860.

𝔇𝔯𝔞𝔪𝔞𝔱𝔦𝔰 𝔓𝔢𝔯𝔰𝔬𝔫𝔞𝔢.　　　　[*See page 22.*

PROLOGUE.—A.D. 1763.

MARQUIS DE ST. EVREMONDE	(Aged 32, the Seducer—Haughty in Manner, and with a Face like a fine Mask)	Mr. Frederick Byefield.
CHEVALIER ST. EVREMONDE	(Aged 28—Brother to the Marquis, who looked on the Sufferer, whose Life was ebbing out)	Mr. Henderson.
DOCTOR MANETTE	(Aged 25—a Young Rising Physician of Beauvais, a good Husband and a Loving Son	Mr. W. Harmer.
SOLOMON BARSAD	(Aged 30—Gamekeeper to the Marquis, Aider and Abettor in his villanies)	Mr. J. Bradshaw.
GABELLE	(His Assistant, Tool, Lacquey, a Man who would do anything for Money)	Mr. N. Harrison.
LUCILLE (The Betrayed—The Dying Victim of St. Evremonde's Amour)		Mrs. E. F. Saville.

No. 780. Dicks' Standard Plays.

Design from Dicks' *Standard Plays*, No. 780, published 1886 friend Rivers; either or both of them may have been employed to copy out the play. Furthermore, *The Tale of Two Cities* was advertised as written expressly for the theatre, and it is unlikely that the management of the Victoria would have given a commission to an actor with no plays to his credit, whereas several pieces by Fox Cooper had been produced there previously.

The reasonable suggestion that Rivers assisted Fox Cooper with the script has been made by Malcolm Morley, who *comme d'habitude* has given the piece a good mauling in *The Dickensian* (December 1954). He is in error, however, in stating that all the scenes were in Paris as in the version by Tom Taylor, because scenes in London occur in Acts II and III. On balance I believe that Fox Cooper wrote it, in spite of the fact that I have found no evidence of his protest at the publication by Davidson. But as Fox Cooper lost his wife less than two months before the production of the play in July 1860, he could have overlooked the minor injury of the attribution to Rivers in Davidson's edition.

Incidentally, the copy of that edition (which is undated) in the B.M. is stamped "19 My 62", and the index gives 1862 as the year of publication. Beyond the implication in the preface I have no direct evidence that it came out in 1860, and the print states that G. H. Davidson's *Actable Drama* was in continuation of Cumberland's *Plays*. A.N. gives the date of the latter as 1826–61, so notwithstanding the claim of priority in the preface, there is some reason to assign Davidson's print of *The Tale of Two Cities* to the year 1862. This still leaves unanswered the question as to why Fox Cooper did not object, and the best reply I can think of is that his mind was at that time in the contemplation of events one hundred years later, as recorded in the previous chapter.

Although notice of the production is contained in the *Daily Director* and *Entr'acte* for 9 July 1860, where about a dozen dramatis personae are mentioned (but not the name of the author) there seems to be no contemporary review. Johnnie Gideon, writing in the *Era* in February 1899, said he well remembered Fox Cooper's splendid adaptation which was wonderfully successful, and in which three of the parts stood out: Solomon Barsad by Jack Bradshaw, Vengeance by

N

F. Wilton, and Miss Pross by Miss Fanny (or Frances) Harrison.
The ending was apparently Fox Cooper's own invention.
Madame Defarge is killed by a pistol, after a struggle with a
more muscular Miss Pross, illustrated both on the cover and
inside Dicks' edition; Sydney Carton, after changing places
with Charles Darnay, escapes the guillotine by drugging the
spy, Barsad, and dressing in his clothes; the victim was thus
Barsad. Malcolm Morley, with some justification, describes
this as banal: a nice choice of word on the ground of derivation.
I feel sure, however, that Fox Cooper was instructed to contrive
a satisfactory ending in order that the patrons of the Victoria
might depart without drying their eyes. If they were not dry,
it would be the result of alcoholic rather than dramatic emotion.

The Corsican Brothers is the third play which provides an
element of mystery. It is printed in Dicks' edition (No. 752)
in three acts: "dramatized from the romance of M. Dumas
by MM E. Grangé and Xavier de Monté Pin, and adapted
to the English stage by F. Cooper." The print purports to
give the cast as represented at the Lyceum under the management of M. Fechter in 1863. There is another version published
by Lacy (Vol. VI) also printed in English. This is described as
the property of T. H. Lacy, and gives the cast of the first
performance in Paris in August 1850 (with M. Fechter alter-
nating with M. Berthollet), and of a production at the Princess's
Theatre in February 1852 with Charles Kean, adapted by
Boucicault. A notable difference between the two versions
is that in Lacy the first act is set in Corsica, and the second act
in Paris, whereas in Dicks' the first act is set in Paris and the
second in Corsica. The general trend of the scenes is similar
but the version attributed to Fox Cooper is less literally taken
from the French, and reads somewhat shorter, although both
prints mention that the play took two hours.

From a study of Lyceum advertisements throughout 1863,
and of playbills at the British Museum and in the Enthoven
Collection, there is no evidence of a production of *The Corsican
Brothers* in that year. There was, however, a production with
M. Fechter at the Princess's in December 1860, and later at the
Lyceum in May 1866. Reviews of both of these productions
indicate that the first act took place in Paris (as in Fox Cooper's

version) but this does not prove that his version was played on either occasion. On the contrary the production in 1860 was stated to be a new version as revised by Fechter. Moreover, in 1866 the advertisement of the play gave the names of the men who were responsible for the scenery, the properties, the dresses, the dances, and the music, but not apparently the adaptation: the natural inference is that the adaptor was M. Fechter himself. The cast as printed in Dicks' proves on examination to be derived partly from the 1860 and partly from the 1866 productions, with some names not in either. This could easily have been the result of Harwood Cooper relying on his memory when editing the play in 1886. Fechter, of course, appears as the twin brothers in all three casts.

In my view the evidence suggests that the same version was used by Fechter for the 1860 and 1866 productions, in spite of some differences in the naming of minor characters. This was not the adaptation by Fox Cooper, but another version which has not been printed.

A note on page 2 of Dicks' print reads:

> In the arrangement of the "Acts" the adaptor adhered to the alterations adopted by M. Fechter at the Lyceum Theatre (as originally produced in Paris). He considered it an improvement upon Mr Charles Kean's version. In the event of any manager wishing to restore the effects as represented at the Princess's Theatre, the transposition of the First and Second Acts will enable him to do so.

These remarks do not provide a clue to the problem; it is possible that Fox Cooper's version was used on some occasions in the provinces, but such productions are difficult to trace.

The above dramas which I have described as problem plays were the three titles published in Dicks', naming Fox Cooper as author, but curiously omitted from the manuscript list in Harwood Cooper's press cutting book. Now, there is a printed list of Dicks' *Standard Plays*, which doubtless Harwood Cooper edited, containing a classification of the plays by authors, in which ten titles are given under the combined heading: "Cooper, Fox and H." Opposite the names of the plays in their numerical order, however, H. Cooper appears only once, namely as the author of the *Stone Jug*. Six plays are undoubtedly by Fox Cooper, with known dates of production, the remaining three being described in this section.

The Stone Jug was produced at the Adelphi in March 1873, and the programme states that it was adapted by J. B. Buckstone from Harrison Ainsworth's *Jack Sheppard*; Harwood Cooper was in the cast. The print of the play in Dicks' (No. 506) does not name Harwood Cooper or even any author, but states that it was compiled and arranged (by authority) from the acting versions of Harrison Ainsworth's *Jack Sheppard*.

One explanation of all this might be that Harwood Cooper —for the purpose of publication by Dicks'—took a hand in some rearrangement of the four plays, i.e. the three problem plays and *The Stone Jug*, and thus justified to himself the inclusion of his name with that of his father over the ten plays contained in the authors' classification. This might also account for Davenport Adams, in a *Dictionary of the Drama*, having credited Fox Cooper with a version of *Jack Sheppard*, and his reference thereunder to *The Stone Jug*.

For the purpose of the list in Appendix II, I have included the three problem plays in the order suggested by their alleged dates of production according to Dicks'.

(b) *The family of Isaac Cooper, and others*

When I first commenced to delve into the family history, I took for granted, because there seemed no reason to disbelieve, the indications of my grandfather Harwood, and my uncle Harwood, that Isaac Cooper, a stockbroker (sometimes described as a pawnbroker) was the father of H. F. Cooper. When I later saw in print the claim by Fox Cooper to be related to Isaac, the wealthy stockbroker, I was almost convinced that it was correct. Moreover, they lived in adjoining parishes. I therefore set about trying to establish the exact relationship, and this is what I have found:

Isaac Cooper was born *circa* 1760, and was married to Mary Sutton in 1783 at St George's, Hanover Square. A William Sutton and an Isaac Cooper were carrying on the business of goldsmiths in Cheapside in the year 1786, so the marriage was evidently within the trade. That may also account for the pawnbroker legend. In 1808, Isaac Cooper appears as a Wine Merchant in Prospect Place, Southwark, and from 1809 to 1825 he was a member of the Stock Exchange. He died in 1825 at Stockwell, worth about £120,000, leaving interests in his property to his wife, four sons and a married daughter. The eldest son, William Henry, who lived in Regent's Park, was a member of the Stock Exchange from 1808–27. Neither he nor the other children (Robert Jones, John Condliff, Mary Lewis) seem to enter into my story, which now converges on the second son, Isaac Sutton.

Isaac Sutton Cooper was born in about 1791, he married Deborah Rhodes at the parish church of St Mary-at-Finchley in 1818, and died at Park Hall, Finchley, in 1875. He was a member of the Stock Exchange from 1819 to 1862. At his death his estate was about £30,000, but he had already given his children considerable sums. I have found that he had at least six sons and three daughters. The elsest son, Isaac Rhodes, born in 1819, went to New Zealand as a soldier, returned to England in about 1856, and died in Sydney in 1889; he wrote *A New Zealand Settler's Guide*, a copy of which is in the B.M. Two other sons, Augustus and Herbert Samuel, were partners on the Stock Exchange in 1861 when the firm got into difficulties. Augustus was apparently "hammered" and his father, who was in some way implicated, resigned in consequence. A cutting on the subject was pasted in his almanack for 1861 by my grandfather. He also preserved another cutting in 1886 recording the death at Brighton of Deborah, the widow of Isaac Sutton; she was about ninety-three and one of her executors was the Reverend Alfred Cooper, a son born in 1821. Finally, on 11 November 1902, the name Isaac Cooper appears in pencil in Harwood's almanack: a cryptic entry.

Nothing that I have uncovered—and I have a lot of ancillary detail—points to a blood relationship between Isaac Cooper and Fox Cooper. It may have been an invention by the latter in 1847, or by the *Theatrical Times* in which the statement appeared.

Another legend recorded in our family notes is that Isaac Cooper's daughter was grandmother of Cecil Rhodes. Now the latter had indeed a grandmother, Margaret Cooper (1780–

1851), but her father's name was Francis, and he came, I believe, from Staffordshire. The fact that Isaac Cooper's son (Isaac Sutton) married a Miss Rhodes may have given birth to this apocryphal story.

A further claim by my grandfather, Harwood, was that he was related to a James Cooper who died at Brixton Hill in January 1853 aged about seventy-seven, and Uncle Harwood, working back to the date of birth, thought James Cooper was a brother of Henry Fox. This, however, is not supported by the names of the children of Henry and Phillis Cooper, which I have given in the Prologue. But it leads into a curious set of circumstances. The above James Cooper had a son, William, who died at the Bristol Hotel, Kemp Town, Brighton, in May 1885, leaving an estate of some £20,000. Another James Cooper, solicitor, formerly of Primrose Hill, died in Brighton in April 1876, aged fifty-two, his address being 23 Upper Rock Gardens, Brighton. Finally, the address of the Reverend Alfred Cooper (already mentioned) in 1886, was 21 Upper Rock Gardens. This concentration of Coopers upon the Eastern borders of Brighton in the 1870–80 period may be no more than a coincidence: but it fails to supply me with the missing link. I am inclined to think that my grandfather was searching for a possible legacy; he could have made good use of it.

Should any of the descendants of persons mentioned in these notes chance to come upon what I have written, I hope they will pardon any inadvertent solecism committed in consequence of my genealogical research.

(c) *A Dictionary of Universal Quotations*

Some months after I had started working on the material obtained from Barry Duncan, he produced several exercise books filled in manuscript with quotations from poets as diverse as Milton and Mrs Hemans. Many of the extracts are by authors who are almost forgotten. Each of the books has a printed sheet pasted on the cover, bearing the name of Fox Cooper, and each has a number: the first of my seven is No. 6, and the last is No. 47. The whole set (including the missing numbers) was designed to contain "10,000 choice extracts from the best Ancient and Modern Poets". The last page in Book 47 is numbered 1810, and as there are about five extracts to a page, it seems there would have been some fifty books in all. Even if Fox Cooper ever completed it, I doubt if it was published; in any event it would have needed a comprehensive index.

An examination of the calligraphy suggests that it was compiled over a long period of time: some of the books are carefully written in at least two different handwritings, the later ones in a scrawl indicative of a person writing hurriedly, and identifiable as that of Fox Cooper. Possibly wife and sons helped to copy out the earlier portions. Printed on the cover-sheet of each book is a quotation from Montaigne: "I have only made a nosegay of culled flowers, and have brought nothing of my own but the thread that binds them." It was probably a task to which Fox Cooper reverted when he had a spare hour or two, which would be frequent in his later years. I have yet to ascertain his sources, and analyse his selection, but it is quite clear that only a genuine love of poetry, coupled with a strong measure of mental discipline, could have yielded even this partial result.

I have mentioned the handwriting in these books. This is a subject which has interested me for some years, and I submitted to an expert a part of the Hughenden letter (see illustration). In the opinion received some of the expressions used about Fox Cooper were:

(*a*) Possessed artistic capabilities.
(*b*) Sincere in all his undertakings.
(*c*) Would help others beyond his means.
(*d*) A sensitiveness for his own sorrows, and the sorrows of others.
(*e*) Intelligent and intellectual above the ordinary.
(*f*) Very proud, also possessed a true humility.
(*g*) Genial, but reticent when considered necessary.
(*h*) The world on the whole could prove too severe at times. Too unworldly to seek for gain.
(*i*) Thrived on friendship.

Much of this is clearly right. But I could not accept (*b*) because I do not look upon sincerity as entirely subjective, and there is not much evidence of (*g*) reticence or (*h*) being unworldly. I think Fox Cooper sought for gain, without ever dreaming of amassing wealth, but merely to live as he would like. He was unpractical, and financially myopic, yet in spite of this he was a man of the world in which he lived.

(d) *Varieties in Verse*

One of the press cuttings kept by my grandfather consists of a few verses of poetry preceded by the words "which will enable the reader to judge of the author's style:" On the cutting I read in ink the words "The Dead Cat", and underneath in pencil Harwood Cooper had written "Fox Cooper", as was his habit when there was no evidence of authorship in what he had preserved.

This suggested to me that Fox Cooper had contributed a poem to a volume of verse, of which the press cutting was a portion of a review. After puzzling over this from time to time I peered through the back of the page against a strong light, and managed to read with difficulty something about the performance of an opera at Covent Garden in June 1861. From the words "*E sei tu*" I realized that it was a review of *Un Ballo in Maschera*, the first performance of which had been given in that month. Greatly encouraged I measured the width of the column and compared it with various newspapers of the time, but failed to find one which exactly tallied. Stimulated by my partial success, I decided with the aid of a boiling kettle to steam the cutting away from the sheet on which it was pasted. This took a long time as it was well and truly stuck, but when it came off, practically intact, the reverse of the cutting proved to be the first part of a review of *Un Ballo* but in a year subsequent to 1861, which was merely mentioned *en passant*. From the four principal singers who were named I was able to establish that the performance took place in the season of 1875: quite definitely during a period of three-and-a-half months, which narrowed down the scope of my further enquiry.

Fortunately, the review of the opera had a heading: "Music and the Drama", in a quaint sort of Gothic lettering not

uncommon at the time, but faintly reminiscent of some newspaper or journal I had seen in the course of my general
researches. That music, and the drama, were coupled together
surely meant that it was not a specialist journal devoted either
to music or to the stage, where the reviews would be separate.
It was possibly a Sunday paper, or a weekly or monthly
periodical. The width of the column was not much different
from that of the *Daily Chronicle*, but the paper had a certain
whiteness about it and a solidity (I hope these are not technical
terms) which dailies at that period did not possess. On my
next visit to Colindale I started looking up (for 1875) all the
journals previously noted, and was lucky in finding the answer
quite early on: the *Court Circular* of 10 April. This was then a
weekly Society journal of especial interest to people in the
Services, containing a lot of contemporary gossip and general
news. I had learnt its name in the first place because my
grandfather preserved from it a small cutting referring to the
death of his mother in May 1860; later I was to find references
to *Garibaldi*, and other activities of Fox Cooper. It was published
between 1856 and 1911, and was a competitor of the *Court
Journal*, published between 1829 and 1925. This concluded
the first leg of my enquiry.

It was an easy matter to turn over the page and see the
whole of the review of which the press cutting formed a small
part. Here, however, was a great disappointment. The review
was of a book of poems called *Varieties in Verse*, published in
London by Smith, Elder & Co., in 1875, but the name of the
author was not given. The review said *inter alia* that "the author
of this volume of unpretending poems writes with a good deal
of culture and refinement, but they are not remarkable for
sustained thought. . . . He is most successful when dealing
with subjects of a grave and sombre nature. As is very
commonly the case in modern poetry the more unpretending
verses are decidedly the best." The preserved extract was
from a poem called, not "The Dead Cat", but "The Dead
Cart", in reference to the plague in 1665. The rapid copy
service at Colindale provided me with a reproduction of the
page forthwith.

The next step was back to the British Museum in London
where I found in the catalogue a reference to *Varieties in Verse*,

which proved to be a neat publication of 189 pages well-bound in a substantial green cloth cover. Many of the folios were uncut, and, with the permission of an official, this I proceeded to remedy, but the contents provided no lead to Fox Cooper's authorship.

The firm of Smith, Elder was acquired by John Murray, the publishers, and although the latter obtained in due course the correspondence with the more eminent authors, Sir John Murray told me with regret that there were no Cooper letters. I also found that Smith, Elder advertised *Varieties in Verse*, without naming the author, on three occasions in the *Athenaeum* in April 1875. A short review appeared in that journal in which it was asserted that the author possessed a genuine fund of poetic feeling, and was no mean master of the forms of poetic expression, but nowhere rose to the height of his subject, e.g. the "Vision of Man", and "Death the Merciful." But some of the verses in "The Power of Nature" were good.

Notwithstanding the uncertainty, I have studied some of the poems and agree with the reviewers that they are far from outstanding, but they are not bad all the same. The subjects are Life and Nature in general: a lot of love, pain, agony, and death. A little Byronic, a little Tennysonian, but mostly without sophistication, and nowhere a reference to the stage except that which is conveyed, either consciously or unconsciously, in the very title of the book. The following verse is from "The Power of Nature":

> For nothing is completed on the earth;
> Our life is but a link 'twixt old and new;
> Age follows youth, and death succeeds to birth,
> As fruit to flower. It were not wise to sue
> To Heav'n to give us endless youth in lieu
> Of growing years, lest haply it might be
> That, wearied for the rest which, overdue,
> Lagged at our bidding, we should hopeless see
> Life's sorrow lengthen out to sad eternity.

The thought in the first four lines of this verse, although far from original, is quite similar to that contained in an article by Fox Cooper in a Christmas annual referred to in the next chapter. A clue to his possible authorship, if not a substantial piece of evidence.

Another stanza I take from a poem entitled "After a Court Ball". The reviewer in the *Court Circular* said that it was written with some passion, although the ideas contained in it had been often expressed before.

> Nay, do I ask too much? If I could hold
> Her hand but once in mine, and feel the beat
> Of her pulse answer mine, and thus unfold
> The secret of my heart; would she repeat
> Softly and slow, as if the words were sweet,
> "I love thee!", I could die; and if one kiss
> Could wed my lips to hers, I dared to meet
> An age of torture for that moment's bliss
> And risk my soul's salvation, could I win but this.

I like "I dared", and the last line but one which seems vaguely familiar. What experience suggested it to Fox Cooper, if, indeed, he wrote it? But the evidence of the relatively lengthy notice in the *Court Circular* is of weight, especially as that journal had been so fulsome about *Garibaldi*, and other activities of Fox Cooper in 1860. In my view the odds are that *Varieties in Verse* was his publication, but one of those like the *Colored News* and *The Times of 1962* in which his name did not appear. After all, Harwood Cooper kept a cutting from the review.

One final thought on this subject: it is not impossible that Fox Cooper (Frederick Fox Cooper), in the knowledge that his own father (Henry Fox Cooper) had published a volume of poems in 1805, had a belated ambition to do likewise. Such an ambition has not appeared in the family since then—at least as far as I am aware.

Chapter 12

The Last Years: 1867–79;
A Brief Summary

A PRESS cutting preserved by Harwood Cooper reviews a production at Astley's Theatre on 2 April 1867 in these opening words: "Mr. Nation encouraged by the success of *The Golden Dustman*, has prepared for the patrons of Astley's a version of another of Mr Dickens's stories. His Easter piece which is taken from *Hard Times* is entitled *Under the Earth, or The Sons of Toil*. It is a clever piece, offering many striking situations." Good audiences were to be expected at Easter and the production was well received. So closely was the plot of the novel followed that one critic remarked that any description of incidents would be superfluous. The name of the adaptor of this play was not specifically given, but Adair Fitz-Gerald states that Mr W. H. C. Nation claimed to have dramatized as well as to have produced the piece.

I thought it worth investigation as this title was contained, and dated 1867, in Harwood Cooper's handwritten list of his father's plays, and published in Dicks' *British Drama* (No. 59), no author being named. Comparison with Fox Cooper's earlier play, *Hard Times*, shows that while the arrangement of the acts and the order of the scenes are different, where the situations are similar the language is almost identical; in fact, *Under the Earth* might be described broadly as a rearrangement to fill out the part of Bitzer, played by Edward Atkins, who was given a lengthy song in the last act, and to exhibit a mine on the stage. This is confirmed by the fact that the "manuscript" as licensed consists only of three new scenes, to be played with the dramatized version of *Hard Times*, as acted at the Strand Theatre in 1854. The new scenes are: Bottom of the Shaft, The Road Side, The Old Shaft; and they form the last part of the drama. There is little fresh composition in *Under the Earth*, and I can only suppose that for licensing it was thought necessary to submit the new scenes and the change of name. As with *Hard Times*, the play ends with Bounderby in a generous mood. Work is suspended at the factory for seven days, while full wages are paid, and a sum of £200 is distributed in gifts.

It is relevant that Nation owned the copyright of *Hard Times* (*vide* Dicks' No. 785), which he had presumably bought from Fox Cooper, as well as that of *Under the Earth*. The probability is that Nation, with the author's assistance, put in some work on the earlier play to produce the later one. It was advertised in the *Era* as an entirely new and original adaptation, but that was what the lawyers would describe as "common form". So I have felt justified in leaving it in the list of Fox Cooper's works, especially as Nation seems to have no other dramatic compositions to his credit.

Harwood Cooper records one other play in 1867. The title, *One Horse Shay*, almost suggests Astley's Theatre, but no evidence of the production has come to my notice. (See note at end of list of plays in Appendix II.)

In August 1868, Astley's Theatre was under the management of an American actress, Miss Agnes Cameron, when Fox Cooper became acting manager for the purpose of producing *Alarcos*, or more explicitly, *The Tragedy of Count Alarcos*. This had been written by Disraeli in 1839, but had never been performed. The suggestion has been made that Disraeli submitted the play to Macready, and published the work only when he had failed to get it accepted for the stage. "It was too strange and terrible for success on the stage, or even to give pleasure as a literary play; horror is piled on horror till the reader has supped too full." (*Life of Disraeli*, Monypenny, Vol. II, 65).

According to a letter in the Hughenden Archives, which I

examined through the courtesy of the National Trust, Mr Grenville Fletcher in 1849 approached Disraeli with the idea of adapting the play, or of writing a play founded upon the tragedy. The writer proposed to call it *The Rose of Castille*, and perhaps somewhat unwisely referred to the need for certain curtailments and judicious emendations with a view to producing a more powerful tragedy as regards the stage effect. Evidently this approach did not appeal to Mr Disraeli, as he then was. But apart from the one letter from Fox Cooper I was unable to find any papers about the arrangements with Astley's Theatre, or the adaptation in 1868. This is curious because Disraeli is reputed to have destroyed very little.

Alarcos was advertised in the *Era* of 2 August as a new and beautiful play from the pen of the Rt Hon Benjamin Disraeli, and Miss Cameron was billed to take the part of the Infanta of Castille. On 9 August an advertisement stated that it had been "a triumphant success". The review in the *Era* remarked, however, that to bring this powerfully written tragedy on the stage, it was essential that modifications should be made. These were judiciously effected by kind permission of the distinguished author; the adaptor was unnamed, but it could easily have been Fox Cooper with his questionable gift for adaptation. Unfortunately, the manuscript, which seems to be in three different handwritings, affords no evidence. Owing to insufficient rehearsals the play did not produce a strong impression, and one critic suggested that the tastes of the multitude were more in the direction of rapidity of action than literary excellence.

A long review appeared in the *Morning Post*, which delivered itself of much philosophy, and from which I quote:

> The failures of the obscure are consigned with themselves to a merciful oblivion; those of the illustrious are remembered as vividly or more so than their triumphs. It was a mad thing in him [Disraeli] to have attempted such writing, and madness in great ones must not unwatched go. The action is assigned to the thirteenth century, and the scene is laid at Burgos, the capital of the kingdom of Castille. "At that time," observes Mr Disraeli, in the preface, "Castille had recently obtained that supremacy in Spain which led to the

political integrity of the country. This state of comparative refinement and civilization permitted the introduction of more complicated motives than the rude manners of the ballad would have authorized." The motives are complicated enough in all conscience, their elaborate involution continually leading to such delay and obscuration of the plot as would kill the interest of the best written play in the world. Alarcos, "the brightest knight that ever waved a lance in old Castille", falls in love with Solissa the Infanta, but finds himself in the painful predicament of being loved most frantically by the lady's mother. He flies to a foreign land, a "hopeless exile", and marries, rather out of vexation than affection, an amiable woman, by whom he has a large family. Returning to Burgos after an absence of some years, when the amorous Queen Mother is happily no more, he finds that the Infanta is as fond of him as ever, and he resolves to possess her. With a view to get rid of his wife he has the baseness to induce a libertine named Sidonia to pay court to her, but nothing can induce the Countess to swerve from the path of honour. Therefore Alarcos slays her in cold blood. But this horrid deed does him no good. The Infanta is killed by a flash of lightning, and her guilty lover thereupon commits suicide. . . . In fact the play is unworthy of its author's fame. . . . It speaks well for his popularity that the audience sat his play out for four mortal hours in this burning weather.

In a final paragraph the *Morning Post* exercised its imagination to the full:

It has been suggested that the revival of *Alarcos* is perhaps to be ascribed, not to a managerial *ruse*, but rather to a deliberate purpose on the part of the Whigs to throw discredit upon the Tories on the eve of a general election. It would be a fine stroke of retaliation to bring out Lord Russell's *Don Carlos* at the Surrey as a set-off against Mr Disraeli's *Alarcos* at Astley's. There could be no finer *tu quoque*.

On 16 August it was claimed that the play had been seen by no less than 60,000 delighted spectators, which seems a very large number. And on 1 September 1868, Fox Cooper wrote the letter to Disraeli preserved at Hughenden, reproduced by courtesy of the National Trust (after page 184).

36 North Street,
Lambeth.

Sir,

I have now performed *Alarcos* for six weeks with the loudest demonstrations of applause from delighted audiences but unfortunately with heavy pecuniary losses to myself arising from the great expense to which I went in the getting up.

I am seeking to reimburse myself a little in the way of a Benefit and I most respectfully desire to learn whether you will graciously honour me so far as to take a few Tickets upon the occasion.

I do not presume to forward any until I know your pleasure upon the subject but I take the liberty of saying that any little aid you may feel disposed to bestow upon me will be most gratefully acknowledged and thankfully received.

I have the honour to be, Sir,
your obedient Servant,
Fredk. Cooper,
Lessee, Astley's Theatre.

The Right Honble
B. Disraeli M.P.

There is no indication of the reaction of the recipient except the brief word "Nil" written in a frail hand at the top of the left-hand corner of the letter. Perhaps Disraeli felt that if 60,000 spectators had witnessed his play, the story of the producer's loss was unconvincing. The whole episode can have brought him little satisfaction, whether or not he actually saw the production at Astley's.

It is interesting that Fox Cooper, as in the letter to *The Times* in 1858, wrote simply as Frederick Cooper; there may have been some notoriety about the Fox, or perhaps on this occasion it were unwise to evoke the spirit of Charles James?

I have a small fly-sheet headed "Mr Cooper's night" which advertises the benefit performance for Friday, 4 September; another, with two minor differences, is framed in the study at Hughenden.* This announced the last representation of the tragedy before the reassembling of Parliament. The entertainment commenced at half past six with *Alarcos*, and a serenade

---

* The study is not always open to the public, but on one of my visits the door was ajar. This led to my further enquiries, and the discovery of the letter now reproduced.

incidental to Act II was composed expressly for the occasion. In the course of the evening Mr Graham, described as a "human piccolo", performed on the grand piano introducing truly wonderful voice accompaniments. After this, there was a performance of *The Spare Bed* with George Yarnold as Pigeon-widdy, and Fox Cooper in the part of the aged French valet. Prior to the burlesque, Miss Cameron, to oblige Mr Cooper, undertook to recite Tennyson's famous poem, *The Charge of the Light Brigade*. Finally, a farce with the title: *Peculiar People —Very*. One can only hope the general support accorded to Fox Cooper on this occasion was more magnanimous than that of the author of *Alarcos*.

Fox Cooper was also connected with Astley's Theatre between April and June 1869, in the capacity of general manager, whatever that title may connote. There was a small attendance on the opening night, 24 April, and the orchestra had not arrived after half an hour from the appointed time. The stage manager (Brandon Ellis) announced that the band had been prevented, but did not disclose the reason. According to the *Era* things improved after the comedietta with a per-formance of *The Field of the Cloth of Gold*. The comedietta was *The Field against the Favourite* by Fox Cooper, but I have no useful details about this piece except that it contained a character, Sir Peckham Wry, played by Mr Liston.

One often looks at quite irrelevant items when searching for pieces of information in the newspapers. Alongside a notice about the opening of Astley's, it was reported that a new work by Wagner, entitled *Rheingold*, was in course of preparation. Wagner had stipulated for a real river on the stage, and Mlle Mallinger, one of the nymphs (we now call them Rhine-maidens) was taking lessons in swimming.

In May, according to a current review, the hippodramatic spectacle of *The Battle of Waterloo** was once again revived at Astley's in a very praiseworthy manner:

> No matter at what season of the year or at what theatre the spectacle is produced, if sufficient is made of the salient points a success is generally the result. On the present occasion Mr Cooper has been at some pains, as well as expense, to

* There were several plays with this title, one of which was produced at Astley's in 1824.

o

make the whole thoroughly effective. Plenty of soldiers, plenty of military tactics, plenty of fighting, plenty of firing and explosions—this is Mr Cooper's programme arranged with a good knowledge of the tastes of those for whom he caters. The band, reinforced and under the direction of Mr Corri, manifestly afforded great pleasure.

On the Thursday a sensation occurred that must have proved an unexpected treat to those who love to see life or limb in danger. In the scene where the inspection of the French Army takes place, one of the mounted officers by some means lost control of his charger, and the animal doubtless feeling somewhat awed by the sight of the Emperor, commenced a retrograde movement which brought him and his rider close to the orchestra. The audience began to get uncomfortable, the musicians left their seats, but the horse still kept backing until at last rider and horse both tumbled into the orchestra. Neither, we are glad to say, was hurt, but Mr Rankin (clarinet) received some injuries, and was taken to the hospital of the Fusilier Guards with a fractured collarbone. The scene caused some commotion. and for a time delayed the action of the piece. When the musicians reappeared they received a hearty cheer, and beguiled the time by playing Mr Maccabe's air of the Galloping Horse.

It is odd that the reviewer had no compunction in expressing greater sympathy with the horse than with the musician. Early in June a special performance of *The Battle of Waterloo* was advertised for 2 p.m. on a Saturday, to commemorate the centenary of the Duke of Wellington, and each visitor would receive a superb medal in honour of the occasion. It was evidently a warm day and one critic said this engendered a craving for ice-cool drinks, and a longing to be in the lovely spots which the scene painter had so admirably transferred to canvas. A domestic drama, *Gentleman Jack*, finished off an entertainment which lasted for five hours. On 21 June Fox Cooper was described as the acting manager, but I can find no later references.

Among the miscellaneous ephemera of Fox Cooper a paper-covered Christmas Annual entitled *Boxing Night* published in December 1869 (price twopence) came to light through Barry Duncan. No example is in the B.M., although it went to a fourth edition in January 1870. This publication contains about a dozen articles extending to twenty pages of written matter, excluding the cover, contents sheet, and advertisements. It is mainly about pantomime and people of the stage. The few illustrations are suitable. Occupying the first page is a prologue by the editor, and a pencilled note by Harwood Cooper on my copy indicates that this was Fox Cooper.* Here it is related how each member of the staff of the theatre thinks himself indispensable: right down (or up) to the perruquier. "A pantaloon without a wig; and do you suppose that Columbine's is all her own?" One sentence in this prologue: "Pantaloon is to clown what abdication is to the throne, age to youth, the workhouse to a home" is reminiscent of the verse quoted from the poem "The Power of Nature" in Chapter 10. But the workhouse is now obsolete, and if it does exist it has another name: just as there are no more board-schools.

In a second article, "The Lessee's Story", Fox Cooper describes an imaginary lessee upon his first day in the manager's chair, when applicants for employment were to come up in rotation. "No. 1. came crawling in, like the half-price at a provincial theatre, on a rainy night. He was a one-armed man, and he had only come to enquire if I wanted another hand." And so on (with omissions) to No. 210, a French gentleman, whose letter of recommendation said he combined the graces of Fechter with the dignity of Talma, but excelled both. He secured his dismissal with a few lines of French Shakespeare. All good journalism, and probably rushed off in a few minutes.

Although the financial position of Fox Cooper could never be described even as comfortable, his son Harwood records the receipt of assistance in 1870–72. Harwood had several children to feed and clothe, so between seasons money would be tight. In spite of a negative financial sense, Fox Cooper might be more resourceful than his son in an emergency. He probably had more friends.

On 23 December 1871, Fox Cooper gave a farewell performance at the Haymarket Theatre. This was lent for the occasion by J. B. Buckstone, a friend of over forty years.

---

* An advertisement for *Boxing Night*, printed in advance, mentions contributions by the author of *The Spare Bed*, and by the editor of *The Times* for 1962.

Unlike the subject of this biography he was a successful man, and became a notable personality in the mid-Victorian theatre.

The performance started at halfpast six precisely. Private boxes were priced up to two guineas, stalls were seven shillings, and reduced prices operated half-way through the performance.

It was stated on the playbill that Fox Cooper had been associated for upwards of sixty years with the press and the stage, a slight exaggeration unless he became a child actor at the age of five. A distinguished company of actors and actresses agreed to assist him, including Mr Buckstone himself, Mr Buckstone Junior, Messrs Kendall, Howe, and Chippendale. On the distaff side were Miss Robertson, Miss Caroline Hill, Miss Merton, and Mrs Chippendale, together with Mrs Herman Vezin, specially engaged for the occasion. The first item on the programme was *The Lady of Lyons*, which must have provided quite a substantial *hors d'œuvre*. The *entr'acte* comprised some original overtures expressly arranged by Alfred Edgar Cooper, in which were incorporated well-known melodies, such as "Should Auld Acquaintance Be Forgot", and "When We Were Boys Together". Following this, at a quarter to nine was a performance of *Pygmalion and Galatea* by W. S. Gilbert. Immediately afterwards Mr Cooper addressed a few last words to his friends in explanation of his reasons for quitting the profession, within a few years of his sixty-sixth birthday. Finally, the performance concluded with Mr Buckstone's farce, *John Jones*. It had been announced that carriages should be at the theatre at a quarter to twelve.

Quantity as well as quality was needed to ensure the success of a benefit, and this rather nice gesture by Buckstone, coupled with the services of well-known players, may have provided an acceptable sum to Fox Cooper who was, no doubt, in need of any cash he could obtain. Regrettably, there was only a brief note of this event in the *Era*, since it coincided with benefits for a number of distinguished actors, better known to that generation, and Fox Cooper's reasons for quitting the profession are unrecorded.

We must now jump another two years. An advertisement in the *Era* on 21 December 1873 refers to a couple of benefit performances for Fox Cooper at the Charing Cross Theatre, in King William Street. The lessee was W. H. C. Nation, who lent the theatre to an old associate in need of assistance. In this advertisement Fox Cooper asked all friends to waive etiquette and ceremony, and rally round him (their old manager) on the stage from eleven o'clock to two o'clock, to prevent the possibility of any omission in the programme as advertised. It was stated that Mr Cooper during forty-five years of management had never once broken faith with the public. Assuming this period—if not the latter part of the statement—to be correct, Fox Cooper's first adventure into theatrical management must have started round about the year 1828. I have a handbill which announces the two grand special performances for 22–23 December, under fashionable and distinguished patronage. Dress boxes were priced at three guineas and two guineas, the stalls at seven shillings. Services were offered gratuitously by various artists of the Theatres Royal, with the permission of their managers. The list commenced with Harwood Cooper, and included Messrs C. J. Smith, Romer, Smithson, and Tomlin; the ladies included Mrs Addie, Miss Maud Howard, Miss Rebecca Isaacs, and Miss Warde.

The performances were due to start with *Hercules*, followed by a comedietta, and a grand concert. Next there was Dibdin's opera, *The Waterman*, prior to which the pleasing task would devolve on Mr Cooper to deliver a few words of gratitude for past and present patronage. Finally there was H. J. Byron's burlesque opera, *Ill-treated Il Trovatore*. The order of the items, however, would depend on the London lessees who were assisting the veteran by allowing the artists to appear. It was a tricky job to fit them all in.

Fox Cooper's theatrical career had not quite come to an end as on one subsequent occasion a new play by him was produced in London: *A Race for a Wife* at the Adelphi on 19 August 1876. This comedietta was originally to have been entitled *A Bunch of Greens*, because it featured three gentlemen named Green, each pursuing the same young lady. The *Era* said mildly that there were many complications, and that before the end much merriment had been created. It was relatively a success as it ran for about ten weeks: not a bad winding up for an output of plays whose first performances covered a span of nearly fifty years.

Just after the end of the run of the final play, Harwood Cooper records that on 4 November 1876 his father met with an accident which he describes as his death blow. I have not discovered the nature of the injury, or whether Fox Cooper was incapacitated, and there is no recorded history of his last two years. He was living at 59 Princes Road, Lambeth, when he died on his seventy-third birthday, 4 January, in the winter of 1878–79. The very cold weather of that season must have aggravated the bronchitis to which he succumbed. It is strange that according to the certificate of death, the informant was not his wife, Selina, but one Emma Plumeridge, of 64 Tyers Street, Lambeth. The funeral took place at Brookwood on 10 January, and Fox Cooper was buried in a second-class private grave in the Actors' Acre, interment number 78605.* The account, made out for "Harriett Fox Cooper", was preserved by Harwood Cooper, which may mean that he settled it in the absence of Selina.

Fox Cooper's will, if he left one, is not entered at Somerset House, so it is a fair assumption that he had no property other than personal chattels, and those of negligible value. I expect he had sold the copyright of his plays, and that there was little provision for Selina. There may have been a separation, which is almost suggested by the absence of her name on the death certificate, and the curious mistake on the funeral account. However, Selina was then only about forty years of age, and young enough to find employment. She subsequently lived in Dublin and let rooms to theatrical folk in around 1887, but perhaps she preferred London after all, as she died in Camberwell in 1892.

The best contemporary sketch of the character of Fox Cooper is contained in E. L. Blanchard's article in the *Glasgow News*. This was reproduced in a theatrical magazine called *Entr'acte* (No. 500) which also contains a little picture of Fox Cooper as an old man with a top hat and a Wellington nose, (see page 218). The article begins:

Closely connected with the amusement world of London is a name now graven on a tombstone but for more than forty years familiar in the mouths of all associated with theatrical and literary pursuits. Frederick Fox Cooper died on his

* I have tried unsuccessfully to locate the exact position.

birthday 4 January last at the age of seventy-three, having through all the strange vicissitudes of his later life outlived his intimate associates of other days, and the memory of talents which, if cultivated with a stricter regard to the responsibility they involved, would have secured for him an enduring reputation. As it was an existence commenced under the brightest auspices, was pursued through many years of strange adventure amidst continual struggles with adversity, and his history, if truly told, would serve as another example of the utter uselessness of intellectual gifts without the ballast of strong moral principles.

This is the history I have tried to tell, although it is incomplete, and lacking in first-hand knowledge of the man himself. Each reader must judge how far it justifies E. L. Blanchard's verdict. For my part I should like to know why, although noted for an excellent memory, he mentions only the vicissitudes of Fox Cooper's *later* life. Ups and downs were the most notable feature of his existence even in his twenties; perhaps some of those in his later years have eluded me. Or they may have been of a purely domestic nature that failed to gain the light of day.

After this beginning many of Blanchard's remarks are factual and he recalls that at various times Fox Cooper was the manager or the lessee of certain London theatres, his tenure of each establishment being very brief "through the shortness of the exchequer".

It was no unjustifiable boast that he made in declaring that he could keep a theatre open for weeks without a treasury and that, though he could hardly be safely trusted as a manager, his company was always sought after by everybody. In those circles where old players may still be found to congregate a characteristic anecdote of Frederick Fox Cooper will be sure to be told in the course of the evening.

Perhaps the following story is typical because it is contained in a press cutting pasted in Harwood Cooper's almanack for 1880, and he has written below: "Fox Cooper to the letter".

Some days ago a tender-hearted stranger of well-to-do exterior passing by the broad stone steps of Warsaw Cathedral perceived a poorly dressed woman crouched at their feet weeping loudly and wringing her hands in deep tribulation. Touched by her evident distress, he stopped and asked what was the matter.

"Kind, gracious sir," replied the sobbing woman, "I am the most unfortunate creature in the world. I want to get my baby christened, and the Pope demands two roubles and I have not a single kopeck."

"Is that all?" observed the pitiful stranger. "Take this five-rouble note, go straight to the Pope, pay him his christening fee and bring me out the three roubles change."

With joyful promptitude the recipient of his bounty entered the church, whence she presently emerged with three silver roubles, which she handed over to her benefactor, expressing her heartfelt gratitude for his timely succour, and her surprise at his apparently disinterested kindness.

"My good woman," answered the philanthropist with a beaming smile, "Your astonishment is uncalled for. You see I am one of those people who cannot bear to contemplate the unhappiness of their fellow creatures. I must always see joyous faces around me. Besides, everybody concerned in this transaction has benefited by it. The Pope has got his fee; your child will be christened; your mind is at ease; and I have derived three good silver roubles from a benevolent action and—a bad five-rouble note."

I suppose Harwood Cooper, having passed his half-century, was in a position to judge his father, and I believe that his life must have been greatly influenced by Fox Cooper's unpredictable and irregular conduct. As a result the son was lacking in confidence, and prone to introspection in his later years. They were very different men, extrovert and introvert. Putting it in terms of auction bridge, I should say that Fox Cooper was a man who always over-called his hand and was unable to pay his losses; Harwood Cooper, on the contrary, was one who invariably underbid and his gains were small. Thus he wrote about himself:

Harwood Cooper was an actor of average merit who formerly performed at the Olympic Theatre (where he was the original Maltby in *The Ticket-of-Leave Man*) and might have been one of the first comedians on the stage of the Adelphi Theatre where he was engaged for twenty-five years, but was repelled by his distrust of his own abilities. The bump of self-conceit was not developed in an extraordinary manner in the cranium of this artist, who never could fancy that he was equal to others whose characters he had played through their absence.

By contrast there was clearly no limit to what Fox Cooper thought he could do. But his achievement so often fell short of the design.

Another press cutting preserved by Harwood Cooper refers to the death (also on 4 January 1879) of Marc Fournier, a Parisian theatrical character: "He was an extraordinary man in his day, and might be termed a cross between Fox Cooper and E. T. Smith." The latter also had a reputation for pursuing a variety of objectives simultaneously, and both were associated in a bid for Drury Lane theatre (Chapter 8). This reputation is reflected in a few lines from Dryden pasted in the same book. They come from *Absolom and Achitophel*, describing George Villiers, Duke of Buckingham.

> A man so various that he seemed to be
> Not one, but all mankind's epitome;
> Stiff in opinions, always in the wrong;
> Was everything by starts, and nothing long;
> But, in the course of one revolving moon,
> Was chymist, fiddler, statesman and buffoon.
> Then all for women, painting, rhyming, drinking,
> Besides ten thousand freaks that died in thinking.

Alongside this quotation Harwood Cooper has written: "in fact your Grandfather's epitaph"; and he has suitably altered some of the words in pencil, now almost illegible. But I can read "loose" for "stiff", and the sixth line became "was editor, manager, playwright. . . ." Of the women I have found no trace, which is perhaps just as well. *Verb. sap.* It is clear that Harwood Cooper intended this book of press cuttings as a memento for his sons; some member of the family must have sold it with various playbills, programmes, and other interesting documents, perhaps when short of funds, or storage space. I was fortunate in buying them back after many years.

Inside the cover of this same book Harwood places on record that it contains all the press cuttings he has appertaining to his dear old Father, bless his memory. On the front cover he has written:

Hamlet: My Father, methinks I see my Father.
Horatio: Where, my Lord?
Hamlet: In my mind's eye, Horatio.

Sometimes I also think that I can see Fox Cooper—in my mind's eye; and that he would thus enjoin his biographer:

Speak of me as I am; nothing extenuate,
Nor set down aught in malice: then, must you speak
Of one that lov'd not wisely but too well.

A Brief Summary

THIS biography would not be complete without an attempt to sum up briefly the character of my subject. I must also try to answer the question, posed in Chapter 4, as to what went astray.

A summary based on gleanings from published sources, and the evidence of manuscripts, without the benefit of personal knowledge, either at first hand or at second, is liable to be deficient in a real understanding of the character of the man himself. For that reason any judgement of my great-grand-father that I might be tempted to undertake is liable to fall into serious error. So this last section will not be a judgement so much as a simplification, in the manner of an artist who has tried to eliminate everything that does not contribute to his final impression of the character he seeks to represent.

As to what went astray, I am inclined to diminish the emphasis placed upon this feature after my first reading of E. L. Blanchard's verdict quoted from the *Glasgow News*. It is difficult to accept that Fox Cooper's existence really commenced under the brightest auspices. His father was a journalist of average distinction, although good enough to be given the nominal, or professional, editorship of *John Bull*. He wrote a book of verse of fair merit, and enjoyed some patronage from the Manchester family, if not that of Charles James Fox. Perhaps he was known to some of the more notable poets and writers of the day. But in the youth of Fox Cooper, his father was imprisoned on two occasions for debt, and on another for the libel in *John Bull*.

There was always comparative penury, and my firm belief is that the wealthy relatives were an hallucination based on the identity of surnames. So Fox Cooper grew up with no basic advantage except perhaps the dubious one of an environment in which the daily bread was earned by wielding a pen rather than a pick-axe. It is true that his earlier work for the stage seems today the most promising: the burlesques and the farces, including *The Spare Bed*, and *Hercules*. The later efforts tended to be adaptations, or amusing trifles related to topical events. But I cannot accept that Fox Cooper failed to live up to a parental reputation, or to the influence of a youth spent constantly with minds of high purpose and social quality. His life followed not unnaturally from that of his father.

Fox Cooper was no complex character. There is plenty of evidence that, although contentious, he was friendly, impulsive, sensitive, imaginative, and proud. He had a great sense of fun and adventure. But he was superficial in action, and lacked profundity of thought. (Thus he attempted little tragedy.) While those qualities would account for his rapid changes of design and purpose, the *causa causans* was his financial myopia. He was never able to store up sufficient capital to tide over the teething troubles which accompany even the brightest ideas, and he failed to realize that it made the slightest difference. With his business partners either he was unlucky in their choice or incompatible when it came to working together. My feeling is that he wanted his own way and that he was best when his own master, as one might read from his portrait.

That he was impulsive is shown by occasions when he said or did something on the spur of the moment, or dashed off a letter which he later regretted: a short temper, but easily forgotten, and no lingering rancour. Unfortunately what has been said is often remembered, and what is written, remains. In this way mere disagreements were inflated into quarrels, and Fox Cooper, who often suffered from Authority, naturally hoped Authority would come to his aid when he felt he was the aggrieved party.

There were times when his imagination ran riot, and Castles

in the Air, Micawber-like delusions—call it what you will—
effectively warped his better judgement. I believe the fact
that he had been secretary to a Duke (later a King), and could
command personal references from Lord Kenyon, Sir Charles
Aldis, and a host of leading editors, induced a kind of mental
intoxication. So in 1841 he could describe Charles Elliott's
printing machinery as his own, and could refer to the owner
as a clever assistant.* In 1847, he could claim to be related to
a millionaire (Isaac Cooper).

A letter in the records of the Lord Chamberlain† states that
Fox Cooper had a glib tongue, and some facility in writing.
His ability to put words together, leaving aside the question
of their meaning, is shown by a letter of reminder to the Secretary of the New Zealand Company about his cabin passages:
"I shall feel greatly indebted to your politeness if you will
inform me what arrangements are contemplated in this respect,
and if compatible with your leisure in the course of the day."

Glib, imaginative, and thoughtless in financial matters, it
is no wonder that Fox Cooper was so frequently at cross
purposes with the law, and his fellow men. In spite of all this,
I decline to believe that he was essentially dishonest: he simply
had a blind spot.

His politics were those of a liberal radical, although he
professed sympathy with the Tories. But *Cerberus* showed he
could write a good case for almost any political party. Despite
a measure of instability he possessed a genuine desire for social
justice and reform, arising partly from his own nature, and
partly from his less fortunate experiences. He was quick to
seize, without much thought, an opportunity for small gain,
but honest enough to correct an error without delay, as in the
case of the misleading playbill for the Strand Theatre (see
Chapter 7).

My most abiding impression is Fox Cooper's quality of
friendship: he thrived on it, according to the analysis of his
handwriting. There is little true friendship in the world, but
it runs through much of this story. Between the lines, one can
sense that he was often helping others, even when the cause
now seems unworthy. He was a good companion, although
in the material sense he had little to offer. Equally, he must

* See letters in Appendix I(a).   † See Chapter 5.

have accepted many a helping hand from his friends after frequent spells of insolvency. They also gave him benefit performances in 1871 and 1873, when his day was done.

Within the family circle little has been handed down, except that Fox Cooper had a weakness for cards, which could well account for his parlous finances: he did not "drink", but he liked champagne. Others have described him as a staunch friend, a kind parent; and his son Harwood, despite some criticism, retained to the end a filial affection for his wayward father. Throughout all the uncertainties of his manner of life he bore aloft Bacon's first fruit of friendship. "For there is no man that imparteth his joys to his friend, but he joyeth the more; and no man that imparteth his griefs to his friend, but he grieveth the less." Of the griefs Fox Cooper would hear more than the joys.

Epilogue: Frederick Harwood Cooper, and the later Generations

THE sons of Fox Cooper who reached maturity, namely, Harwood and Alfred Edgar, have been mentioned from time to time. They had no sister. To conclude the story and thus to bring it into this century, a little more about Harwood, my grandfather, may not be out of place.

The records he left show that after his marriage in 1855 he lived in Tenison Street for about six and a half years. He then moved to Cumberland Row, where he lived for over thirteen years (1862–75). This was followed by Cleaver Street, where he remained for twenty-one years (1875–96) until the death of his wife. These addresses were all in or near Lambeth. He played at the Olympic Theatre between 1853 and 1869; and at the Adelphi Theatre between 1869 and 1894. At each of these he was a member of the stock company, and received a modest but regular salary.

Thus three private addresses sufficed for over forty years, and apart from occasional weeks out of season, two basic theatrical engagements covered a similar period. What a contrast to the restless movements of his father: and what an amazing record for a poor comedian!

I have mentioned that Harwood Cooper was Editor of Dicks' *Standard Plays*, from October 1881 until some time in 1889. Almost as evidence, he kept the telegram from H. Dicks inviting him to discuss the proposal in the first instance. Under the name of "The Old Stager", he wrote the *Actor's Hand-book*,

published by Dicks in 1884, which A.N. found of interest.
There are also a few plays to his credit, and he occasionally
dabbled in "penny dreadfuls". In this way he supplemented
his salary from the theatre, and by some would have been
accounted fortunate.

Harwood Cooper appeared at Windsor Castle, by command
before Her Majesty, on three occasions: in 1854, 1855, and
1860. I have a programme of the last of these, which says:
"Her Majesty's servants will perform . . . a Drama entitled
Daddy Hardacre, and a Dramatic Sketch called *B.B.*" The
latter were the initials of the principal character Mr Benjamin
Bobbin, and Harwood Cooper took the part of Joe. The whole
entertainment was under the direction of Mr W. B. Donne,
the licensor of plays, if I am not mistaken.

In his almanack for 1889, Harwood wrote that there were
nine children born to him, but I can count only eight. Two
died in infancy, and another daughter (my aunt Anne) married
after a short period on the stage; her grand-daughter, Nancy
Burne, was an accomplished actress in musical comedy who
died in 1954 at the comparatively early age of forty-six. The
other five children of Harwood, all sons, made their careers
on the stage.

Emma Cooper, the well-loved wife of Harwood, died in
1896. He was then financially supported by his sons, who moved
him away from Cleaver Street, Lambeth. Stage folk at that
time rarely had holidays as we now understand them; they
merely rested during periods of enforced leisure. So Harwood
recorded that for the first time for thirty-one years, he was
sleeping out of London. This was at Tooting, where he ended
his days in a small house, but in reasonable comfort attended
by his daughter-in-law and a housekeeper whom he called
"Dutch-oven Overy". She probably had to exercise economy.
Harwood Cooper died in 1905, at the age of seventy-eight, but
his careful nature had given way to anxiety in his later years,
and he was a victim of introspection. On numerous occasions
he wrote in his almanack his own obituary notice, the best of
which is quoted towards the end of Chapter 12. The main
cause of his death was given as senile decay, but of this there
can be little complaint from a man who recorded in 1864 that
his health had broken down.

The five actor sons of Harwood Cooper were: Reynard, Charles Newton, Frederick Donald (my father), another Harwood, and Cecil Barrett. The first three were professionally known as the brothers Renad. After varying periods in vaudeville in this country, and extensively in Europe, they produced an English version of *Le Voyage en Suisse* in December 1891, at the Princess's Theatre in London. Unfortunately Reynard took poison by accident in the following year, but the remaining two carried on, and were joined by their younger brothers in due course. The latter were known on the stage as Harwood Cooper, and Cecil Barrett. Including continental performances *The Swiss Express* was played 4,123 times, before it was laid to rest in 1910. It sustained the family.

My father, who gave me Renad as a second name, said it was obtained by translating Fox into French, and eliminating one letter. It was first used as the Lucien Renads in 1881, for a troupe of four performers which included Reynard and Charles. The complete story of the Renad brothers I may attempt to relate in the future, *deo favente*.

So I come to my own generation. My cousin, Charles, the senior male representative, is well known in the world of automobiles. He has laid foundations which will not be soon forgotten. I will not weary the reader with my own affairs: except for one period in which I finished a piece of work my father had begun, my world has been far removed from the stage and journalism. Perhaps this is strange after at least four generations in those two professions. But my father would have it thus, and I expect he was right. He often was.

In conclusion, and by way of postscript, here is my own direct line of descent on the Cooper side to A.D. 1963 from as far back as I can reach:

Henry Cooper—Phillis . . .
Henry Fox Cooper—Harriett . . .
(*circa* 1771–1838)
Frederick Fox Cooper—Ann Foxall
(1806–79)   m. 1823
Frederick Harwood Cooper—Emma Barrett
(1826–1905)   m. 1855
Frederick Donald Cooper—Winifred Calamaro(*née* Hubbard)
(1865–1939)   m. 1902

P

Frederick Renad Cooper—Catherine Grenville Eves
        (1902–   )   m. 1930
    Antony Fox Cooper—
        (1938–   )

Perhaps in a hundred years or so, a later Cooper will continue the table. In the dedication of his play to Fox Cooper
in 1838, T. P. Taylor wrote of this busy world of trouble and
anxiety. What would he say today? But I still hope that in
2063 some ageing Cooper will have the desire, and the strength.

Appendix I

(NOTE: Fox Cooper's occasionally hasty composition
        has been left unedited)

(a) *Letters written to the New Zealand Company in 1841*

12 Great Union Street,
Newington, May 6th. 1841.

Gentlemen,
    I have long had a wish to proceed to New Zealand for the
purpose of establishing a Paper in that Country but have
hitherto been prevented from carrying my intention into
execution in consequence of the Capital for Type, Paper,
and the Material of a Printing Office being more than I can
at present command.
    Wishing to embrace the opportunity afforded by the pro-
posed Second Colony, and having been informed that upon a
proper representation of the Case, you might possibly be
induced to lend some pecuniary assistance towards the above
object, I beg leave respectfully to ask whether the information
I have received is correct, as in the event of its being so, I
shall forthwith lay before you such Testimonials of qualifications
etc., as shall, I flatter myself, convince the Company that its
liberality will not be unworthily bestowed.
    In soliciting the favour of an answer permit me to state that
I am married—have a family of children—am thirty-four

years of age—intend to take my clever married assistant in my business and will study at all times to advance the interests of the New Zealand Company to the best of my ability and power.

I have the honour to be,
Gentlemen,
your obedient Servant
F. F. Cooper

The Directors of the
New Zealand Company, etc.

(*Printed heading of notepaper:*)
SECOND COLONY OF NEW ZEALAND

The First or Specimen Number of THE NELSON ADVERTISER and ECHO OF NEW ZEALAND (a newspaper to be printed weekly in Port Nelson, the second colony of New Zealand,) will be issued to the subscribers on Saturday the 4th of September next. Advertisements and Communications are requested to be forwarded to the office of publication on or before the 30th instant. The Specimen of the Nelson Advertiser will furnish the latest news from New Zealand, and much valuable and exclusive information for the use of Settlers. It will also contain an article showing the Rise and Progress of Port Nicholson, illustrated with a spirited engraving of, and key to, that flourishing Colony; Statistics of the country, &c., &c.— Published for the Proprietor by John Chappell, 84 Lombard-street.

19 Prospect Place, London
Aug. 21st. 1841

Gentlemen,

Being desirous of taking one allotment of 201 Acres in the proposed Settlement of Nelson I wish to learn whether in the event of my doing so the Company would allow the purchase money to remain on mortgage for 2 years.

I am compelled to make this application at the eleventh hour having expended rather more than I intended in ready money on the purchase of Types, Printing Paper and the Stock in trade of a general Librarian and Bookseller the trade I purpose carrying on in New Zealand.

Permit me to Solicit your earliest consideration of the above as I particularly wish to take my chance of the ballot for choice of situation on the 30th. of August as per public Advertisement.

I embrace the present opportunity of tendering to you my grateful acknowledgements for the liberal intentions (conveyed to me through the medium of R. D. Mangles Esqre·) which you have signified you are ready to carry into effect with reference to the formation of my proposed Newspaper.

I have the honour to be,
Gentlemen,
your obedient Servant
F. F. Cooper

The Directors
of the New Zealand Company,
etc.

46 Liverpool Street,
New Broad Street,
November 10th· 1841

To I. Ward Esqre·
Sir,

In asking for the compensation which I feel I have a just right to expect from the Company in consideration of the serious losses I have sustained through the inadvertence (to use no harsher term) of certain parties at New Zealand House, I am guided by no vindictive recollection of the past and therefore proceed at once to name the lowest sum which will reimburse me.

In the first place I am fully justified in asking the Directors to refund to me the amount I paid for the passage of myself & family. In sanctioning this act of pecuniary justice the Company will suffer no loss inasmuch as the Directors have only to pay the Captain of the Mary Ann for such Cabin & other passengers as are actually landed in New Zealand.

Upon this point the Company will bear in mind that the whole of my printing property valued by their own Agent at £1,500 is consigned to Capt. Wakefield under a warrant of attorney to cover the amount & that I agreed in conjunction with my partner in the business to furnish Advertisements for the Company to the full amount of the loan, in the Nelson Advertiser when publishing in the Colony.

Mr Elliott having been supplied by me with the requisite means and instructions for establishing the Newspaper, the Directors have a guarantee that this debt will be fully liquidated and their best interests advocated in the Columns of the paper.

In common fairness the Directors cannot hesitate to refund to me the amount of my passage money.

Secondly, my original demand for Advertisements inserted in, and copies taken of, the first No. of the "Nelson Advertiser" remains unpaid. The bill exceeds £41 and, as I am given to understand on the ground of no orders have been given. The papers and Advertisements were duly authorized by the Agent of the Company, and the proof sheet containing the Advertisements sent to Mr Bell before the Paper was issued to the Public. Mr Bell did not countermand the original order but on the contrary wrote me a Letter requesting me to keep 300 copies for the Directors and also to publish a Second Edition of my paper for the purpose of advertising some additional terms of purchase.

Thirdly, and lastly, I think I am fairly and equitably entitled to some award at the hands of the Directors for the miseries I have endured in the course of six weeks incarceration in a Common Gaol for a debt which the Company's Agent gave a written undertaking to pay.

It is not for me now to descant upon what has passed. Suffice it to say that your Directors would not have had a more zealous advocate than myself in the Colony, nor indeed (be the upshot of this affair what it may) will the pages of the Nelson Advertiser be permitted by me to be made the vehicle of any comments by its Editor on the annoyances to which its Proprietor has been subjected in this Country.

If I am driven to seek redress I shall adopt no other course than what is open to me by a jury of my Countrymen.

I still, however, feel that I am in the hands of gentlemen who will meet my wishes and thus bury in oblivion the painful recollections of the last month.

I have been thus prolix in justice to my family who are the sufferers in this affair—in justice to Mr Garratt who furnished me with my original Capital—and in justice to my own honour which is somewhat compromised.

> I am Sir
> your obedient Servant,
> Fredk. F. Cooper.

(Printed heading of notepaper:)
SECOND COLONY OF NEW ZEALAND

Now Publishing, price 1s., or £2 10s. per annum, the First or Specimen Number, of THE NELSON ADVERTISER and ECHO OF NEW ZEALAND, a newspaper to be printed weekly in Port Nelson, the second colony of New Zealand, The Specimen of the Nelson Advertiser furnishes the latest news from New

Zealand, and much valuable and exclusive information for the use of Settlers. It also contains an article. showing the Rise and Progress of Port Nicholson, illustrated with a spirited engraving of, and key to, that flourishing colony, Statistics of the country, &c., &c. Published for the Proprietors by John Chappell, 84 Lombard-street.

In order to ensure to Subscribers in England the certain and early importation of their files of this journal, duplicate copies will be sent by different ships.

> 46 Liverpool Street,
> November 15th. 1841.

Gentlemen,

I receive the names of your Solicitors with much pain because upon reflection common sense points out to me that you cannot take my claims for compensation into consideration whilst under a threat of hostile proceedings.

I now hasten to address you in a more equitable light confident that the request I make—based as it is on an appeal to your justice—will be granted.

Gentlemen, throwing aside all the pecuniary points of my case, I find from Mr Arthur Willis, Mr Alderman Copeland and others, that my integrity stands impeached under the worst stigma which can be thrown upon any individual—I allude to the non payment of M. Manning's demand.

I owe it to the children who are looking up to me as their guide and mentor through life—I owe it to the many kind Noblemen and friends who gave vouchers for my character—and I owe it to the New Zealand Company itself, to ask you immediately to appoint a Court of Investigation amongst yourselves as to my affairs, and thus enable me to meet my accusers face to face.

If, Gentlemen, you will do this, and I do not doubt but as men of business and strict impartiality, you will, I am confident that I shall prove to your satisfaction that the whole of this unpleasant business originated in the very negligent manner in which certain official parties at New Zealand House did their duty.

In conclusion believe I court the fullest enquiry and, though suffering dreadfully in a mental and pecuniary sense, I am resolved not to let this matter rest until I prove my own innocence and am restored to your favour.

Soliciting the favour of a reply at your earliest convenience,

> I am Gentlemen,
> your obedient Servant,
> F. F. Cooper

46 Liverpool Street
November 25th. 1841.

Gentlemen,

Having agreed to abide by your decision and take whatever your liberality may award to me I am placed in rather a delicate position in being called upon to name the amount which under all the circumstances would compensate me for my late unfortunate losses, but encouraged by the very kind manner in which I was received by the Committee yesterday, and gratified by the peculiar feelings of commiseration exhibited by the Directors present, I am emboldened to submit for re-consideration my original application, viz for the payment of my bill for papers &c ($£41$)—for the return of the freight with which I was charged ($£36$) and my own personal passage money ($£100$) in all $£177$—being about one fourth of what I have really lost by the late unfortunate transaction.

I think it my duty to inform you that I was released from Dover Castle on consenting to a judge's order for the payment of Mr Manning's claim by three instalments of 3, 6 and 9 months date.

In the termination of this affair I pray it may be most distinctly understood that I repudiate all charges of having spoken disrespectfully of any member of your honourable Court.

From the first I had but one opinion of the New Zealand Company, and the pages of the Nelson Advertiser will give henceforward that proof of my Sincerity, which the brief limits of this hastily penned letter preclude.

I have the honour to be
Gentlemen
your obliged Servant
F. F. Cooper

The Directors
of the New Zealand Company
&c.

(b) *Letters written to the Lord Chamberlain in 1844 and 1846*
17 Walcot Place
Lambeth
Tuesday night, June 18th. 1844

My Lord,

Permit me to submit the following brief statement of facts for your Lordship's humane and impartial consideration.

For the moment I find myself most unjustifiably ejected

from the occupancy of the Royal City of London Theatre by Christopher Cockerton but I find that an application to the Court of Chancery will immediately reinstate me in possession and therefore the more important object of this communication is to solicit your Lordship to refrain from depriving me of my Licence until your Lordship is apprised of the Lord High Chancellor's decision.

Your Lordship will recollect that you granted me the Licence on the 22nd. of April last consequently I have not yet been one quarter of a year in the tenancy and therefore cannot owe a legal quarter's rent to the Landlord (indeed I am prepared to prove I do not owe him one Shilling) but my Lord the most serious and unjust part of this business is that I have already caused to be expended upwards of Eight Hundred Pounds in repairing and embellishing the theatre both before and behind the "Curtain" and it is to recover some compensation for this outlay that I now petition your Lordship to pause before you sanction an act of great injustice and oppression to an individual, humble though he be, who never yet wronged his fellow creatures.

I am, my Lord, in this peculiar and unfortunate situation. All the members of my dramatic company are engaged by me up to the latest period named in your Licence to me and whether they play or not I am responsible to them for the amount of this liability.

I have already offered Mr Cockerton the power of deducting his Rent nightly from the money taken at the doors for admission, and having availed himself of my empowerment to the extent of the sum I have mentioned what more does he require.

Everybody it appears has been perfectly well satisfied with my mode of conducting the Theatre and in the absence of a Certificate which when completed will contain 100,000 signatures I forward a letter to me* from the Gentleman who is Surety for me as required by Act of Parliament and I do not presume to make any comments upon his observations. Your Lordship did me the honor to accept his Surety and I am proud of his written opinion of my Management up to the present hour.

Under all the Circumstances I have again to implore your Lordship to ponder before you deprive me of a Licence until I shall have been released by the Company from liabilities in Salaries alone to the extent of £8000.

* From Mr Passmore, 40 Brook St., 18 June 1844.

Soliciting your merciful consideration I have to implore you not to decide too hastily. I am ready to resume the management and to allow Mr Cockerton his nightly Rent—the Company are willing to act under me, and Mr Passmore having consented the majority favour his opinion.

Finally, my Lord, it will be obvious to your Lordship that unless your Lordship fully looks into this affair in all its bearing your Lordship will be made the medium of enforcing the Landlord's rent under a threat from him to the Tenant in possession that he will apply for a Licence in person. Did the legislation, my Lord, ever contemplate such an abuse of the Act of Parliament.

> I have the honour to be
> your Lordship's
> grateful and obliged Servant
> F. Fox Cooper

The Right Honble.
The Lord Chamberlain.

> 17 Walcot Place, Lambeth
> 20 Nov. 1846

My Lord,
I respectfully approach your Lordship for permission to enact Stage plays for a limited season in the Building known as the National Baths, Westminster Bridge Road, Lambeth. The eligibility of the situation—the respectability of the Proprietor and the immense population of the surrounding neighbourhood are considerations which I flatter myself will entitle me to your acquiescence.

But my Lord I have a claim of a far more serious nature and which stated to your Lordship will convince you at once that I have sustained a grievous wrong by the Lord Chamberlain's office. The fact is this—and I am sure it needs only to be named to be remedied—I was last year and had been for two years previously Lessee and Manager of the Royal City of London Theatre, and in consequence of the poverty of the district and the Competition of the cheap Saloons I was compelled to reduce my charges for Admission to 1/- the Boxes—6^d the Pit and 3^d the gallery—but by means of Tickets admitting Two persons on payment of the original price for one viz 2/- the Boxes—1/- the Pit and 6^d the Gallery. This being communicated to your Office I received an order from the Authorities to discontinue the issue of these free Admissions. I did so and then applied for permission to take the reduced prices at the doors instead. I was distinctly forbidden to do this and told that any reduction from the established prices of Admission would endanger the licence. The consequence of this mandate—from which there was no appeal—was my utter ruin. The public would not pay the old prices and I was compelled to give up the Theatre. It has since been taken by a Mr Honner who is nightly admitting the Public at the obnoxious prices of admission and is as I am credibly informed making a fortune by it. Now my Lord is this equity or justice towards myself. Am I to be driven from a property in which I had invested the hard earnings of a laborious Life by the mandate of a Lord Chamberlain which is revoked in favour of my Successor the moment I am fairly ousted. I dare not trust myself to make a comment upon the injustice of the proceeding but if it is to be tolerated and allowed Surely some compensation ought to be given me for the loss I sustained in obeying the orders which originally issued from the office over which your Lordship now so ably and impartially presides. The instruction to which I allude took place in July 1845 and I have not yet recovered from its effects.

As regards my present application I beg to state that I am fully prepared to carry out the very proper stipulations of the Act of Parliament for the regulation of Theatres

Soliciting your Lordship's answer

I remain

My Lord

your respectful Servant

F. Fox Cooper

The Lord Spencer
&c.

17 Walcot Place,
Lambeth, Dec. 5th. 1846.

My Lord,
Permit me to call your Lordship's attention to a Letter which I forwarded to the Lord Chamberlain's office on the 20th. of April last and in which I took the liberty of throwing out a variety of suggestions for the better regulation of the Public Theatres.

I perceive by an order having been sent to the different Managers requiring them to forward their Bills regularly—that some of my suggestions are being carried out.

Now having devoted much of my time in devising means for curing all the evils of the present System and which must

be constantly annoying your Lordship I crave to be admitted
to the honor of an Interview for the purpose of submitting to
the Authorities my plans in detail.

I am My Lord
most respectfully your
humble Servant
F. Fox Cooper

The Earl Spencer
&c.

17 Walcot Place, Lambeth,
Dec. 8th. 1846.

My Lord,
  I have the honor to acknowledge your answer to my note of
the 5th. inst. communicated to me at your Lordship's desire
by Mr E. M. Browell, and from the tenor of that answer I
fear that the Authorities of the Lord Chamberlain's office
have forgotten my earlier suggestions.

  In a long Letter of the 18th. of April I called the attention
of the Lord Chamberlain to the then (and now) existing abuses
of the law and I pointed out what I believed would be a full
remedy.

  To that Letter I received the following reply

"Lord Chamberlain's office
April 23rd. 1846.

"Sir,
  "I have received your letter of the 18th. inst. and beg to
"thank you for the information contained in it. There is no
"intention at present of making such an Appointment as
"that you allude to.

I am, Sir,
your obedient Sert.
(Signed) De la Warr.

"F. F. Cooper Esqre.
  17 Walcot Place
    Lambeth."

  The evil state continued—plays appeared and were acted
in violence of the established law and when your Lordship
received the appointment of Lord Chamberlain I took the
liberty of embodying the contents of my letter to your Predecessor and transmitted another on the same subject addressed
to your Lordship on the 19th of the month of July. To this
communication your Lordship was pleased to send me the
following answer

"Lord Chamberlain's office
                                                           July 22nd 1846
"Sir,
    "I beg to acknowledge the receipt of your letter of the
"19th the contents of which will receive due attention. As
"regards the appointment you allude to, I have only to
"repeat what was communicated to you in the letter of my
"Predecessor herewith returned.

                                                  I am, Sir
                                        your obedient Servant
"F. F. Cooper Esqre.   (Signed)   Spencer
    17 Walcot Place
        Lambeth."

The above correspondence will at least convince your Lordship
that before the present stir in Theatrical matters I was alive
to the abuses which existed and humbly hoped to succeed in
pointing out a remedy. Daily I find cause for enquiry and only
the other night had the pain to hear the Sacred name of her
Majesty made a common vulgar jest of by the Buffoon at a
properly licensed Theatre.

    In asking to be admitted to the honor of an Interview I had
none other wish than to state the errors (in person) to your
Lordship which a long acquaintance with the dramatic world
had enabled me to find out, and, if any such appointment as
the one I had previously alluded to had in your Lordship's
wisdom been determined upon, to put in a claim to be considered upon the occasion of carrying it out.

    In conclusion I crave permission to state to your Lordship
again that when I obeyed the mandate of your Predecessor
and returned to the old prices of Admission at the City of
London Theatre I became a ruined man.

    The manifest injustice to me therefore of allowing the present
low prices of admission to the various Theatres is self apparent.

    And, with the respect I bear your Lordship and your office,
I also beg to mention that I do not select the Public Press as
a means of addressing your Lordship, like other writers.

                                I am My Lord
                                    your obedient Servant
                                            F. Fox Cooper
                        (Late Lessee of the City of London Theatre.)
The Right Honble.
    The Lord Chamberlain
        &c.

(c) *Open letter in the* Sunday Times *of 6 December, 1846, attributed to Fox Cooper by the Lord Chamberlain's department.*

THEATRICALS AND MUSIC
THREEPENNY THEATRES

TO THE LORD CHAMBERLAIN

My Lord,—When the monopolies of the old patent theatres and the restrictions which private interests had placed on the free representation of the drama were abolished by the legislature, in your hands was placed the full and absolute power of licensing, directing, and controlling all the metropolitan theatres. This is a high and honourable office, but it is, also, one of serious responsibility; for it constitutes you the sole censor of public morals, and the conservator of good manners and decorum in all those places of dramatic entertainment, of which there are upwards of *twenty-four* under your jurisdiction, without including a vast number of public-houses licensed for singing, &c. Thousands upon thousands of people flock to these theatres nightly, and it is as much your duty to interpose your authority whenever the arrangements at any of them are likely to promote or lead to public immorality, as it is incumbent on you to prohibit the utterance of improper language on the stage. You are entrusted with extraordinary powers for maintaining order and decency at these establishments. How, we ask you, have you fulfilled this duty? A visit to any of *the threepenny theatres*—as the theatres are termed where the price of admission to the gallery has been reduced to threepence, and in some instances to twopence—must convince any one that these extremely low prices are a direct encouragement to vice and profligacy, by affording strong inducements and great facilities for young people of both sexes to assemble promiscuously, under circumstances peculiarly dangerous to their morals. We speak from actual observation. The pit and gallery at these houses are now crammed to suffocation nightly with an audience composed chiefly of boys and girls, associated with the most abandoned wretches—thieves, and prostitutes—the very dregs and scum of London. The galleries, in particular, are thronged by these juvenile recruits for Newgate, apprentice lads, young servant girls, children of humble mechanics, who, tempted by the smallness of the price of admission, rob their parents or employers to obtain it, and thus make their first step towards the gallows, and plunge into an atmosphere of moral contamination, which speedily destroys

every spark of virtue in their breasts. The language openly
spoken by the depraved portion of the audience at these houses
is of the most disgusting and abominable description; and, to
complete this revolting picture, the physical sensibilities are
not less outraged than the moral feelings, by the fetid effluvia
arising from a mass of people, filthy in attire and person, being
crowded together in a close heated theatre. These are unexag-
gerated facts, which exhibit in a lamentable light the degraded
state of some of those minor theatres that, under the sanction of
your Lordship's licence, are doing incalculable mischief to
public morals, and to the real interests of the drama. The
remedy for the evil is in your own hands, and, on behalf of all
true lovers of the drama, we call upon you to apply that remedy
effectively by closing every theatre where the prices of admission
are so low as to render them dens of infamy, instead of being
places for intellectual recreation. The magistrates of the metropolis have exerted themselves successfully in putting down the
unlicensed penny theatres, which were notoriously the hotbed
of juvenile profligacy. The galleries of the *threepenny theatres*
are equally pregnant with iniquity, but, shielded by your
Lordship's licence, they cannot be suppressed by magisterial
power. Private interests may suffer by the closing of these
theatres; but it is better that it should be so than that the moral
atmosphere of society should be tainted by the pollution which
the existence of such places must necessarily spread amongst
the youthful portion of the lower classes. However, while we
condemn the practice and deplore the results of the *threepenny*
admission system, we must admit that the managers who have
adopted it are not wholly without an apology for their conduct.

We last week inserted a letter from Messrs Johnson and Lee,
of the Standard Theatre, Shoreditch. It is *explanatory* as to
that which we *never* inferred, and *refutatory* of that which we
never asserted. In speaking of the threepenny theatres we
attacked the system, not the men. What necessity had driven
Messrs Johnson, Lee, Honner, Thorne, Osbaldiston, and
James to such a course was a matter best known to themselves.
We looked, as public curators, at the result—we did not inquire
into the cause, we did not seek to injure or annoy any individual
but we deemed it right to attempt to awaken your Lordship to a
sense of the situation of the drama. Messrs Johnson and Lee
complain of the saloons. Will they be pleased to remember that
they are "saloons", and do not arrogate to themselves the title
of "theatres". They complain that these places have tavern

sources of profit. Why do not Messrs J. and L. know that the saloon of every playhouse in the metropolis is, to all intents and purposes, a tavern? Why do Mr Notter, Mrs Watts, and others, pay £10 per week for a saloon, but to use it in that capacity? Does not every manager in London let his saloon, and is he not aware whilst letting it that it is only by the sale of wine (ay, and spirits, too) that the saloon keeper can pay him this exorbitant rent?

The complaint of Messrs Johnson and Lee comes with a peculiarly bad grace; they came to their opponents, not their opponents to them. The Grecian, the Albert, and other places existed long before Messrs Johnson and Lee dreamt of building the Standard Theatre.

We have before said, and we repeat it now, that the fact is, the theatres are opposing the saloons, not the saloons the theatres. Any one conversant with this class of theatricals knows that a performer requires more for appearing at a saloon than a theatre; he puts a price upon his loss of caste. It has pleased certain speculators to decrease their prices rather than increase their expenses; the two courses lay open to them, and they chose the former. Suppose, for an instant, that a saloon procures a better company than a certain theatre, and that the said saloon plays at half the price—the obvious policy of the theatre should be to improve their company, and make it more desirable to be delighted for one shilling than nauseated for sixpence; on the contrary, the late movement in the east was to come down to the prices of the saloons, and to use a market phrase, by the force of the name "theatre", undersell them.

When Mr Fox Cooper had the City Theatre your Lordship interfered, and put an end to an order system that involved admission at a very low rate. Now the rate is advertised, and taken in so many halfpence at the door, and you are silent. That steps are about to be taken in this matter we *know*. All we desire is—however your Lordship has broken down the line of demarcation—to see theatres hold their position, and saloons retain their pristine character. If prices and entertainments are to be the same, why enforce upon them different appellations? There is *one* theatre—and the prices are only 2*s.*, 1*s.*, and 6*d.*—the proprietress of which has presented the highest English talent in tragedy, comedy, and opera. How she has made those prices remunerative we know not; but does any person believe she could attempt it at 1*s.*, 6*d.*, and 3*d.*?

Persons who are fonder of argument than fact say, "You advocate cheap literature, why not support cheap theatres?" The cases are not parallel. A book may obtain 100,000 readers, a theatre cannot contain 10,000 auditors; bricks and mortar have limits—type, and paper none.

We will not say that the fact of the increase of theatres swelling the purse of the Deputy Licensor has had any effect upon the minds of the higher powers, but it is clear that pieces that are unsuccessful are a great source of profit to him. Knowles's *Hunchback* or *William Tell* returned him no more, though running their hundred nights each, than Mr Witless's comedy that was never repeated. As regards the fees, the Deputy may well exclaim "the more the merrier"; and, therefore, the duller the play the better *his* chance.

For one piece licensed fifteen years ago there are at least twenty now. It is true the fee is less, but "small profits and quick returns" is an old commercial axiom.

To return to the threepenny theatres, which your Lordship is, or will be, called upon to repress, we can only iterate our former opinion—price is not the *criterion* of respectability, but usually its *concomitant*. Below sixpence, for the poorer classes, we believe a theatre cannot be properly conducted; and, in the name of all respectable authors and performers, managers and ground-landlords, we protest against any attempt at reduction.

The reasons we have urged for the suppression of all *threepenny nuisances*, therefore, remain undisturbed. If theatres cannot be maintained upon a respectable basis, let them be closed; public morality and decency require this, and we trust that your Lordship will see the necessity for carrying it into execution.

(d) *Paragraphs in the* Standard *of Saturday, 12 December 1846, attributed to Fox Cooper by the Lord Chamberlain's department.*

THE MINOR THEATRES

The authorities at the Lord Chamberlain's office are in communication with the managers of those theatres who have lately reduced their prices of admission, in order to compete with the musical and dramatic saloons and concert rooms in and about the metropolis. The attention of Earl Spencer, the Lord Chamberlain, was called to the subject by Mr F. F. Cooper, ex-lessee of the City of London Theatre, who received the following in reply to his note:

"Lord Chamberlain's Office, Dec. 3, 1846.

"Sir,—In reply to your letter of the 1st. inst., I am desired to inform you that the Lord Chamberlain has not sanctioned the lowering of the prices in the theatres alluded to by you.

"I am, Sir, your obedient servant

"E. M. BROWELL

"To Mr. F. Fox Cooper, 17, Walcot-place, Lambeth."

Mr Cooper states, that when lessee of the City of London in July last year, he lowered his prices of admission, and on the bills announcing the reduction appearing, he received the following summons from Earl Delawarr, then Lord Chamberlain:

"The Manager of the City of London Theatre is requested to be at the Lord Chamberlain's office at half past two this day.

"Lord Chamberlain's office, Monday, July 28, 1845."

Mr Cooper accordingly waited on the authorities, and was informed that if he persisted in his reduction of prices, the Lord Chamberlain would most certainly interfere. Mr Cooper, therefore, was compelled to give up the management, close the theatre, and discharge his company. Under these circumstances, he addressed Earl Spencer, which elicited the above reply.

On Friday last, Dec. 4, the day following the receipt of the letter, Mr Osbaldiston, lessee of the Victoria; Mr Robert Honner, lessee of the City of London; Mr Richard Thorne, lessee of the Pavilion; Mr C. J. James, lessee of the Queen's; and Messrs Johnson and Nelson Lee, lessees of the Standard, were summoned to attend at the Lord Chamberlain's office, to explain to his Lordship the reasons which had induced them to alter the prices of admission to their theatres. These gentlemen, or their solicitors, accordingly attended and represented that it was in consequence of the low theatrical saloons and concert-rooms being now licensed by his Lordship as places of dramatic entertainment, and possessing advantages which were refused to theatres—the sale of wines and spirits, for instance, the profit on which alone would enable their proprietors to open their establishments without charge for admission.

The several statements were taken down in writing, to be submitted to the Lord Chamberlain.

On the next day the following circular was issued:

Q

"Lord Chamberlain's Office, Dec. 5, 1846

"Sir,—The Lord Chamberlain is desirous that the play-bills from all places licensed by him, either theatres or saloons, shall be sent every week to this office; and in conveying to you his Lordship's directions, I am desired to ascertain whether in so doing it will cost you much.

"I am Sir, your obedient servant,

"E. M. BROWELL

"To the Manager of the —— Theatre."

Appendix II

Plays by Frederick Fox Cooper

NOTES: Breaking with convention, but for the sake of simplicity, only a comma and the word "or" separate the title of each play from the sub-title, if given. I have included all sub-titles which have come to my notice.

The names of the theatres, and the dates given, relate to the production, or first performance of which I have traced a record.

The word "Royal" is omitted from London theatre names.

References to Dicks', and other printed editions of plays, have been made according to A.N., and my own researches.

L.C. = Manuscript submitted to the Lord Chamberlain: followed by date of licensing where known, and, in brackets, reference to B.M. Department of Manuscripts, where applicable.

SONS OF THESPIS, an interlude, said by the author to have been produced at the Surrey in 1827. Not traced.

THE ELBOW-SHAKERS, or *Thirty years of a Rattler's Life*, a burlesque
extravaganza. Adelphi, 3 December 1827. Richardson's
New Minor Drama, Vol. I, 1828. L.C. 30 November 1827
(42887: 127–43).

BLACK-EYED SUKEY, or *All in the Dumps*, a burlesque extra-
vaganza. Olympic, 30 November 1829. Richardson's *New
Minor Drama*, Vol. III, 1830; Cumberland's *Minor Theatre*,
Vol. XIV. L.C. 21 November 1829 (42898: 163–206).

LOVES OF THE LIONS, or *Hyder Ali's Squad*, a burlesque opera.
Sadler's Wells, 21 November 1831. Title and theatre
recorded by Harwood Cooper; A.N. has theatre, with date
8 November 1831, author unknown.

FIEND OF MANY SHAPES. Title recorded by Harwood Cooper,
and dated 1832, with the word "Paris". This date is
close to the year of Fox Cooper's visit (1831), which might
have had some connexion with the production of this play.
Otherwise untraced.

THE SPARE BED, or *The Shower Bath*, a farce. Victoria, 8 July
1833. Cumberland's *Minor Theatre*, Vol. VIII; Dicks'
786 (1886). Written *circa* 1828. The B.M. has the Cumberland print (42964: 891–911). In 1854 this play was
advertised as *Pigeonwiddy's Perils*, or *The Spare Bed*.

REJECTED ADDRESSES, or *The M.P.'s Lodging*, a burlesque.
Clarence, 6 August 1833.

MR. SIMPSON, M.C., or *Vauxhall Gardens*, a local extravaganza.
Victoria, 26 September 1833.

THE DESERTED VILLAGE, a burletta suggested by Goldsmith's
poem. Adelphi, 28 October 1833. Duncombe's *British
Theatre*, Vol. XV, 1834; Dicks' 727 (1886). L.C. 29 October 1833 (42924: 71–129). Sub-title used at the Effing-
ham Saloon in 1851: *The Prodigal Daughter*.

THE COURT JESTER, a broad farcical interlude in two scenes.
Garrick, 22 September 1834.

THE WHITE TOWER, a romantic melodrama in two acts. Garrick,
22 September 1834. Recorded by Harwood Cooper as
The Castle of Glenwar.

ANGELO, or *The Tyrant of Padua*, a tragedy, adapted or trans-
lated from the French of Victor Hugo. Victoria, 15 June
1835.

HERCULES, KING OF CLUBS, a farce. Strand, 7 July 1836. Cumberland's *Minor Theatre*, Vol. XIII, 1837; Lacy, Vol.
LXXXIX, 1870; Dicks' 387 (1882). L.C. 6 July 1835
(42937: 377–90).

Q*

WAITING FOR BAIL, or *Sponge in a Sponging House*, a farce. Possibly produced at the English Opera House (Lyceum) 1836 (see text).

JEWESS, TRAVESTIE, or *The Fatal Gridiron*, a burlesque of the work by Scribe. Victoria, 5 September 1836.

ION, TRAVESTIE, a burlesque of the tragedy by Sir Thomas Talfourd. Garrick, 9 November 1836. Cumberland's *Minor Theatre*, Vol. XII, 1837.

THE SARCOPHAGUS, a laughable interlude. Garrick, 30 November 1836.

IVANHOE (*The Lists of Ashby, or The Conquests of Ivanhoe*), an historical drama based on the novel by Sir Walter Scott. Astley's, Easter Monday, 27 March 1837. Also at Astley's, Easter Monday, 25 April 1859, then described as a spectacle. Dicks' 385 (1882). L.C. 23 April 1859 (see text).

THE QUEEN'S VISIT, or *Guildhall Banquet*, a comedietta. City of London, 6 November 1837. Pattie's *Penny Play*, Vol. I, No. 2 (but advertised on back cover as No. 3), 1838. Reviewed by several journals as *The Queen's Visit to the City*.

PERILS OF THE MAIN. Title recorded by Harwood Cooper: 1837. Not traced.

JENNY JONES, or *The Valley of Llangollen*, an operetta. St James's, 1 March 1838. Pattie's *Penny Play*, Vol. I, No. 1, 1838. L.C. 28 February 1838 (42945: 480–500).

CROMWELL, a tragedy. Part produced at Marylebone, 21 December 1838. Full title possibly *Oliver Cromwell*, or *The Days of the Commonwealth* (see text).

IRISH ABSENTEE. Title recorded by Harwood Cooper: 1838. Not traced.

THE TRIUMPH OF VENUS, or *Cupid and Capers*, a burlesque. Marylebone, 23 May 1839.

MASTER HUMPHREY'S CLOCK, or *The· Old Curiosity Shop* (sub-title used at Theatre Royal, Dover, December 1841), a domestic drama, "founded on the first story in the work of Charles Dickens". Victoria, 26 May 1840. Duncombe's *British Theatre*, Vol. XLI (*circa* 1840); Dicks' 724 (1886). Revived as *The Daughter of Mystery*, Marylebone Theatre, 2 June 1845.

THE BLACK SENTINEL, a vaudeville. Grecian, August 1840. A.N. has theatre and date, but author unknown. Also advertised in *Dover Chronicle* for Theatre Royal on Boxing Day, 27 December 1841, under Fox Cooper's management. An earlier unattributed advertisement appears for City of London Theatre, 12 February 1839.

OLD ST PAUL'S, or *The Perils of the Plague*, a drama based on the novel by Harrison Ainsworth. Queen's, 22 February 1841.

HARLEQUIN AND THE MEN OF KENT, or *The Fairy of the Magic Rose*, a pantomime. Theatre Royal, Dover, 27 December 1841. (With a Mr. Walbourn.)

THE BLACK GUARD, or *Love and War*, a laughable farce. Royal Pavilion, 8 April 1844.

BURNT AT SEA, or *The Fate of the Falcon*, a drama. City of London, 3 June 1844.

LONDON BY NIGHT, a romantic drama, from an epoch in the writings of "Boz". City of London, 5 May 1845. Sub-title used at the Garrick in April 1856: *The Fatal Fire*.

THE OLD FLEETE PRISON, or *The Widow and her Suitors*, an historical domestic drama. Surrey, 12 May 1845. L.C. 9 May 1845 (42985: 61–101).

WELLINGTON (*Wellington, Nelson and Napoleon*), an equestrian spectacle. City of London, 12 May 1845.

THE SEA WOLF, or *The Old Well of the Manor Lands*, a nautical melodrama. City of London, 21 July 1845.

DEALINGS WITH THE FIRM OF GAMP AND HARRIS (*Mrs. Gamp*), a farce with characters based on *Martin Chuzzlewit* by Charles Dickens. Queen's, 16 November 1846. L.C. 27 November 1846 (42997: 1044–70).

ARE YOU COMING TO BED?, an interlude. Strand, 26 April 1847.

THE BOTTLE, or *The Drunkard's Doom*, a domestic drama. Strand, 11 October 1847. The *Colored Acting Drama*, (published by F. Mitchell, Holywell Street, Strand) 1855. Probably revived as: THE WORSHIP OF BACCHUS, or *Death in the Glass*. Bower, 18 February 1865 (see text).

MAN IN THE MOON, or *Harlequin and the World of Waggery*, a pantomime. Strand, 27 December 1847. (With Vandeightone.)

VICAR OF WAKEFIELD. Gravesend Theatre, 21 September 1850.

SHOOTING THE MOON, or *The Cove of Cork*, a comedietta. Strand, 29 October 1850. Lacy's *New British Theatre*, No. 548, 1854; French's acting edition: Vol. 135, No. 2017. L.C. 21 October 1847 (43007: 43–86).

OVINGDEAN GRANGE: A Tale of the South Downs, a romantic drama founded on the novel by Harrison Ainsworth. Dicks' 1019 (*circa* 1889). L.C. 5 January 1863. Stated

on print to have been performed at the Surrey Theatre
29 September 1851. Production untraced. (See text.)

TRIP TO PARIS. Harwood Cooper records title and year, 1852.
Not traced.

HARD TIMES, a domestic drama, adapted from the novel by
Charles Dickens which appeared as a serial in *Household
Words*. Strand, 14 August 1854. The printed play was
advertised in the *Era* in the same month by H. Pownceby,
Leman Street, Whitechapel. Dicks' 785 (1886). L.C. 10
August 1854.

NEW WAGS OF WINDSOR, or *Trial by Jury-women*, a farce. Strand,
18 September 1854. L.C. 11 September 1854. (With J.
H. Tully, who probably contributed music.)

WHO'S A TRAVELLER?, a farce. Strand, 30 October 1854. L.C.
25 October 1854. (With J. H. Tully.)

WHERE'S CRUVELLI?, a sketch. Strand, 6 November 1854. L.C.
6 November 1854. (With J. H. Tully.)

THE SOLDIER'S WIFE, or *The Heights of Alma*, a drama. Strand,
20 November 1854. L.C. 17 November 1854.

CHRISTMAS CAROL, a fantasy, founded on the work by Charles
Dickens. Strand, 11 December 1854.

WHO'LL SERVE THE QUEEN? a comedietta, or "New local
drama". Strand, 8 January 1855.

THE SEVEN POOR TRAVELLERS, or *Heart-strings and Purse-strings*,
a dramatic version of a story in the Christmas number
of *Household Words*, 1854. Grecian, 12 March 1855. The
Colored Acting Drama, No. 2, 1855. L.C. 14 March 1855.

SISTER OF MERCY, or *The Ruined Cloister*, a drama taken from
the life of Fénelon. Garrick, Easter Monday, 24 March
1856.

LITTLE DORRIT, a drama founded on the work by Charles
Dickens. Strand, 10 November 1856. *Penny Pictorial Play*,
No. 28 (see text). L.C. 12 November 1856.

HARLEQUIN AND THE MAGIC NEEDLE, a pantomime. Ramsgate,
Christmas 1856.

SILVER STORE ISLAND, or *The British Flag of the South American
Pirate*, a drama adapted from the Christmas tale in *Household Words*. Strand, 15 February 1858. L.C. 13 February
1858. For the production the sub-title was: *Perils of
Certain English Prisoners*.

THE TALE OF TWO CITIES, or *The Incarcerated Victim of the Bastille*,
an historical drama adapted from the story by Charles
Dickens. Victoria, 9 July 1860. Dicks' 780 (1886).

GARIBALDI, THE ITALIAN LIBERATOR, an opera founded on an epoch in the life of the Italian liberator, with music by J. H. Tully. Surrey, 9 July 1860. Some of the principal songs, duets, trios, and choruses are printed (anon.). L.C. 7 July 1860.

THE CORSICAN BROTHERS, a dramatic romance, adapted to the English stage from the romance of M Dumas dramatized by MM E. Grangé and Xavier de Monté Pin. Dicks' 752 (1886). Stated on print to have been represented at the Lyceum Theatre in 1863: not verified. (See text.)

GIOVANNI REDIVIVUS, or *Harlequin in a Fix, and Pantaloon on Horseback*, a pantomime. Bower, 26 December 1864.

UNDER THE EARTH, or *The Sons of Toil*, a drama adapted from *Hard Times* by Charles Dickens. Astley's, 22 April 1867. The authorship of this work has been claimed by and credited to Mr W. H. C. Nation, lessee of Astley's in 1867. (See text.) Dicks' *British Drama*, No. 59. L.C. (three scenes only) April 1867.

ONE HORSE SHAY. Harwood Cooper records title and year 1867. Not traced, but see note at end.

THE FIELD AGAINST THE FAVOURITE, a comedietta. Astley's, 24 April 1869.

A RACE FOR A WIFE, a comedietta. Adelphi, 19 August 1876. Title originally intended was: *A Bunch of Greens*.

Additional undated titles from Harwood Cooper's list, which have not been corroborated from other sources:

Royal Consort
I won't be a Nun
*King Death**
John Howard—This is the name of an actor who appeared in at least three of Fox Cooper's plays at the Strand theatre in 1854.
Modern Chrichton
Robin Adair
Uncle Tom's Cabin—in 1852–53 there were several dramatic versions of this story.
Hand and Glove
Friend of the Family
Bevis Marks

* A drama by this title, with the sub-title, *The Infidel and the Peri*, was produced by Osbaldiston at the City of London theatre in January 1839. (See text.)

Siege of London
No Concealments
Monks of Old
Private Theatricals (possibly a descriptive title).

On the print (1855) of *The Bottle* already mentioned, it is stated that Fox Cooper was the author of several plays including *Wapping Old Stairs*: not otherwise verified, although several plays of this title are on record, one of which was produced at the Strand Theatre, under Fox Cooper's management in 1847 (Harwood Cooper's notebook).

Davenport Adams in *A Dictionary of the Drama* (A–G, 1904). attributes to Fox Cooper a version of *Jack Sheppard*, undated. A play of this name was produced by him at the City of London in June 1845, but described as the original *Jack Sheppard*, presumably by Moncrieff (1825), or Buckstone (1839).

A fragment of a paybill (undated) contains the cast of Fox Cooper's irresistible extravaganza in one act, entitled *Eight Hours at Brighton*. The principal character, played by George Yarnold, was Mr Bubb, of Farringdon Within, and owner of the "Von Oss Shay". This piece may be the *One Horse Shay* recorded by Harwood Cooper, 1867. During that year Yarnold played at the Victoria and the City of London Theatres, but the production is untraced.

In addition to the above there could be added a number of titles from the *Penny Pictorial Plays* published under the editorship of Fox Cooper (see Chapter 8). In most cases these seem to have been adapted specially for that edition, and it is a fair assumption that the editor took a hand in their preparation.

Appendix III

A Chronology of the Life of Frederick Fox Cooper

		Family, and office, addresses
1806	Birth, 4 January.	Delahay Street, Westminster.
1821	Articles published in *Drama*.	Family living in Blackfriars.
1823	Marriage to Ann Foxall, 9 August.	(Both of the parish of Camberwell.)
1826	Birth of Harwood, 24 November.	Mount Gardens, Lambeth.
1827	Two plays produced.	
1828		Earl Street, Blackfriars.
1829	One play produced.	Pilgrim Lane, Ludgate Hill.
1830	Birth of Henry Fox, the younger, 1 July (?).	Fetter Lane, City.
	Paul Pry, newspaper (February–September).	Brook Street, Lambeth. Office at 13 Wellington Street, Strand.
	In Paris (December, 1830–31).	Rue des Marchés.
1831		Wood Street, Cheapside.
	In North Wales.	Segontium Terrace, Caernarvon.
		Edmund Place, Aldersgate Street.
	In Fleet Prison (December 1831–June 1832). One play produced.	Union Row, Kent Road.
1832	One play produced (?).	Surrey Street, Strand (?).
1833	Secretary to Duke of Cumberland. (Orange Lodge activities), 1833–35. Five plays produced.	Bridge Court, Westminster.

1834   Walnut Tree Walk, Lambeth.

Partnership with Robson   Office at Titchbourne Street,
Harrison.   Piccadilly.

1835 Reference to work as
      dramatic critic.   Clattern Bridge, Kingston.
      Evidence before Select   Sloane Street, Brompton.
      Committee of the House
      of Commons (August).

                                Palace New Road, Lambeth.
                                Garden Row, Southwark.
One play produced.

1836 In Horsemonger Lane
      prison   (February–
      April).
      Five plays produced.   Swan Street, Old Kent Road.
                                Sutton   Street,   Waterloo
                                  Road.
                                Wood   Street,   Millbank,
                                  Westminster.

1837 Three plays produced.   Manor Place (Surrey Gar-
                                  dens), Walworth.
                                Edmund Place, Aldersgate
                                  Street, City.

1838 *Crim. Con. Gazette* (1838– Office at Wellington Street,
      40).   Strand.
                                Goswell Street, City Road.
      Four plays produced.

1839 In Fleet prison (Febru-
      ary–April).
      Marylebone   Theatre   Lisson Grove, N.
      (May–July).
      One play produced.

                                Canterbury Place, Lambeth.

1840 Birth of Alfred Edgar,
      1 February.
      Two plays produced.   Meads Place, Lambeth.
                                Gt. Union Street, Newington
                                  Causeway, Lambeth.

Family, and office, addresses

1841	Launching of *Nelson Examiner*.	Prospect Place, Lambeth.
	In Dover Castle prison (October–November).	Liverpool Street, New Broad Street, City.
	Theatre Royal, Dover, (December 1841–August 1842).	Bench Street, Dover.
	Two plays produced.	
1842		Paris Street, Lambeth.
		Tower Wall Street, Dover.
		Pedlar's Acre, Belvedere Road, Lambeth.
1843	*Cerberus*, newspaper (June–November).	Office at 164 Strand.
		Walcot Place, Lambeth (until 1849).
1844	City of London Theatre (April–June).	
	In Queen's Prison (July–September).	
	Two plays produced.	
1845	Royal Kent Theatre, Kensington (January–?).	
	City of London Theatre (March–September)	
	Deptford Theatre (winter 1845–46)	
	Four plays produced.	
1846	In Horsemonger Lane Prison (May–July).	
	One play produced.	
1847	Strand Theatre (March 1847–February 1848).	
	Three plays produced.	
1848	Editorship of *Theatrical Chronicle* (September 1848–March 1849).	

Family, and office, addresses

1849   Gravesend Theatre and   Commercial Road, Lambeth.
       Terrace Pier Gardens.
       (May 1849–September
       1850).

                              New Road, Gravesend.
                              Fountain Place, City Road.

1850   In Maidstone Prison
       (May–July).

                              Milton Road, Gravesend.
       Strand Theatre (Octo- Britannia Street, City Road.
       ber–November).
       Two plays produced.

1851   Royal Chinese Junk
       (June–October).
       One play produced (?).

1852   Singleton Street, City Road.
       One play produced.   Newington Causeway, Lam-
                                beth.
                              Hercules Buildings, Lambeth
                              Brook Street, Lambeth.

1854   Strand Theatre (July   New Street, Kennington.
       1854–January 1855).
       Six plays produced.

1855   Grecian Theatre (March– Hercules Place, Lambeth.
       April).
       Marriage of Harwood
       Cooper, 9 August.
       The   *Colored   News* Office at 183 Fleet Street.
       (August–September).
       Two plays produced.

1856   Garrick Theatre
       (March–May).
       Ramsgate Theatre (Nov- Hardres Street, Ramsgate.
       ember 1856–January
       1857).
       Two plays produced.

1857   Hercules Place, Lambeth.

1858   Astley's Theatre (?
       –December).
       One play produced.

Family, and office, addresses

1859	*Ivanhoe* revived as new play.

1860 Death of first wife, Ann, 2 May.

Two plays produced.

Hercules Buildings, Lambeth (possibly the same as Hercules Place).

1862 *The Times of 1962* (*circa* March–May).

Office at 5 Catherine Street, Strand.

Second Marriage, to Selina Gallagher, 12 July.

Chester Place, Kennington Road.

Bankruptcy (December).

1863 One play produced (?).

1864 Bower Operetta House (December 1864–June 1865).
One play produced.

1867 Astley's Theatre (?).
Two plays produced.

1868 Astley's Theatre (August–September).

North Street, Lambeth.

1869 Astley's Theatre (April–June).
Boxing Night Annual.
One play produced.

1871 Benefit performance at Haymarket Theatre, (December).

1873 Benefit performances at Charing Cross Theatre, (December).

1875 *Varieties in Verse.*

1876 Last play produced.

1879 Death of Fox Cooper.   Princes Road, Lambeth.

R.I.P.

Index